D0089657

MILLER'S
P O C K E T
ANTIQUES
FACT FILE

ESSENTIAL INFORMATION FOR, DEALERS, COLLECTORS AND ENTHUSIASTS

compiled by
JUDITH and MARTIN MILLER

MILLER'S

MILLER'S POCKET ANTIQUES FACT FILE

First published in 1988 by Miller's
an imprint of Reed Consumer Books Limited
Michelin House
81 Fulham Road
London SW3 6RB
and Auckland, Melbourne, Singapore and Toronto

General Editor Judith Miller
Editor Alan Folly
Art Editor Nigel O'Gorman
Design Assistant Christopher Howson
Researcher/contributor Christopher Carling
Additional material by Paul Holberton
Artwork by Karen Cochrane, John Hutchinson and
Hard Lines, Oxford, England
Map by Lovell Johns Ltd, Oxford, England
Production Barbara Hond, Stewart Bowling

ISBN 0 85533 689 7

Typeset by Bookworm Typesetting, Manchester,
England
Reproduction and camera work by M. & E.
Reproduction North Fambridge, Essex
Produced by Mandarin Offset
Printed and bound in Malaysia

CONTENTS

INTRODUCTION
How to use this book 5
Factors affecting price 6
Where to buy Antiques 6
How to buy Antiques 8

FURNITURE
Glossary 10
Woods used in furniture 12
Periods and styles 14
What to look for:
   Drawers 16
   Veneers 17
   Repairs, alterations,
   marriages and fakes 18
What you should know
about:
   Beds 20
   Bookcases 21
   Bureaux 22
   Cabinets and sideboards 23
   Canterburies 24
   Commodes 24
   Chairs 25
   Chests 27
   Cupboards 28
   Desks 29
   Dumbwaiters 30
   Early oak furniture 31
   Mirrors 32
   Stools 32
   Tables 33
   Walnut furniture 35
   Wine coolers 35
Recognition and dating
   English chair backs 36
   Continental chair backs 39
   American chair backs 40
   Legs and feet 42
   Sofas & settees 45
   Handles 46
   Pediments 48
   Mouldings 49
Furniture makers
and designers 50

PORCELAIN and POTTERY
The crucial questions 52
What to look for 54
Glossary 56

English and Continental
marks 58
The Major Factories 82

ORIENTAL WARE
Glossary 90
Dynasties and their
marks 92
Chinese pronunciation 94
Japanese periods 94
What you should know
about oriental porcelain 95

METALWARE
Glossary 96
British silver marks 98
Gold marks 111
British silversmiths 112
Continental silver
marks 114
Old Sheffield plate 115
Silver shapes and dates 116
   Teapots 116
   Coffee pots 116
   Tankards 116
   Jugs 117
   Sauceboats 117
   Candlesticks 117
   Spoons 118
American silver
shapes and dates 119
What you should know
about silver 120
What you should know
about pewter and other
metals 121
Marks on pewter 122

CLOCKS and BAROMETERS
Glossary 124
What you should know
about clocks and
barometers 128
Recognition and dating 130
   Hour and minute hands 130
   Bracket clocks 131
   Longcase clocks 132
   Wall clocks 133
Clockmakers and their
dates 134

GLASS

Glossary 136
What you should know
about glass 138
Glass engraving 139
Drinking glasses: dates and
shapes 140

ART NOUVEAU and ART DECO

Glossary of names
and terms 144
What you should know
about Art Nouveau and
Art Deco 148

RUGS

Glossary 150
Regions, makers and
styles 152
Pronunciation guide 154
What you should know
about rugs 155

ARMS and ARMOUR

Glossary 156
Armour 160
Edged weapons 162
General militaria 164
Firearms 166
Gunmaking 168
Leading gunsmiths &
gunmakers 168
The chronology of
arms 169

DOLLS and TOYS

Glossary 170
Doll makers 171

What you should know
about Dolls and Toys 173

OTHER COLLECTABLES

Antiquities 174
Jewellery 174
Netsuke 175
Bottles 175
Scent bottles 176
Potlids 176
Boxes 176
Papier Mâché 177
Sewing antiques 177
Scientific instruments 178
Medical instruments 179
Cameras and
photographs 179
Musical boxes, phonographs
and gramophones 180
Typewriters 180
Pop ephemera 181
Posters 181
Cigarette cards 182
Postcards 182
Costume 182
Goss & Crested Ware 183
Fairings 183
Wemyss Ware 183
Tins 184
Tools 184
Fishing tackle 184
Railway antiques 185
Treen 185
Mauchline Ware 185

INDEX 186

ACKNOWLEDGEMENTS and CREDITS 191

HOW to USE this BOOK

Miller's Pocket Antiques Fact File has been devised to help both specialist and novice, collector and dealer. A great deal of research has been carried out to find the most useful facts to be included. Every effort has been made to reflect pieces which are in the market place and available to the antiques public – avoiding, wherever possible, museum pieces and the most expensive items. As a result, most facts included deal with 18th, 19th and early 20th century pieces. For this we make no apology. From the many thousands of facts accumulated, we feel that those presented in this book most reflect buyers' needs.

The book is split into natural collecting areas and general discussion has been kept to a minimum. Accordingly, this is a book of solid facts, with charts, marks, dates, shapes and glossaries to assist with identification and dating. This is a book to take with you when you attend an auction, fair or go on a browse round antique shops.

It is important to state that marks alone cannot guarantee an item. This book cannot make you an instant antiques expert. What it does provide is the basic tools. To learn more you have to work – you have to educate your eye. You have to visit collections and museums; you have to spend time in antique shops; you have to ask specialists, and more than anything you have to handle the items. The joy of exploring the field of antiques is that it can take you a lifetime to discover and to learn. We all have to make mistakes but that is part of the learning process.

This book is designed to give you, ready at hand, the basic facts that we all find impossible instantly to remember.

The best advice on how to use this book is: make sure you have it with you all the time!

Judith H Miller

Factors Affecting the price of Antiques

The problem of fixing prices for antiques is a never-ending one, and one which we constantly address in producing *Miller's Antiques Price Guide*. A price can be affected by many factors, for example:

Condition

This is always an important factor when dealing with antiques and the best way to learn what a "perfect" piece should look like is to visit a museum such as the Metropolitan Museum in New York or the Victoria & Albert Museum in London. This is especially useful if one is looking to buy an expensive item of furniture, as you will see fine examples of wood colour and patination. Perfect examples will, obviously, cost more. Damage and restoration is always to be regretted and the price must reflect this.

Desirability and rarity

Although a piece may be extremely rare, unless it is also desirable it will not necessarily command a high price. A relatively common form in good condition is sometimes more pleasing than a rare piece in poor condition.

Size

In general terms smaller pieces are favoured by the majority of buyers, with particular attention being paid to usability rather than to mere decoration. Thus, items such as chairs, small tables and desks can fetch higher prices than perhaps a rarer but larger object that would not comfortably fit in the home.

Museum buying power

Museums are often guilty of encouraging prices to soar. They normally only purchase the more expensive items, but prices are lifted as a consequence.

Buyer's power

One can often be surprised at an auction by a piece selling for many times its estimated value. There can be several reasons for this. Perhaps the estimated price was incorrect but it is also likely that two or more people were determined to have the piece and by bidding against each other, carried the sale price well above the true value of the object.

Investment value

Another interesting point to bear in mind when buying items for the home (furniture being a prime example), is that once a new item has left the shop its value decreases dramatically, but with an antique it will hold its value and in most cases the value of the piece will increase even though it is in use.

Public appeal

The factors affecting the prices of antiques are therefore numerous, but media response should also not be underestimated – for example, the mere fact that items or collections have been given exposure on prime time television will arouse great public interest, and substantially increase demand.

Location

As a large percentage of sales of antiques takes place from dealer to dealer, it is obvious that prices vary. Many dealers buy at auction but it is also possible (though to be honest unusual) to pay more at a provincial auction than in a specialist shop in London or New York.

Where to Buy Antiques

There are a number of choices when it comes to buying antiques. Before we look more closely at some, a word of warning. Don't rush into buying antiques; learn as much as you can about your subject and beware of the obvious bargain. Some antique dealers and auctioneers are not as scrupulous or as knowledgeable as they might be. Some dealers' stocks and some auction lots are what could euphemistically be called "unreliable", furniture in particular.

Antique Dealers: Shops, Markets and Fairs

Buying from an antique shop is probably where most people start. The entire spectrum is covered, from the luxurious showrooms and galleries of London's West End and New York's 57th Street to the bric-a-brac, secondhand dealer found almost anywhere. There are two professional organisations which you will come across in Britain: BADA (British Antique Dealers Association) and LAPADA (London and Provincial Antique Dealers Association). In the United States there is NAADAAI (National Antique and Art Dealers' Association of America Inc.). Members of these Trade Associations are bound by their various codes of practice which are based on providing a reliable and trustworthy service to customers in accordance with consumer protection legislation. Look for their signs normally displayed on store door or windows.

Other shops are harder to categorize; each has its own good buying points. An old dealer once told me that if you really know what you are doing, you should be able to buy anywhere. I list below a couple of examples:

The pretty village high street shop is always worth visiting for two reasons: firstly the owner cannot possibly be an expert on every subject. He or she may be an expert on early English silver but be less certain on red anchor Chelsea porcelain. Secondly, there is a chance that the owner has had to buy stock in lots, some of which may not be saleable in that particular shop. For example, a dealer in period walnut furniture could have a storeroom of Victorian mahogany that he will be very pleased to move on at a reasonable price.

The bric-a-brac or junk shop: certainly, I have made many good purchases from such shops but I have also found that when they obtain a saleable but mediocre piece, it can be very over-priced. It is probably the best item they've had in stock for a year. Fairs, markets and fleamarkets are like shops in that they can vary from the highly prestigious to the car boot fair in a local farmer's field. Remember what my old friend said: if you know your subject you should be able to buy anywhere! A good point to remember is that if you always ask for a full invoice you are then covered by consumer protection legislation.

Auctions

Auctions rooms, if you are careful and knowledgeable can be an excellent source for all kinds of antiques.

Don't be overawed by the jargon or by anything else. View the sale carefully and fix your price limit. Do try to stick to this and don't get carried away. And don't think that because you've outbid "the trade" it's necessarily a bargain. It could have belonged to the man you've just outbid!

Selling

Finally, a cautionary word about selling. BADA and LAPADA dealers (NAADAAI in the U.S.), also auctioneers, particularly members of SOFAA (Society of Fine Art Auctioneers) are your best source of good advice. Please beware of the plausible, polite and seemingly very generous people who knock on your door. "Knockers" are invariably up to no good. Always get a second opinion. The best advice is never to let them inside the house.

How to Buy Antiques

Buying your first antique can be quite a nerve racking process. Even seasoned professionals who are totally hooked on buying antiques still recall the first time they bid at auction, the first time they managed to walk into an antique shop or fought for a piece of china at a jumble or rummage sale.

The main advice for anyone just starting to buy antiques is: Do your research first and don't get hustled into hasty decisions. We have already discussed the many ways of buying antiques; what I want to deal with here is how to do it.

Antique Dealers

Probably the first contact most people have with antiques is gazing into the shop window of the local antique shop. The various categories of antique dealer has been explained, but how do you approach one? Firstly, do cultivate a "pet" dealer. Most specialist dealers are fascinated with, and fascinating about, their subject and are very willing to talk to an interested listener – who may well one day become a customer. But don't plague a dealer – especially when there is a potential customer in the shop. I have gained most of my knowledge about actual pieces from experts, either dealers or auctioneers. Don't be intimidated by any expert; everyone had to learn sometime. Don't, however, pretend to know more than you do. A dealer will know. Bluffing your way in antiques can be fun, but also dangerous.

Do your own research. I really can't emphasise that enough. The more museums you visit, books you read, auctions you go to , dealers you cultivate, the easier deciding what to buy will become. You also need to buy your *Miller's Antiques Price Guide* every year to build up your own photographic reference library and give you a "ball-park" figure of what you will have to pay.

If you want to buy a specific type of antique go to an area where there are lots of specialist shops. You may find these shops charge slightly more than the one piece which just might come up in the local auction, but if time is money – choice can be cheaper. Don't think that specialist dealers are necessarily more expensive. A specialist knows what to charge and although that can on occasion be more expensive, someone who is guessing may well charge more. You can ask a dealer what is his best price but if he won't shift, leave it.

Auctions

Auctions can be the most exciting place to buy antiques but the general public do tend to be worried about attending auctions which are still dominated by the trade.

The first point to make is that some expensive item will *not*, repeat not, be knocked down to you if you scratch your nose or take out a handkerchief! It is actually very difficult to attract the auctioneer's attention to take your initial bid.

Secondly always view an auction properly. Obtain a catalogue and really examine the pieces in which you may be interested. If there isn't a printed estimate list, ask one of the staff for a price guide. If the piece you are considering is reasonably expensive ask the auctioneer for advice about it. They can be very helpful, so don't be put off if you find an unhelpful auctioneer – every trade has them. Always check the condition of a piece carefully and remember that restoration can be very, very expensive. Now before you think of going to the actual auction set your own limit of how much you will pay and DON'T go above it . . . and remember that in a large number of auctions you have to add a "buyer's premium" onto the hammer price.

Now the actual bid. As I've already intimated, it can be quite difficult as an unknown buyer to attract the auctioneer's attention. This is not a time for the faint-hearted ... wave your catalogue in the air and if that doesn't work I'm afraid you have to shout "Sir" or "Madam". Once you have the auctioneer's attention, bid in a clear way. Ignore the fact that some dealers seem to have odd ways of bidding. Just keep it simple. Where to start bidding is very much a personal decision. I start quite early on in the proceedings and hope to stop others bidding. My husband leaves it to the last minute!

You can, of course, leave a bid with the auction house. Most have bidder's forms which are either in the back of the catalogue or available at the front desk. Or you can cultivate a porter to bid on your behalf. (Do remember that if the porter gets you something – give him a tip! It works wonders). There is one small problem which should be mentioned here. An auctioneer has a duty not to run up bids, but it has been known to happen. I must say that when I leave bids I often find the piece is knocked down to me for less than I indicated on the form but do watch this. If you are nervous, leave your bids but still try to attend the auction, as there is nothing quite like the excitement. But don't bid above your limit, even though it is tempting to think that the next bid will succeed!

Be ready to pick up a bargain, but only if you remember the piece from the viewing. Some sales are very poorly attended and bargains can abound. Don't feel that city auctions and specialist auctions will automatically be more expensive. Some of the minor lots at important sales go quite cheaply.

Make arrangements for the auction house to accept your cheque if you are not paying cash. If you can't clear your lot or lots on the day you may have a storage charge. Most auction houses will arrange delivery but this can be expensive.

Some auctions require you to register and obtain a bidding number, so do that before the auction starts. If this system is not in operation you need to shout out your name when a piece has been knocked down to you then fill in a form with your address etc. Obtain this from a member of the auction staff.

Most people have heard stories about dealers' rings which supposedly control auctions. In my experience this is not a problem. The auctioneer has a responsibility to give the vendor advice on a sensible reserve. If some dealers have grouped together and agreed not to bid against each other it is the vendor who suffers, not someone else bidding in the room. So ignore it.

My only other advice on auctions is go early, and do check the state of the auction room as you may well need a cushion, a rug, a vacuum flask with a hot drink, a sandwich and even a hot water bottle. Have fun!

Important: when you have purchased a piece you value, no matter how small or seemingly insignificant, make a point of following this procedure:

1. Photograph the piece; a Polaroid will be fine – and easy.
2. Write a full description of the piece in a book kept for the purpose, with date of purchase.
3. Also, record the price you paid for it, and where the purchase was made.
4. Always obtain a receipt, and keep it safely, where you know you can find it if required.

This information will be vital when making an insurance claim, or if the tax man requests a statement of assets.

apron Decorative skirt of wood set between the legs of a chair or cabinet.

armoire French term for a press, wardrobe or any similarly large cupboard.

associated Not original, but of same period and style. Losses are often made good with "associated" parts.

baluster One of set of upright posts supporting a balustrade. Baluster shapes (e.g. baluster splat) always have a dominant convex swell at the base terminating in a smaller concave one at the neck.

barley-sugar twist Colloquial name for spiral turned legs and rails, popular from mid C17.

block front Front shaped from thick boards, so allowing recessed centre section.

bobbin In the shape of a bobbin or reel: in furniture usually a turned element resembling a row of connected spheres.

bombé Outswelling (e.g. the front of a cabinet which is not flush, but curves forward).

bonheur du jour Small writing table, sometimes with a cupboard above, introduced in France, second half C18.

bracket foot The foot itself is plain, but where it is joined to the rail or stretcher it is carved or stepped like an ornamental bracket.

breakfront With a central section that projects or "breaks" forward.

bun feet Feet shaped like flattened globe. Introduced late C17.

burr Deformation to a tree caused e.g. by the stunted growth of a branch: used in veneer, it gives a decorative pattern or "figure".

cabriole leg Leg, often for a chair, that curves out at the foot and in at the top. The point of change from outer to inner curve is termed the "knee". Introduced in C17, the cabriole leg was fundamental to the development of furniture, revolutionizing not only style, but the way furniture could be constructed.

carcase The inner frame or "chassis" of a piece of furniture, commonly made of an inferior wood and veneered.

cavetto Moulding making an inward curve across a right angle.

chamfer An angle that has been bevelled or flattened off, e.g. an octagon is a chamfered square. A "sunk" or "hollow" chamfer has a trough or groove in it.

chauffeuse Low fireside chair.

chiffonnier A low or side cupboard. Original C18 pieces had solid doors replaced in C19 with lattice or glass doors.

cornice The horizontal top part or cresting of a piece of furniture.

cross-banding Decorative edging, in which the veneer is cross-grained.

davenport In Britain a small writing desk, usually with drawers at side; in the U.S. a bed-couch or sofa.

dentil Small moulding in the shape of a block, usually found under a cornice. Properly an element of the Corinthian Order.

deudarn Welsh name for two tier press or hall cupboard.

ebonize To stain a light-coloured wood to the colour of ebony.

escritoire Cabinet with a fall front which lowers to form a writing surface.

fauteuil Upholstered armchair with open sides and padded elbows. Popular in Britain and America mid C19.

fielded With a raised central area or "field", usually set off by a frame or surround, e.g. fielded panel.

figure The pattern made by the grain through a wood.

frieze Any long ornamental strip.

gadroon Type of carved edge decoration or moulding, consisting of a series of grooves or "flutes" ending in a curved lip, with a ridge between them.

girandole Shaped wall mirror in carved gilt frame with candle branches.

herringbone banding Decorative edging, in which the veneer is laid down in a series of oblique stripes.

inlay The setting of one material (e.g. wood, metal, tortoiseshell, mother-of-pearl) in or over another. Inlay techniques include **marquetry**.

marquetry The use of **veneer** and often other **inlays** to make decorative patterns.

moulding Decorative shaped band e.g. around a panel.

mount Fitting mounted on or attached to furniture, almost invariably of metal, sometimes **ormolu**.

ogee (ogive) Any S-curve shape. An ogee arch is composed of two meeting S-curves.

ormolu Any mount, sconce or article, that is gilt or at least gold-coloured. "Or moulu" is French for "powdered gold".

ovolo Moulding making an outward curve across a right angle.

oyster veneer Veneer with a concentric grain resembling an open oyster-shell. Achieved by making a slanting cut across the grain of a branch.

pediment The equivalent in classical architecture of a gable: a triangular head or topping. A "broken" pediment has the apex of the triangle removed.

rail A horizontal member, running between the legs or outer uprights of a piece.

rosewood Exotic hardwood, not rose but blackish brown in colour, with an attractive stripe or ripple. Commonly used in veneer from C18. When cut the wood has an attractive rose-like fragrance.

satinwood Exotic close-grained hardwood, used from c1750 in veneer, also for panels and turnery. Yellow to golden.

scroll Any membrane (e.g. paper) that has been rolled up. In practice, the shape meant is usually that of a curling tongue. Chair legs or backs are often carved with a relief scroll curling at their foot or top.

spindle In the shape of a spinner's spindle. Specifically the upright bars of a spindle-back chair.

splat The central upright of a chair back. This may take various decorative shapes (e.g. baluster splat).

squab Detachable or loose cushion for a bench or seat.

stile Old name for an upright. A stile foot is plain and square-cut.

strapwork In furniture, a low-relief ornament resembling a series of thongs, rings and buckles, C16, C17 and revived.

stretcher The rail joining and stabilizing the legs of a chair or table.

Sycamore Hard, even-grained maple, light yellow in colour. Often stained and used for veneering *see* hardwood.

turnery Anything "turned" on a lathe and so cut with a circular form of decoration.

veneer Thin sheet or band of wood laid over another (the **carcase**) as part of a **marquetry** pattern, or simply for its decorative grain, colour and **figure**.

wainscot Quarter-cut oak of any kind, but usually in panels.

Woods used in furniture making

acacia Hardwood used for inlay and bandings end C18. Dull yellow with brown markings.

alder Used in C18 for country style furniture esp. chairs. Orange yellow.

amboyna West Indian wood much used for veneers, marquetry and inlay in C18. Warm light brown with speckled grain.

applewood *See* fruitwood

ash Hardwood used both in the solid (in country furniture) and in veneer (it makes a good burr, and can be stained). White. Closely resembles oak.

beech Workable but not a "superior" hardwood (such as walnut or mahogany). It is particularly common in country furniture, esp. the Windsor chair, since it not only turns but also bends well. From C17 it was widely used in gilt and japanned furniture. Later it was stained, as a substitute for mahogany. Brownish white with speckled grain.

birch Hardwood of no great quality, used for carcase work and in C18 country furniture. Sometimes used as a light-coloured veneer. Pale yellow with fine grain.

bird's eye maple Wood of the sugar maple with a distinctive figure created by aborted buds. Good for veneers. Gold/brown.

boxwood Very close-grained hardwood, esp. good for carving and turning. Not generally used in furniture except for inlay or in pattern veneers taken from roots or branches. Pale yellow.

cedarwood American hardwood (Virginia Cedar) resembling mahogany, not to be confused with "cedar of Lebanon". Used in C18 and C19 mostly for carcase work, esp. for drawers. Reddish-brown.

cherrywood *See* fruitwood

deal Name generally given to sawn wood of fir and pine trees.

ebony Lustrous black exotic hardwood. Ebonized woods (i.e. stained to imitate ebony) are much more common than ebony itself. It was used in veneer in ancient Egyptian and Roman furniture and again in Europe from C17.

elm Hardwood, best known for its use for coffins. Neither attractive nor very workable, but serves well for chair-seats, etc. Makes a burr veneer. Light brown.

fruitwood Generic term for the wood of fruit-bearing trees, typically applewood, cherrywood or pearwood. Fruitwoods are hard, close-grained and even in texture, so good for turning and carving. Not usually attractive, they were ebonized from C17 or, commonly, gilt: picture frames are often of fruitwood.

harewood Either: sycamore or maple dyed grey, used in veneer from C17; or: a variety of satinwood that seasons to grey, used from C19.

kingwood Exotic hardwood, not dissimilar from rosewood, but more purplish. Found usually in veneer.

mahogany Exotic hardwood, which became extremely common in England from the 1720s, so that C18 and C19 are sometimes called the "Age of Mahogany". Most attractive when its rich brown retains some of the pink it has when fresh. Used in the solid and then in veneer as it became scarcer in C19.

maple Hardwood with a distinctive pale colour, with wavy darker lines through it. One of the first North American woods to be used for furniture and exported. Turns and works well, and produces a variety of pattern veneers.

oak Hardwood, yellow when fresh, aging to deep dark brown. There are many types of oak. English oak is the oak of the "Age of Oak" in English furniture (the period up to 1660). In later periods American oak was used, and in this century the lighter-coloured Japanese oak.

padoukwood Exotic hardwood, used from C18 in veneer, turnery and similar high-class work. Reddish.

pearwood *See* fruitwood

pine Softwood used almost exclusively for carcase work until this century. White. Scots pine is wood most commonly known as deal.

purpleheart Exotic hardwood, purplish, used mostly in veneer.

rosewood Exotic hardwood, not rose but blackish brown in colour, with an attractive stripe or ripple. Commonly used in veneer from C18. When cut the wood has a rose-like fragrance.

satinwood Exotic close-grained hardwood, used from c1750 in

Types of grain

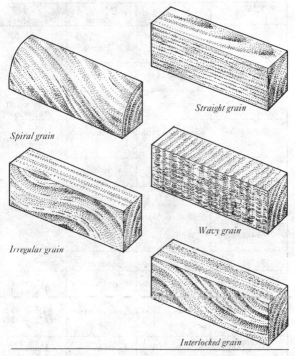

Spiral grain

Straight grain

Irregular grain

Wavy grain

Interlocked grain

veneer, also for panels and turnery. Yellow to golden.

Sycamore Hard, even-grained maple, light yellow in colour. Often stained and used for veneering. *See* harewood.

tulipwood Exotic hardwood, generally pinkish but with varied stripes, used in veneer since C18.

walnut Hardwood, synonymous with a change of fashion following the Restoration of the monarchy in England (1660 onwards), the "Age of Walnut" displacing the "Age of Oak". Commonly used in the solid until C18, and from C17 in veneer, esp. in burr veneer. Rich brown shaded with darker brown or black. American black walnut was used for a wide range of American furniture throughout most of the C19.

yew A close-grained hardwood, tough and pliable. Turns well, so used for chair-legs, etc. Also used in the solid, esp. in C17 and C18, or in veneer (with or without burr). Golden to reddish brown.

Patination

* Patination is the word describing the layers of polish, dirt, grease etc., which build up over the surface of a piece of wood in the course of time.

* It varies considerably on different woods, but the same wood will basically colour to the same extent, except where sunlight affects certain surfaces.

* C18 walnut furniture often had an oil varnish applied as a base to take wax polish. This gives a lovely yellow patina practically impossible to fake.

* Grease and dirt from handling (especially under drawer handles, on chair arms, etc.) gives a darker colour to the areas affected. If this is lacking, be suspicious.

* In the same way, grime will have accumulated in carving and crevices.

* Patination is extremely difficult to fake, but beware of heavily applied wax polishes designed to remove evidence of patination and so conceal conversion or replacement.

Dates	British Monarch	U.K. Period	French Period
1558–1603	Elizabeth I	Elizabethan	Renaissance
1603–1625	James I	Jacobean	
1625–1649	Charles I	Carolean	Louis XIII (1610–1643)
1649–1660	Commonwealth	Cromwellian	Louis XIV (1643–1715)
1660–1685	Charles II	Restoration	
1685–1689	James II	Restoration	
1689–1694	William & Mary	William & Mary	
1694–1702	William III	William III	
1702–1714	Anne	Queen Anne	
1714–1727	George I	Early Georgian	Régence (1715–1723)
1727–1760	George II	Early Georgian	Louis XV (1723–1774)
1760–1811	George III	Late Georgian	Louis XVI (1774–1793) Directoire (1793–1799) Empire (1799–1815)
1812–1820	George III	Regency	Restauration (1815–1830)
1820–1830	George IV	Regency	
1830–1837	William IV	William IV	Louis Philippe (1830–1848)
1837–1901	Victoria	Victorian	2nd Empire (1848–1870) 3rd Republic (1871–1940)
1901–1910	Edward VII	Edwardian	

German Period	U.S. Period	Style	Woods
Renaissance (to c1650)		Gothic	Oak period (to c1670)
	Early Colonial	Baroque (c1620–1700)	
Renaissance/ Baroque (c1650–1700)			Walnut period (c1670–1735)
	William & Mary		
	Dutch Colonial	Rococo (c1695–1760)	
Baroque (c1700–1730)	Queen Anne		
	Chippendale (from 1750)		
Rococo (c1730–1760)			Early mahogany period (c1735–1770)
Neoclassicism (c1760–1800)		Neoclassical (c1755–1805)	Late mahogany period (c1770–1810)
	Early Federal (1790–1810)		
Empire (c1800–1815)	American Directoire (1798–1804)	Empire (c1799–1815)	
	American Empire (1804–1815)		
Biedermeier (c1815–1848)	Later Federal (1810–1830)	Regency (c1812–1830)	
Revivale (c1830–1880)		Eclectic (c1830–1880)	
	Victorian		
Jugendstil (c1880–1920)		Arts & Crafts (1880–1900)	
		Art Nouveau (c1900–1920)	

Drawers

Coming into general use in the early C17, the drawer has become an important factor in dating and authenticating antique furniture. Construction, woods and furnishings (handles, escutcheons etc.) all provide useful clues. However, as with all pointers in the pages that follow, remember that dates are always approximate and that rules invariably have exceptions. Early craftsmen, while following basic trends and fashion, often varied the detail. New ideas took time to travel, even in England, while North America could be 10–30 years behind London.

What to look for:
17th Century drawers
* Early C17 drawers were nailed together, the side runners fitting into deep side grooves.
* Runners could be nailed to side of carcase on inside.
* Bottom runners, usually of oak, appeared c1680.
* Look for signs of wear on runners: they may have been replaced in course of time.
* Check handles. If these have not been tampered with the surrounding wood will be darker, and show slight indentations.
* From mid-C17 dovetails were concealed by mouldings (beading and reeding).
* Linings of white or red pine indicate Continental origin.
* Check for signs of secret wooden spring on underside of many C17 drawers.

18th Century (Georgian) drawers

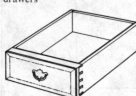

Veneer-fronted drawer, C18

* Drawer linings oak until mid-C18.
* Good quality drawers had oak sides, with top edges rounded.
* Bottom boards made from 2 or 3 pieces of same wood, and grooved to form bottom runners.
* To 1770 grain in bottom boards ran from front to back; after 1770 from side to side, often with central bearer for extra support.
* No C18 drawer exactly fitted space between front and back, a space always being left for ventilation.

19th Century drawers
* Corner mouldings on drawers introduced by Sheraton, so giving date after 1790.
* Victorians made bottom boards from one piece of wood, usually screwed to sides.
* Machine-made dovetails indicate piece was made after 1880s.

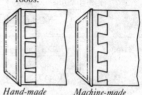

Hand-made   *Machine-made*

Beware
If the dovetailing in all drawers in a piece do not match.
If handles have been moved or changed: drawer may have been reduced in width. Check reverse of front for filled holes. If no corresponding holes on front, veneer almost certainly later than drawer.

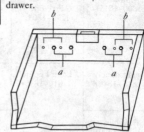

Check inside drawer front for (a) new holes; (b) old, filled-in holes where width reduced

If dovetails at back of drawer show signs of alteration: drawer has probably been reduced in depth.
If wood of carcase is not same age as base and back of drawer: look closely at rest of piece.
If you find one replacement, alteration or restoration: look for others!

Veneers

Veneering has been an essential part of the cabinet-maker's art since the early C18. Basically, a thin sheet of quality wood was applied to the visible surfaces of a piece of furniture whose carcase was of a coarser wood. The intention was both decorative and to mask the construction. Veneers could be cut to display the grain in a way impossible with solid wood.

What to look for

* The earliest veneers were of walnut, followed by the superbly patterned mahogany veneers of the late C18 and early C19.
* Note, however, that walnut returned to favour in the Victorian period.
* Many other woods were also used as veneers, notably satinwood, rosewood and maple.
* Early veneers were always handcut with a *minimum* thickness of about ¹⁄₁₆in (1.5mm) and more usually around ⅛in (3mm). Therefore any veneer uniformly thinner than this has been machine-cut *not earlier* than the early C19.
* If the carcase itself is genuine C18, then any veneer thinner than ¹⁄₁₆ in (1.5mm) was either added considerably later or the piece has been re-veneered. This happened most commonly with early C18 oak furniture, which is often found with a later walnut veneer.
* If a veneered piece has a drawer or drawers, look carefully at the inside drawer front. Part of this should be made of the coarser carcase softwood if the veneer is original.
* If, however, the front is solid oak, then any veneer was almost certainly added later.
* Cross-cut veneers set at 45° indicate a likely date of late C17 or very early C18, as does cross-grain combined with herringbone. Cross-grain banding alone is probably after 1710.
* Feather-banding on drawers should be continuous.

Beware

* Plain veneer panels on an otherwise decorated piece could indicate replacement of the original veneer.
* Look at hinges on doors: if there is very little dirt or grime around them, then the veneer has probably been steamed off to repair the carcase wood beneath, and subsequently replaced.
* Hand-cut veneers show saw marks when viewed from above; a machine-cut veneer appears much smoother.
* C19 machine-cut veneers are wafer thin and almost lacking in "figure".
* Veneers occasionally "bubble"; if this bubble can easily be pressed in with the finger, it is either machine-cut, or the surface has been sanded down, probably to obliterate signs of damage.
* FINAL WARNING: A vast number of pieces have been re-veneered at some time in their lives. This significantly reduces their value, so take the trouble to check.

Marquetry

Marquetry, an extension of veneering, is the art of inlaying elaborate designs in wood, with wood of other colours or graining, or with other materials such as ivory, shell or metals. It originated in Europe and was particularly popular in Holland from end C17.

Correct feather-banding

What to look for

* In England marquetry flourished in the late C18, with intricate detail engraved rather than cut as on the Continent.
* Marquetry on walnut fetches more than marquetry on mahogany; and the latter more than marquetry on oak.
* Particularly desirable is marquetry which includes bone and/or mother-of-pearl. Birds and insects are much more rare as subjects than flowers.

Beware

* Some pieces have marquetry panels added later. If a panel appears very slightly *lower* than the surrounding wood, be suspicious. A genuine original will usually have *raised* ridges of either glue or grain which can be detected by the finger-tips.

Repairs, alterations, restoration, marriages, copies and fakes

With furniture, pieces are all too often not what they seem at first sight. This is not surprising since wood, by its very nature, is subject to wear, tear and time, is easily damaged, yet responds to careful doctoring. It is this "doctoring" which concerns us here, and which can be separated into five main types: Repairs; Alterations and restoration; Marriages; Copies; Fakes.

Repairs

* This heading covers work carried out to restore the effects of normal wear or damage occurring during the useful lifetime of a piece of furniture.
* Few pieces of antique furniture escape the need for some form of repair. Such repairs can often be crude, unskilled and of considerable age. However, they need not affect the value to any great extent.
* Careful repairs by a modern restorer can often produce a piece of furniture that is pleasingly near its original condition. Provided this restoration is pointed out to any potential customer, such repair is quite acceptable.
* Other recognized repairs include the removal of French polish applied later by some Victorian "improver", or the stripping of any coat/coats of paint not on the original.

Alterations and restoration

* Alterations were often made with no dishonest intent, but to conform with changing fashion, personal needs or taste, or simply to fit available space.
* Structural alterations include tallboys split up to make two chests, with a top added to the base piece and feet to the top.
* Such "domestic" alterations to early C18 walnut pieces can be valuable.
* Look for marks of saw cuts on rails, stretchers or backs. However, these marks could also point to a deliberate attempt at deception (see *Fakes* below).
* Some later (C19) "restoration" was certainly designed to "improve" a piece to make it a more saleable item.
* Such improvements could include embellishing the existing legs and feet, carving the original plain wood, replacing tops and doors, re-veneering and adding inlaid or carved panels.
* In mid C19 large Tudor or Elizabethan pieces were frequently cut down to fit the Victorian parlour or dining room. Look for "new" frame members and saw marks on panelling.
* The C19 also saw much other restoration work of this nature, large numbers of such pieces being sold to America. They have now achieved the status of antiques in their own right, but do not have the re-sale value of the originals.

Marriages

* A "marriage" is the union of two separate pieces (e.g. writing bureau and bookcase) to produce a more saleable two-part piece (e.g. bureau-bookcase).
* Many kinds of pieces can be "married off" in this way. There is no objection to this if the two pieces are of the same period and the result is openly sold as a marriage – though this should be reflected in a lower price.
* Always look carefully at two-part pieces for signs of a possible "marriage". Check that carcase wood, veneer, colour, proportions and general "feel" all match top and bottom.
* Different styles of construction for base and top would indicate a marriage. So do old screw holes in the base which do not match up with the top.
* When a top was intended to sit on a base, it was made smaller so that it could fit within a moulding on the base top. And that base top, being hidden, would not have been veneered.
* Accordingly a marriage is probable if the top sets flush on the base, or if the base top is veneered.
* Marriages are usually very evident when viewed from the back, so check that the backboards match on both pieces. If they do not, then take a closer look at the pieces as a whole. The same is true with made-up bottoms and tops.

Copies

* Copies of C18 pieces were frequently made in the C19 and are not easy to detect when skilfully constructed in quality materials, particularly as they will now have "aged" naturally.
* Most, however, lack the form and style of the originals, often displaying a plodding heaviness in construction and execution.
* Old wood was frequently used in such copies, but the evidence of saw marks on old panels etc., should reveal the truth.
* French polish was not in general use until the C19, though sadly the Victorians sometimes applied it to genuine C18 pieces, with a consequent loss in value. It can therefore indicate a possible copy.
* "Reproductions" are (or should be) copies of earlier styles made with no intention to deceive. Those made in the second quarter of the C19 (of Georgian and Regency furniture) are now sought after in their own right.
* Late C19 and modern reproductions are usually "in the style of" rather than exact copies, and are not difficult to distinguish.

Fakes

* Faking is the construction of a piece of furniture so that in all respects it resembles the original piece it fraudulently claims to be.
* Faking demands considerable skill and the right materials. Since these are not always available, check each individual point carefully if there is the slightest doubt as to authenticity.
* Is the wood – carcase and decoration – correct for the piece? Particularly check drawers and backs. The edges of period timbers at the back should be black. Look out for pieces of replaced timber.
* Is the veneer hand-cut? Thin machine-cut veneers are an instant give-away, but are frequently used by the faker because of the expense and scarcity of the genuine hand-cut veneers. Note also that it is difficult to fake herringbone inlay. On fakes it usually lies completely flat, whereas on a genuine piece the effect of time and humidity causes the inlay to lift slightly. This is extremely difficult to simulate.
* Are the handles, escutcheons, locks, screws, hinges and castors right? Do they look as if they have been attached to the piece for the whole of its life?
* C18 brass had a "softer" feel and more subtle colour due to a high copper content. Modern brass cannot be made to duplicate this.
* The faker also finds it difficult to simulate realistic looking patches of discoloration round the heads of screws and nails.
* C18 beading was all done from one piece of wood, hence the grain always runs true. With Victorian and later beading, the beads are glued on.
* Is the "evidence" of wear on stretchers, rails, doors, etc., totally convincing? The faker "distresses" his work to simulate such natural wear, but this is extremely difficult to achieve. If it doesn't feel right, it probably isn't.
* Are the proportions and decoration right for the period? In fakes they are often wrong.
* French polish is sometimes applied and rubbed down to simulate the old finish obtained with the beeswax and turpentine. The result is unconvincing and should be easy to detect.
* Some pieces are not outright fakes, since they were originally genuine pieces that have subsequently been rebuilt to look like other more desirable items. These are known as "pastiches".
* Pastiches retain much of their original carcase, and consequently appear genuine at first sight. Once again, look carefully at decoration, veneer, feet, drawers and fittings. And for replaced timber.
* Dressing tables, kneehole desks, writing tables and commodes are all pieces that have been "made up" in this way. Sets of eight or more chairs can be made up from just five or six originals.
* Large pieces of furniture are frequently "cut down" to make smaller, more saleable items. Examples are tallboys, secretaires, chests-of-drawers and break-front bookcases. The same checks apply.
* Carving is a common subject for the faker. If original, it should always stand "proud" of the piece. Flat or incised carving has almost certainly been added later, and detracts from the value. Beware shallow carvings.

What you should know about:
Beds

Main types of bed

Four poster	Daybed
Tester	Brass bed
Half-tester	Cradle

General pointers

* The four poster, either with a full canopy over it (tester) and rails for bed curtains, or with a canopy over the head only (half-tester), was the commonest form of bed until C19.
* Very few such beds have survived in their original state. From the 1850s onwards, old beds were taken apart and rebuilt because room sizes had changed and people were taller.
* Because owners want to be able to use a bed they have purchased, a skilfully lengthened or widened piece can fetch more than a short and narrow bed in original condition.
* The bed should, however, retain its original members, with any additions compatible.
* A bed made up of different parts should not command premium prices, especially if the decorative elements are ill-matched.
* Early alterations were executed skilfully and have had time to age. From c1850, oak beds were widened, lengthened and reduced in height; look for newer carving to the bedstead and canopy where panels have been added and check that the decoration is right.
* C18 mahogany beds escaped modification until the 1920s, when it was common to cut down or replace the canopy to create a half-tester or torchère. Provided they retain their elegant posts, often fluted or turned, such pieces are in demand.
* Drapery was an integral part of the bed and of bedroom decoration. Beds which retain good drapes are rare and very expensive. When buying a bed without its drapes, remember that replacement is costly.

American beds

* Early American beds, whilst following English and Continental styles, were made larger from the start. Less likely to have been rebuilt, because treasured as family heirlooms, good examples are both rare and valuable.

Cradles

* Any repair or alteration to these should be reflected in a lower price, since many more have survived in original condition than their adult counterparts. Cradle rockers are, however, susceptible to wear; check to see if they have been removed or replaced.
* Good pieces command high prices. Often beautifully carved or painted to reflect a family's social position, they are fashionable and in demand.

Early C19 mahogany cradle

Daybeds

* Early versions reflect contemporary chair styles. Later, under French Empire influence, they became increasingly elaborate with rich upholstery, gilding, paint and exotic motifs.

Brass beds

* All good quality and usable beds are now very saleable, including the once despised brass bed. Original examples are sought after, but there are many "made-up" brass bedsteads on offer which should be viewed with some suspicion if the asking price is high.

Beware

* Whilst skilful alteration is acceptable, this is very different to a "made-up" bed, of which few of the parts are original. Beds which consist of two original front posts only, the rest newly made, are very common and of little antique value. They are, however, still good pieces of furniture and command reasonable prices.

What you should know about:
Bookcases

Main types of bookcases _____

Breakfront	Open
Bureau	Secretaire
Dwarf	Pedestal
Library	Revolving

General pointers

* Freestanding bookcases were introduced in C17 and perfected in C18.
  * Early pieces were large, being intended for libraries in wealthy houses. When buying check height against that of your lower modern ceiling.
* The small (dwarf) bookcase without doors became fashionable in late C18, and Regency and Federal pieces are in demand because of their size and craftsmanship.
* In glass-fronted bookcases, glazing bars should match rest of piece in quality, timber and age.
* Earliest adjustable shelving on quality bookcases was achieved by cutting rabbets in sides of cabinet into which shelves could slide. Then came a toothed "ladder" at each side with removable "rungs" forming shelf rests. By end C18 movable pegs which fitted into holes were in general use. These often of brass or gilt metal.
* Edges to doors and flaps are normally flush on veneered pieces.
* Locks and doorbolts of brass, other bolts and levers of steel.
* Early pediments were curved, rounded and broken; in late C18 fashion changed to triangular shape, often with central ornament.
* Remember C18 love of proportion. In an original piece, if the groove for the first shelf is 6in (15cm) from the bottom of the piece, then the groove for the top shelf should be 6in (15cm) from the top.
* C19 reproduction bookcases usually have less height and were made in Virginia walnut, not mahogany.

Bureau-bookcases/Secretaire bookcases

* The evolution of the bookcase or cabinet standing on a bureau or secretaire base was a natural one from late C17 and early C18.
* Decorative elements such as cornice and finials, pediments and shape of the glazing bars are all keys to assessing date and place of origin from the basic style.
* Mahogany pieces should have good colour and patination, good mouldings, good "fitted" interiors and original feet and brasses.
* A bureau-bookcase should have 3 separate components: bureau base, bookcase and pediment. Veneers should match on all three.
* Bookcase should be slightly smaller than base, with moulding fitted to base not top.
* It is most unlikely that top of base would have been veneered in original.
* The sides of base and bookcase should therefore not be flush or joined.
* Backs of base and bookcase should match for wood, patination and colour.
* If piece *is* flush-sided without moulding between top and base, this could indicate a "cut-down" from a larger library bookcase.
* If handles and escutcheons are out of proportion, the piece could have been made up from a larger piece.
  THE RULE IS: always look closely at all 2– and 3–part pieces!
* On secretaire bookcases an original interior and secret drawers add considerably to value.

Breakfront bookcases

* Many "breakfront bookcases" on the market started life as ordinary C19 breakfront wardrobes. Look for signs of up to 8in (20cm) having been cut off the depth, and check glazing in frames.

Beware _____

* As with many pieces of furniture, bookcases have often been adapted. They may have been reduced in height or had pediments added.
* A pair of dwarf bookcases may have been constructed out of one large original bookcase.
* In a breakfront bookcase always examine the breakfront to ensure that it is not a library bookcase that has been cut down.
* Examine the drawers in a secretaire: many have been replaced. Or a "secret" drawer may have been added.

What you should know about:
Bureaux

Main types of bureaux

Fall front	Bureau cabinet
Cylinder	Bureau on stand
Bureau de dame	Bureau bookcase

General pointers

* Bureaux, first made in the 1680s of oak, were usually in two parts, each with carrying handles, and a moulding to cover the join.
* Early fall fronts are supported on square sectioned bearers with fan-shaped pulls, and sit above a pair of drawers.
* Most had bun feet, but the original feet rarely survive.
* From early C18, bureaux were more commonly made in solid walnut or walnut veneer on Baltic pine, often with fine marquetry or inlay.
* Writing flap bearers were rectangular with brass knobs; interiors are stepped with arched pigeon holes above drawers.
* C18 bureaux often have a single shallow top drawer, or a well reached from the inside and covered by a slide.
* Bracket feet are common from 1710, with an apron from 1720.
* Mahogany was introduced c1720 and became the norm from 1750.
* Two piece construction was briefly revived, but by 1760 all bureaux sides were made in one piece.
* Desk slopes were made steeper; consequently vertical interiors superseded stepped.
* From 1780 on the writing flap has a lip moulding.
* Continental bureaux of C18/C19 are often much more elaborate in shape and decoration than British counterparts. The French tambour fronted cylinder bureau became popular late C18.
* Dutch manufacturers revived C17 marquetry styles in the mid C19. Marquetry was often applied to earlier, unadorned bureaux. As a rule marquetry on walnut is more valuable than on mahogany, both of which fetch more than on oak.
* Bone, mother-of-pearl, bird and insect patterns are all worth looking out for.
* Size is critical to value. Bureaux fetch considerably more if under 38in (96.5cm) in width; 36in (91.5cm) is the ideal size.

* Fall front bureaux are in greater demand than tambour fronted.
* Stepped interiors with a central cupboard, fitted well with cover slide, secret drawers and oak drawer linings all add to the value, as do original handles, escutcheons and feet.
* Above all condition, patination, quality of construction and good proportion are crucial.

Bureau cabinets

* Bureau cabinets are prone to marriage or separation. A bureau intended to bear a cabinet will normally have a steeper fall than one intended to stand alone. This was in order to provide a larger top for the cabinet to stand on.
* The retaining moulding will be on the top of the bureau, not on the foot of the cabinet. Moulding attached to the cabinet will suggest a possible marriage.

Beware

* Bureaux may be reduced in width to try and increase their value. Look for multiple sets of screw holes on the inside of drawer front where handles have been realigned.
* Victorian oak bureaux were commonly veneered later to pass off as Regency. Check that the back panels are of unveneered oak, mahogany, or pine planking. Look at the inside of drawers: original pieces should have a top lip of oak with pine below. Solid oak usually indicates later veneering.
* Unrelated pieces may have been combined to create a cabinet bureau or bureau bookcase. Check that the back panelling, the veneer and the decoration matches on both pieces. The top of the bureau should not be veneered and should have a retaining moulding for the upper part.
* Even if the two parts are unrelated the value is not necessarily reduced, provided the two parts are still contemporaneous, the veneer and decoration are compatible and the overall proportions are harmonious.
* Avoid any bureau with cracks and splits, particularly to the flap and sides; avoid bureaux with replaced flaps.

What you should know about: Cabinets and sideboards

Main types of cabinets

Wall cabinet	Credenza
Cabinet on stand	Chiffonier
Bureau cabinet	Sideboard
Display cabinet	

General pointers
* Made for show, many of these pieces were lavishly decorated with fine veneer and inlay, ornate handles and legs, serpentine and bow fronts and ingenious fittings.
* Nevertheless, early pieces are elegant and harmonious, and much in demand, compared to the over-rich and ungainly products of the mid C19 onwards.
* Size affects demand; early pieces often had generous depth, and buyers now prefer narrower pieces, under 4ft (122cm), which fit better into modern rooms. One cut down from a larger piece should not be mistaken for one in original condition.

Sideboards
* Dining room furniture, popularized by Robert Adam from c1770, with six square tapering legs. Turned legs are either *very* early or, more likely, Victorian.
* Central drawer should be baize-lined with compartments. Side drawers or cupboards should have containers, racks or cellarets intact. Removal reduces value.
* Top should be of one timber; two-or three-piece tops are Victorian.

Cabinets
* Ostentation is the essence; cabinets were designed to be ornamental, and to display the owner's prized pieces.
* Thus, while original condition, elaborate interiors, quality of decoration all add to value, individual taste is also a factor in assessing demand.
* Glazed display cabinets are more popular than solid or blind doors, allowing objects to be permanently on show.
* Early pieces have small rectangular panes and astragal mouldings. By c1750, easily cut crown glass enabled more elaborate shapes, often with finely detailed mahogany glazing bars.
* Cabinets were commonly made from wardrobes in the early C20. Signs are drawers instead of cupboards, low base in proportion to top, modern glass and, often, adjustable shelving on "ladders".

Side cabinets/credenzas
* The term "credenza" usually means an ornate Italianate or French-style piece. Look for good work, particularly on serpentine-fronted pieces with shaped sides. The quality of craftsmanship can be surprisingly poor.
* Regency cabinets are desirable and many Victorian mass-produced chiffonniers have been made to look like earlier pieces by the addition of gilt mounts, brass grilles and pleated silk fronts.
* Damaged tops were sometimes replaced in marble; the value of the resulting piece will depend on the quality and attractiveness of the marble.

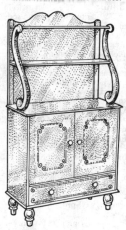

Upright chiffonier, early C19

Beware
* Cutting an early piece down to suit modern size preferences has devalued many fine sideboards. Look for a join on the top undersurface.
* Many items of furniture lend themselves to conversion to cabinets: chests, bookcases, wardrobes have all been modified. If the proportions seem suspect, seek advice before paying a high price.

What you should know about:

Canterburies

* The first canterburies were made c1700, originally as plate-holders to stand by the supper table.
* Sheraton attributed the name to the first piece having supposedly been commissioned by an Archbishop of Canterbury.
* The earliest canterburies are of mahogany but satinwood examples are known.
* The number of divisions varies, though four is common. Tops are square or slightly convex with a drawer below.
* Early pieces are pleasingly simple with decoration generally limited to the legs and corner supports, sometimes with stringing. Rare "colonnaded" examples in which all the supports are carved to resemble pillars are highly desirable.
* Square legs are an indication of an early date; round tapered and turned legs appeared c1810.
* In C19 canterburies were used to hold sheet music, and the Victorians' passion for the piano accounts for the large number of such pieces surviving.
* C19 canterburies became increasingly elaborate with barley-twist supports, fretwork side panels and ingeniously shaped racking.
* Later still, it was common to add a superstructure to the racks, so combining the functions of canterbury and étagère, sometimes with a music stand in the top tier.
* Elegance is the quality most sought after by collectors, and elaborate pieces often do not command such good prices as a simple, well-proportioned piece.
* High prices are paid for rare shapes, crisp deep carving and canterburies decorated with musical motifs e.g. lyre sides. Rosewood pieces often achieve better prices than walnut.

Beware _____

* Canterburies made from a cut down whatnot or étagère will show signs of recent finishing and new members.
* Many canterburies on the market are modern reproductions; they will lack patination and turned members will be too regular.

Commodes

* The Commode is a chest of drawers in the French style, fashionable from mid C18, but never produced in great quantity because their elaborate shapes and decorative detail were always expensive to achieve.
* Prudery caused the Victorians to call any piece of furniture designed to conceal a chamber pot a commode. The bedside type was produced in great quantity and has little antique value, though early examples and the more curious and elaborate pieces are now collectable.
* All chest of drawer commodes are now valuable and the more delicate pieces in good condition fetch high prices.
* Serpentine and bombé shapes are the commonest, but commodes are also found in rectangular, demi-lune and kettle shapes. Rarest of all is the secretaire commode with the tall front disguised as the top drawer, and with a fitted interior.
* Commodes are highly decorative, using finely figured and coloured veneers for inlay and marquetry, with ormolu mounts and heavy brass or gilt metal handles and escutcheons.
* Sheer flamboyance is not, however, a guarantee of value. The decoration must feel integral to the piece, helping to articulate the shape and outlines, not merely applied.
* No rules are absolute in distinguishing between an early piece and a later copy, but the latter tend to be scaled down in size to suit smaller rooms, more elaborately decorated and with thinner marbletops. White Carrara marble was most popular for C18 pieces; coloured marble is commoner in the C19.
* Drawers in C19 pieces are often more finely finished than in C18 pieces – sometimes even veneered or polished.

Beware _____

* The cheap C19 and C20 reproductions are not likely to confuse a knowledgeable buyer. Obvious signs are regular machine cut dovetailing to the drawers, and steam shaped softwood carcases with thin veneers.

What you should know about:
Chairs

Main types of chair	
Armchairs	Hall, corner and
Dining chairs	side chairs
Windsor chairs	Fancy chairs

General pointers

* Copying was so widespread in C19 that care is needed to identify genuine early chairs. In general, look for signs of wear to feet, back and seat.
* Stretcher rails close to ground may indicate that worn feet have been cut down; this need not affect value if seat is at least 18in (46cm) from ground.
* Repairs can reduce value. Look for members with different patination to rest; these may have been replaced.
* Pre C19 corner braces are rectangular blocks let into seat frame from top, creating an open triangle in each corner. Solid corner blocks fixed with screws indicate replacements or that the chair is a copy.

A George II style mahogany "carver" (i.e. with arms) from a set of dining chairs. The "carver" to such a set will always be wider across the seat than the "singles".

* The earlier a set of chairs and the more pieces in it, the greater the value; especially if the set includes a carver or, better still two. The carver seat should be at least 2in (5cm) wider than the others in a set. Use the following ratios to assess the value of sets of average quality compared with the single chair price:
  A Pair: 3 times
  Set of 4: 6/7 times
  Set of 6: 10/12 times
  Set of 8: 15 plus times

Armchairs

* To mid C17 chairs square, with carved oak panel backs.
* Copies, common in C19, have back panel of even thickness because sawn, not split, uniform dark varnish, carved arms, and stretchers same distance off the ground.
* Back panels may be replaced. Look for inconsistency of decoration with rest of piece. Some backs "improved" in C19 with a spurious date or anachronistic heraldic symbols.
* After 1660, easily carved walnut became principal material. Chairs elaborately decorated with fretwork, H or X-shaped stretchers, characteristic "barley twist".
* C19 copies usually have upholstered backs and seats instead of carving. Twists are regular and run in opposite directions, whereas early turning should be uneven in depth, twists all running in same directions.
* Chairs with extant carving are valuable; original carving is square; early oval carving is even rarer and more desirable. Modern carving has a diamond weave.
* The introduction of the cabriole leg in c1710, and the widespread use of mahogany after 1730 resulted in lighter, stronger chairs in a variety of styles. The common denominator is a back splat which fits into a shoe which is separate from the back seat rail. If shoe and rail are one piece of timber, the chair is a C19 copy.
* The perennial wing armchair was introduced early C18, since when design has remained unchanged.
* In an early piece, cabriole legs should form corners of seat frame. Backlegs should continue seat to form back frame; S-curved arms ending in rounded arm rests. All curves should contribute to a graceful, flowing piece.
* Most frequently replaced members are legs and arms. Check carefully for colour and patination match. Original upholstery is very rare, but the earlier the re-upholstery the better.
* Button-back refers to upholstery style popular from c1830. Early pieces are of

"black" Virginia walnut, rosewood or mahogany, with front leg and arm supports of one timber, carved with scroll and foliage. Later versions tend to be less decorative, of inferior materials.

* Deep buttoning should be to back only, and stop at the "waist-line" where the arms join the back.
* Original upholstery will be of worsted damask, cotton and worsted, silk and worsted or heavy velvet; dark plain colour or stripes, floral patterns or imitation tapestry. New upholstery is common and diminishes value.

Dining Chairs
* In last half of C18 (Chippendale, Hepplewhite) chairs became lighter, simpler and cheaper to make in quantity for a growing middle class.
* Early pieces have characteristic silky feel; mahogany was oiled or rubbed smooth, not varnished.

Check that the seat rails are the same, with equal patination, and that the top rail does not overhang the sides.

* Back splats fit into shoe piece separate from seat frame. Integral shoe piece and seat frame indicates post 1830 date.
* C19 copies can be sometimes valuable depending on quality of workmanship, style and materials. Avoid those with skimpy legs.
* Victorians often re-carved side-rails and front legs of early dining chairs with inappropriate relief carving. Unspoiled pieces should have carved legs.
* Hepplewhite shield and lyre

back chairs had frames of beech, overstuffed and never intended to be seen. Later copies have seats of pink birch or solid mahogany.

Side, hall and corner chairs
* These decorative chairs often painted, ebonized, gilded and/or inlaid. Though early chairs are usually delicate, legs often plain.
* C19 copies popular for boudoirs and drawing rooms, increasingly ostentatious and in mahogany rather than earlier beech, birch or satinwood. Many are good, but bulbous, bowed or serpentine legs are less popular than plain.

Fancy chairs
* In America, late C18 early C19 Hepplewhite and Sheraton style chairs were often hand-painted by their owners. Good original pieces are much in demand.

Windsor chairs
* Introduced 1720s as tavern or coffee house chairs, and in continuous production since; good handmade pieces much in demand.
* Clues to date are: cabriole legs 1740–70, hooped back after 1740, wheel splat after 1790, gothic splat and pointed arch back 1760–1800, bulbous turning largely post 1830.
* Avoid machine-cut pieces. Seat should be adzed into saddle shape, centre splat hand carved.
* Due to wear, members often replaced. Look for consistent rich patination on all parts.

Beware
* The practice of "scrambling" is widespread. One or more members are replaced in each chair to make up new ones to increase number in a set. The process is theoretically reversible, but costly, and price should reflect this.
* Be suspicious of any piece that has been upholstered so as to hide the underframe which conveys important information on condition and date.
* Be alert for damage. It can be repaired but affects value. Walnut is particularly prone to splitting and woodworm. Check that additional coverings to a drop-in seat has not forced frames apart and damaged leg/seat rail junctions.

What you should know about:
Chests

Main types of chest

Coffer	Military chest
Mule chest	Chest on chest
Chest of drawers	Chest on stand
Tallboy	

General pointers

* Coffers with hinged lids were in use from C13 to early C18 and much copied in C19.
* The Mule chest, with drawer beneath coffer, introduced end C16. First chests fitted entirely with drawers date from about the mid C17.
* Flat fronted chests of walnut made in early C18 and revived by Hepplewhite. Curved and serpentine shapes dominate mid C18.
* C19 chests mass produced in large quantities, often poor in quality and bulky.
* Pieces in original condition, of good colour and patination, with original feet, fittings and high quality decoration, fetch best prices.

Coffers

* Pre-Jacobean coffers are rare; more have survived from C17, but C19 copies are commonest.
* Genuine coffers will be made of split or quarter-sawn timbers with rounded edges; will never show saw marks, and any splintering along the grain will have been worn smooth with age.
* Lids should be bowed or curved with shrinkage between the planks. Expect worn feet, panels loose from shrinkage and good patination inside lid from handling.
* Coffers made up from antique panels in the C19 can be attractive if the panelling looks harmonious and not obviously cut down, but will never be as desirable as genuine pieces in good condition with original hinges, lock, candlebox, reasonably tall feet and fine decoration.

Mule Chest

* C17 chests with one or two drawers below a hinged lid are rare and valuable if found in good and original condition.

Chest of drawers

* Drawers are particularly diagnostic in recognizing the best pieces. Up to c1660 drawers ran on side bearers,

afterwards on bottom runners. Look for wear to drawers and bearers consistent with age.
* C18 drawers never run the full depth of the chest and should be oak-lined.
* Drawers without locks will be C19 or later. Check also for blackening of the grain of drawer timber, characteristic of Victorian oak.
* A top flight of three drawers indicates the piece was originally the top half of a tallboy. Check also for a new top with edge mouldings out of character with the rest, or a deep cornice.
* Walnut pieces and serpentine shapes, including commodes, are more likely to be original since they were expensive to mass produce.
* Chests of drawers from the end of C17 and through C18 are generally less heavy in construction, with lighter drawer linings and finer dovetailing.
* C19 saw a gradual increase in size and decrease in quality in the attempt to satisfy growing demand. Pine, mahogany, walnut and rosewood were among the woods used.
* Original feet and handles add value. Bun feet were common until the late C17, thereafter brackets. Drop handles were used up to c1700, ring handles until end C18 when fine and small turned wood knobs became fashionable.

Beware

* Re-carving, particularly of early unadorned coffers, in the C19, distinguished by sharp edges to the grooves.
* Georgian chests re-veneered and inlaid in the C19 with thin lifeless veneer and end grain visible in the inlay panels.
* Later oak chests veneered to imitate Regency styles. The inside front drawer panel should not be of solid oak in a genuine piece.
* The marriage of unrelated pieces to create a tallboy or chest-on-stand. Check that the dovetailing of the drawers, the back panels, veneers and decoration match satisfactorily on both pieces.
* As a general rule, avoid "improvements" but accept competent restoration.

What you should know about: Cupboards

Main types of cupboard

Court cupboard	Armoire
Corner cupboard	Dresser
Clothes press	Step-back
Kas	cupboard
Wardrobe	

General pointers

* Court cupboards date from C16; others from the C18; wardrobes are Victorian or later.
* Cupboards were functional and more liable to wear and damage than other furniture, consequently most pieces have been repaired or modified.
* Original untouched pieces in good condition are rare and valuable, particularly those of fruitwood.
* As the C18 progressed, the use of glass in the manufacture of cabinet furniture became more common, with glazed doors replacing the blind-door type. This happened both with new furniture and with older pieces which were thus "improved".

Court cupboards

* Even skilful repair affects value substantially. All timber should have the same colour and patination. Plain planks at the back should be fixed to the frame with clout nails and show signs of shrinking. The bottom, often replaced, should be worn smooth and a similar colour to the back.
* A two-tier cupboard may have been cut down from one of three tiers. Check that the top timber is of the same age as the rest and shows no signs of dowel holes.
* *Vice versa*, a third tier may have been added or panels replaced. Look for differences in timber colour and hardness and decorative inconsistencies.
* Victorian copies lack the patination, hardness and wear characteristic of age. C19 recarving on an earlier piece will feel raw or inappropriately crisp.

Corner cupboards

* Cupboards with glazed fronts are more in demand than oak, walnut or mahogany fronted, but are rarer and more expensive. Bow fronted pieces fetch more than the commoner flat fronted.
* Few early walnut pieces were glazed. Unless the glazing is Vauxhall mirror glass, suspect that the original front has been replaced.
* Genuine early pieces should have serpentine or elegantly curving shelves. Those fitted with two or three small drawers are especially desirable.
* Backs are often replaced; all pre-Victorian cupboards were backed in unfinished wood and painted. Look for signs of original paint.
* Double height cupboards are often broken up to create two hanging cupboards. The underside of a genuine hanging cupboard should be polished and not show signs of recent finishing.
* *Vice versa* marriages to create a standing cupboard can be detected if the back planks do not match or the timbers differ in colour and style.

Clothes presses

* Typically a low chest with a cupboard above containing shelves, trays on runners or trays and a hanging space.
* Many fine Regency presses were gutted to make wardrobes; a mid C19 invention. Best prices are paid for those which still retain good quality oak fittings.

Dressers

* Country furniture of oak, ash or elm until mid C19 when most were made in pine. Early pieces with a decorative canopy or frieze and turned legs, or late C19 Arts and Crafts designs are most sought after.
* Dressers suffered domestic wear and tear and only a tiny number of those on the market have not been repaired (often with sawn timber), wire brushed, and polished to look old. Check that all timbers have consistent colour, patination and hardness.
* American step-back cupboards, being usually two-part pieces, are subject to marriage. As always check to see that timber and construction match up in both parts.

Beware

* Look at all cupboards with great care. Repair, modification and even marriages may be acceptable but should be declared and reflected in a lower price.

What you should know about:
Desks

Main types of desk

Davenport	Carlton House
Pedestal	Roll-top
Kneehole	Partners'

General pointers

* Kneehole desks are the earliest and date from as early as c1710. The pedestal desk was not made until c1765 and the design is similar. The Carlton House desk was first published between 1791-4, whilst Davenports were a late C18 early C19 development.

* Good craftsman-made pieces all share one basic quality: they are rock solid. Lack of this quality is a reliable indicator of a marriage or of second rate materials and workmanship.

* Carcase material is often a clue to date and quality. Good period desks are of close-grained and heavy woods; look for mahogany, red or white Baltic pine and baywood. Victorian desks are often of coarse-grained American oak, not intended to be veneered. Cheap mass produced desks are of softwood, such as pine, and the veneer will often part from the carcase in course of time.

Kneehole

* Kneehole desks were originally developed as furniture for a gentleman's bed or dressing room and provided both a writing surface and dressing table combined.

* The usual arrangement is three drawers across the top, and three down each pedestal. Between the pedestals there was a recessed cupboard, said to be used for storing boots and shoes.

* Because of their small size and elegant proportions, kneehole desks are in great demand. This has led to a great number of fakes and conversions.

* Most pieces had six bracket feet, but some have four only, one at each corner. This latter type is easiest to fake by converting a chest of drawers. Always check the inner sides of the pedestals for veneers that do not match the rest of the piece. Also check inside the carcase around the drawer opening for lack of wear to the kneehole side.

* Also check the frieze between the pedestals for sawmarks which would indicate recent manufacture.

* It is not usual to have a brushing slide in a kneehole desk. This too could point to a conversion.

* A kneehole desk with drawers on one side only is almost certainly a converted Victorian washstand.

Davenport

* Not to be confused with an American type of sofa, these small desks derive from a design first ordered by Captain Davenport in late 1790s.

* Popular throughout C19 and still highly sought after; especially well-carved Victorian walnut, though others prefer more severe Regency.

* Qualities which add substantially to the value of a Davenport are fine veneering in figured walnut, bird's eye amboyna, tulip wood, kingwood, rosewood or specialist veneer: crisp deep carving to the brackets, brass stringing to the writing surface and ingenious fittings such as a rising top and concealed drawers.

* Mass produced versions in bleached oak, elm, Virginia walnut or light mahogany are considerably less valuable.

* Careful examination is vital since marriages are commonplace. Check veneer match and colour between desk top and base, backs, side and front.

* Look for evidence of replaced desk supports, rising top and drawer knobs. In particular, a plain writing top may have been replaced with a piano top to increase value.

Pedestal

* Made from c1765 onwards. Earliest are larger and more ornate, with all-over dark veneer on mahogany, baywood or red pine carcase. Later ones have inferior timber carcase, or veneered oak.

* Built in three pieces, therefore susceptible to marriage of unrelated parts; check veneer colour and consistency; marriage often results in lack of solidity.

* Tops often replaced with solid wood. Originals should have stud-fixed leather panel (three panels on large desks) in a

* frame of cross-cut veneer with overhanging lip moulding.
* Tooled leather panels are late C19/C20. Original tops in good condition are desirable but a fine replacement is better than a bad old one.
* When the fashion was for smaller desks, early ones were cut down: length reduction will show in handle repositioning in central drawer; to detect depth reduction, feel for a cut in the desk top under the lip moulding.
* Damaged kneehole desks were adapted to pedestals. Look for new timber and veneer on the inner face of the pedestal.
* Detect mass produced fake Regency by thin veneer on wrong carcase wood.

Carlton House
* First made late C18 for Prince of Wales' house in Carlton House Terrace, of table base and U-shaped superstructure of drawers and pigeon holes.
* No carving. All embellishment is in the veneer, inlay and mounts, though some later designs have turned legs.

* Highly decorated C18 and C19 pieces are very valuable, Edwardian reproductions much less so. These later pieces often have clumsily painted decoration instead of inlay, substitute birch veneer for satinwood and bird's eye maple for speckled amboyna.
* Most pieces measure over 60 in (153 cm) in width. Rare smaller pieces, under 48 in (122 cm), usually command a premium.
* Some late C19 and Edwardian pieces have a central third tier. Sometimes this is removed to pass the piece off as earlier.
* Be wary of a newly veneered top. Even if the veneer seems authentic, always check the carcase wood. Later C19 reproductions with pine drawers and light coloured, soft carcase wood are sometimes reveneered to pass as period pieces.

Beware
* There are far more reproductions, improved, married and faked pieces on the market than genuine period pieces. Seek expert help before paying high prices.

What you should know about:
Dumb waiters

* Defined by Sheraton (*Cabinet Dictionary* 1803) as "a useful piece of furniture, to serve in some respects the place of a waiter, whence it is so named!"
* Dumb waiters were produced in the 1720s but not in great quantity until the 1750s.
* The earliest dumb waiters are generally of three tiers, though two tier examples are occasionally found.
* Early examples are usually made from mahogany. Examples in a mixture of mahogany and satinwood can command a premium.
* Chippendale period dumb waiters often have finely carved supports decorated with fluting, foliage, acanthus leaves and broken scrolls.
* Styles changed with Robert Adam's neo-classical designs. Pillars and supports became plainer towards the end of the C18 with turned collars at top and bottom.
* Dumb waiters with brass supports and pierced rims to the trays were introduced in late C18 and became popular in

C19. Some were also made of rosewood.
* A matching pair of dumb waiters is worth considerably more than singles.
* Pieces with three or four supports around the tray circumference are considered more desirable than those with a central column.
* Drop leaves, ormolu mounts and well proportioned legs all enhance the value.

Beware
* Dumb waiters are relatively easy to adapt to a more desirable piece. Marriages are common so check for differences in turning between the different column sections.
* Two-tier examples should be examined closely to establish that they have not been cut down from a three tier piece or made up from unrelated parts. Check for inconsistent turning, and judge whether the proportions look right.
* Pieces which feel light, lack patina and have shallow carving are probably C19 or later copies.

What you should know about:
Early Oak Furniture

Main types
Armchairs	Cupboards
Chests	Tables
Stools	Dressers

* Oak was the principal material for all furniture up to c1670 and well into the C19 for country furniture.
* Early oak has character and although originally a golden honey colour, it will have aged to a warm chestnut to black colour, with a rich patination from centuries of polish and handling. Stripping and refurbishing destroys colour and sheen, and substantially devalues a piece.
* Wear and damage consistent with use is inevitable, but avoid pieces so damaged as to require repair, which reduces value.
* Avoid pieces which have been "embellished" at a later date. Victorian carving will be in relief with sharp edges. Original carving stands proud and will be worn smooth. Later veneering and inlay is thin, machine-cut, often distinguished by insensitive treatment of grain or anachronistic patterns.
* Rarity is not, of itself, a guarantee of value. Best prices are paid for exceptional condition, even if the piece is of relatively common type.
* Before buying a heavily restored period piece or a C19 copy compare with the costs of a new piece made today in seasoned oak by a good maker. Ask yourself whether the premium to be paid for patina and antiquity is always worthwhile, bearing in mind the use to which the piece is to be put.

Tables
* Oak Tables can be dated with some accuracy by their legs and stretchers. The earliest are simple and square; lathe turning was mastered c1640 and more decorative legs with twists, bobbins and balusters were introduced. C18 turning is more restrained and architectural in style. Later oak furniture often has heavy bulbous mouldings or over elaborate imitations of earlier styles, especially barley-sugar twist.
* Many early oak tables are small and therefore popular since they fit modern room sizes. Avoid, though, tables reduced in size which will lack patination to the cut edges.

Chests
* Period chests in solid, well-worn oak with good decoration, are highly desirable.
* Some were made up in the C16 and C17 from timber from panelled rooms or churches, and though attractive should not command as high a price as rarer pieces made from original timbers.
* Chests with drawers and original decoration fetch the best prices, with linenfold panelling next. Plain board chests should be comparatively inexpensive.
* Early oak chests of drawers usually have four flights of drawers (the uppermost being shallow), drawers on bottom runners, and plain block or bun feet. Decoration is of fielded or coffered panels, with mouldings to disguise joints.
* Check mouldings carefully for brass pins – usually a sign that a piece is C19 or that mouldings have been added at a late date.

Dressers
* The best dressers are C17 and C18, made for the parlour and elegantly proportioned. By C19 dressers tended to be relegated to the kitchen, and were constructed of pine. However, the occasional fine later oak piece may still be found in country areas made up of surplus architectural panelling from carpenters' workshops.

Beware
* The fashion for stripping painted furniture has ruined some fine pieces. Always seek expert advice. Early painted pieces are more valuable in original condition.
* Not all C19 furniture is of equal value. Mass producers used poorly-seasoned oak which has split and looks old to an inexperienced eye. Check for characteristic black lines in the grain, saw marks on hidden edges, thin timbers and machine carving. Pieces with these flaws are much less valuable than furniture of the same period displaying good materials and craftsmanship.

What you should know about:
Mirrors

Main types of mirror

Looking glass	Pier glass
Mirror overmantel	Cheval
Toilet mirror	mirror

General pointers

* Until 1773 looking glass was blown from cylinders of glass, which accordingly limited the size. Thus early mirrors are either small, or made of 2 or 3 pieces covered by astragal bars at the join. After 1773 large single piece mirrors became possible.
* Old glass has a different reflective quality from modern. The image is dark rather than luminous, and the glass viewed at an angle appears grey in tone, compared to the greenish hue of modern glass.
* Early glass is thinner at the top of the frame than at the bottom, and thinner overall than modern mirror plate. Check the thickness by placing a pencil on the glass and judging the distance between the point and its image.
* Until the C19, frames were generally of wood covered with gilt gesso or carved giltwood.
* C19 frames tended to be of stucco built up on a wire frame. Some are excellent but worth considerably less than wooden frames, and even less if the stucco is cracked with age.
* Test for stucco with a needle on the reverse of the frame. It will penetrate wood but not stucco.
* Best prices are paid for mirrors with finely detailed, but not over-elaborate, frames and unusual shapes. Leaves, shells, swags, fruit, scrolls and flames are popular motifs.
* Candle arms on pier glasses and sconces on cheval mirrors add considerably to their value.
* Regency convex mirrors attract very good prices, and toilet mirrors in unusual shapes, or with fitted interiors to the drawers, always find a ready market.

Beware

* Be suspicious of any mirror in perfect condition. All old mirrors will have deteriorated and have non-reflective spots. Resilvering reduces the value, particularly that of toilet and cheval mirrors. Mirror glass can be replaced but the original glass should be carefully stored.

Stools

Main types of stool

Joint stool	Music stool
Box stool	Tender stool
Upholstered stool	X-frame stool

General pointers

* Apart from benches, stools were the main form of seating until chairs took over from the late C17 onwards. Joint stools were however, made well into the C18 and mass produced during the Victorian "Jacobean revival" period.
* The joint, or "joyned" stool is the commonest form, so called because of its simple mortise-and-tenon joint construction
* Church or box stools have solid sides with a V slot or trefoil shape to form "legs" and a hinged seat covering a box.
* In both cases the earlier the piece and the better its condition and colour the greater the value. Most are of oak, and yew wood examples are highly desirable.
* Signs of an early piece are coarse cut timbers, curving seat of split, not sawn, timber at least 1in (2.5cm) thick, good overhang, wear to stretchers, legs and feet, and all-over polish and patination.
* Finely turned legs and a decorated frieze add to the value. Ensure that the legs have not been replaced with staircase balusters in an attempt to enhance value.
* C18 stools are of walnut first, then mahogany and follow contemporary chair styles, often having stretchers and upholstery and, from the mid C18 drop in seats. The exception is the X-framed stool, often with finely carved feet and terminals.

Beware

* Tops and legs are often replaced. Be suspicious of absence of: 1. shininess due to wear; 2. damage; and 3. shrinkage. Look for regular shaped dowels from tops of legs through the seat.
* Victorian joint stools are very common. Look for thin flat seat timber of even thickness and regular shallow carving to the seat edge and frieze.
* Hessian under an upholstered seat indicates a post 1840 date or may conceal alterations on an earlier piece.

What you should know about:
Tables

Main types of table

Breakfast	Library	Side
Card	Loo	Serving
Centre	Lowboy	Sofa
Console	Occasional	Sutherland
Dining	Pedestal	Tea
Display	Pembroke	Supper
Drum	Pier	Tilt-top
Dropleaf	Pillar	Tripod
Games	and claw	Work
Gateleg	Refectory	Writing

General pointers

* The oak refectory table was the only type until gateleg tables and side tables appeared in the early C17. From the turn of the C18 tables were increasingly designed to serve a specific purpose.

Refectory table

* Original pieces are one or two planks wide, never three; from c1660 often cleat framed with mitred corners; richly carved bulbous legs.
* None has survived without repair, and value depends on the extent of the restoration: replacement of stretchers or feet is less serious if done well than loss of legs, bearers or top. An early replacement which has had time to mellow is better than recent work.
* Reproductions all have sawn tops, not split, and regular machine-made dowels. Legs have exaggerated mouldings and large melon-shaped bulbs.
* Good reproductions are collectable in their own right if skilfully made, as distinct from made-up pieces, often using floorboards for tops. These lack patination and will have holes where previously nailed to joists.

Side table

* Early C17 versions are of oak, but sometimes of fruitwood, plane or cypress. Later of solid walnut or walnut veneer on oak. Period piece in pine indicates Dutch origin.
* Top overhangs on front and side with simple lip moulding; none to back edge.
* Legs twist-turned, often with serpentine stretchers.
* Legs can be in darker wood than top; not to be confused with replaced legs which will show as a break in the grain at the join.

* Old pieces should be well patinated on underside of top. In walnut, patination here but not on top indicates planing to remove wormholes. No patination indicates a Victorian copy.

Gate leg table

* Derived from side table with addition of semi-circular flaps on gate-legs.
* Very early versions have square legs. Turning comes in 1640–1660.
* Walnut and fruitwood are scarcer than oak and command higher prices.
* Better prices for early barley twist, for double action gatelegs, and for larger tables to seat 8 to 10.
* Flaps are frequently replaced; look for difference in colour and patination. Originals should be at least 1in (2.5cm) thick, of a single piece of timber, uneven in thickness due to hand cutting.
* Copies will be of thinner timber with uniformly regular turning.

Lowboy

* Used as dressing tables to stand before a mirror. Rarely copied, but check for drawers from another piece of furniture cut to fit. Best prices for cabriole legs so check they have not been replaced to enhance value; look for break in grain at join.
* A period piece with only one drawer, instead of three, may be a sidetable with added frieze.

Drop-leaf table

* Came in with the widespread use of mahogany c1750. Some were made earlier of walnut which proved problematical for large tables, but if found in good condition is very valuable.
* Circular tables were superseded by square c1740 and are now more valuable. A rectangular leaf cut to the more desirable oval will lack patination on the underside.
* The underframe should be of oak or red pine, the top of heavy mahogany at least 1in (2.5cm) thick. Lighter mahogany may indicate a Victorian copy.
* Gates and flaps are prone to damage at the hinge; this can be repaired but weakens the table.

Card table

* Commonest C18 form has fold-over top supported on hinged back leg. Better is the version in which both legs hinge to open at 45 degrees from the frame. Best is the late C18 concertina action, which folds back into the wider frame.
* Last version before card tables were supplanted by compartmented games and loo tables had a swivel top on a central column, often decorated with Boulle marquetry.
* Later inlay will show as more highly polished than rest of piece when viewed obliquely against the light.
* Original carving should stand proud of the curve of the cabriole legs, not within the outline.
* Matching pairs are very valuable, hence always check that both are original by looking for patination on the underframe.

Rosewood work table, early C19

Occasional table

* These tables, with a tray top and tripod base, are valuable in original condition but faked, restored, cannibalized and reproduction versions far outnumber fine period pieces in shops or at auction.
* Commonly a period drinks tray is married to a base from a fire-screen; the tray underside will show inappropriate-distressing and breaks in the column grain indicate the shaft is from another piece, given a collar for extra height.
* Lightweight mahogany or reddish mahogany plus shallow carving indicate a C19 copy.
* Reproductions lack patination to the tray underside and the legs undersides often show saw marks.

Dining table

* Large, multi-pedestal tables with free-standing D-ends were common in C18 and C19, but broken up when unfashionable in C20. Many pieces on the market are made up.
* Look particularly for original square legs; later turned legs are less valuable.
* Any piece which has disguised screwholes, new fixings or unmatching timbers is unlikely to be in original condition. So make further checks.

Tilt-top table

* Usually rectangular with rounded corners. Oval and circular are rarer. Sometimes an oval top is added to a period base. Overall proportions will not look right.
* Tops were intricately inlaid from c1830. Some earlier unadorned tops have later inlay; grain running all in one direction provides a clue.

Pembroke table

* Early square-legged better than later turned and reeded.
* Rounded flaps more desirable than square; satinwood and marquetry increase value.

Sofa table

* Rosewood especially desirable, so are lyre end supports or those carved with Egyptian heads.
* Some are marriages of a period top to a cheval mirror stand; look for supports set too close, a turned stretcher with central square block, disguised screwholes.
* Drawers should be shallow but long drawers better than those later cut down.

Beware

* Commonest form of "improvement" is cutting a round or oval top from a square table. Always check that underside patination is continuous. There should be 2in (5cm) minimum overhang between legs and outer edge.
* Filled holes, signs of previous fixings, un-oxidized areas where timbers removed, all indicate repair or modification which should be treated with caution.

What you should know about:
Walnut Furniture

* Walnut imported from France and Spain became the principal material for furniture from c1670 until c1730 when France prohibited further walnut exports.
* The period coincides with the Restoration of Charles II in England; the plain Puritan styles of the previous 20 years were superseded as the exiled aristocracy returned to England with a taste for continental flamboyance.
* Walnut lent itself to the new taste because of its rich golden brown colour, with darker brown figuring, and its suitability for veneer work.
* Walnut is easily carved. Characteristically, early walnut furniture has twist turned legs and stretchers and detailed mouldings.
* English walnut furniture which makes subtle use of the figuring and grain for embellishment, is more desirable than continental which can be over-decorated.
* English furniture is generally stronger. Joints were mortised and tenon pegged and dowelled. Continental furniture is often simply pegged and legs have additional stretchers to provide stability.
* The carcase on English veneered furniture is close-grained yellow Baltic pine; Continental makers used coarser grained pine and softwood.
* All walnut pieces are desirable and fetch good prices if in prime unrestored condition. Particularly valuable are small chests and bureaux, secretaires, bureau bookcases, and chests on stands.
* To detect restoration on walnut chairs, look for new seat frames, joints where new legs have been attached to back seat rail, added arms and later carving which does not stand proud of the surrounding wood.

Beware _____
* Walnut is especially prone to woodworm and, being soft, easily splits. Avoid damaged pieces.
* Do not confuse early walnut with "black" or Virginia walnut. Some later C17/early C18 pieces were made in the latter, but it was mostly used in quantity from 1830.

Wine Coolers

* Wine coolers, generally of mahogany, were popular as objects of furniture from c1730 until the late C19.
* Cisterns have open tops, whilst cellarets are fitted with a locking lid.
* There are two main types: those with integral feet or a pedestal which were made to stand on a sideboard; and those with legs or a separate stand, made to stand on the floor.
* Coolers of coopered construction are commoner than jointed forms. Round, oval hexagonal and octagonal shapes are all found in coopered form, with an upper and a lower brass ring.
* A cooler made to stand on a pedestal usually has the lowest brass band close to the base. The band is further up the body on a cooler made to fit into a stand. Discrepancies may indicate a marriage between cooler and stand.
* The earliest coolers have plain square or turned tapering legs. After 1800 large carved paw feet are commoner, and the sarcophagus shape then became popular.
* From c1820 coolers were made in highly figured veneers, with inlaid lines and crossbanding.
* All period wine coolers are much in demand. Octagonal shapes on a stand command a slightly higher price than hexagonal, which in turn commands more than oval or round.
* All mounts must be original and in good condition. Lion mask ring handles attract a slight premium.
* Check that casters on stands are original; small concealed casters should have a wheel made of leather discs. Cup casters should have a brass wheel. Lion's paw casters and cast, gilt decorative casters are C19 or modern.

Beware _____
* Avoid pieces in poor condition or with replaced mounts, though the absence of the old lead lining is less serious.
* For best prices the cooler and stand should have been made for each other. Even for second best, the two pieces should be contemporary and represent a good marriage.

"Bullet wood" armchair with carved cresting and back panel. Early C17.

Jacobean oak straight-back side chair. Early C17.

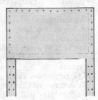

Cromwellian oak dining chair with padded open back. Mid C17.

Derbyshire chair, oak, with carved back. Mid C17.

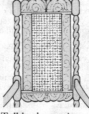

Tall-back carved walnut armchair, Charles II, c1680.

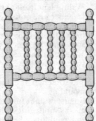

Fruitwood joined chair with ball turning. Mid C17.

Hoop-back Queen Anne walnut chair with urn-shape splat. Early C18.

Chippendale armchair with flattened top back rail. c1775.

Chippendale style side chair with carved splat. c1760.

Ladder-back armchair with horizontal pierced splats. c1760.

Chippendale "Chinese" chair with lattice work and carved cresting. c1760.

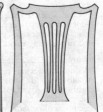

Plain mahogany chair, Chippendale style but without expensive carving. c1760–1770.

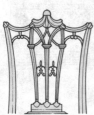

"Gothic"
Chippendale with
waved and carved top
rail and interleaved
splats. Late C18.

**"Prince of Wales'
Feathers"** motif on a
Hepplewhite shield-
back chair. Late C18.

Shield-back with
plain splats, in
Hepplewhite style.
Late C18.

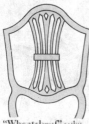

"Wheatsheaf" splat
on modified shield-
back chair. Late C18.

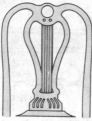

Lyre-back dining
chair with arched top
rail. Hepplewhite.
Late C18.

Elm ladder-back
country chair. Late
C18.

Wheelback dining
chair with radiating
leaf splats. Late C18.

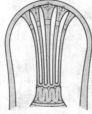

Hoop-back dining
chair, with pierced
wheatsheaf splat.
Late C18.

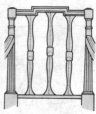

Sheraton armchair
with triple stick back
and decorated top
rail. c1790.

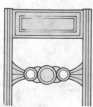

Square-framed
mahogany Sheraton
dining chair. Late
C18.

Sheraton mahogany
chair with arched top
rail and Prince of
Wales' Feathers splat.
Late C18.

Plain spindle-back
country chair with
braces. Early C19.

Hoop-back Windsor armchair with pierced splat. Late C18-mid C19.

Sheraton beechwood armchair with fretted splat and rails with painted panels. Early C19.

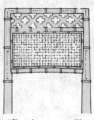

"Bamboo turned" (to imitate bamboo) beechwood chair with cane back. Early C19.

Gothic square-backed armchair. Early C19.

Rail-back Regency dining chair. Early C19.

William IV rosewood dining chair with heavily carved and arched top rail. c1830.

Painted papier-mâché side chair with spoon-shape splat. Early Victorian.

Spoon-back open armchair with carved walnut frame. Mid C19.

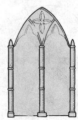

"Gothic" style hall chair with imitation bamboo supports. Mid C19

Balloon-back Victorian dining chair with scroll carved splats. C19.

Victorian mahogany dining chair. c1880.

Straight-back padded Victorian chair with carved top and bottom rails. Late C19.

Continental chair backs

Walnut side chair with padded back. Italian C17.

Carved walnut chair with barleytwist supports. Flemish. Late C17.

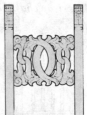

Walnut chair with carved panel of entwined leaves. Tuscan. Late C16.

Painted and gilt side chair with inverted vase-shaped splat. Italian. Mid C18.

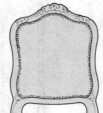

Louis XV giltwood chauffeuse with padded back and carved crest rail. French. Mid C18.

Chaise à canne, painted and gilt, with carved back. Italian. Mid C18.

Moulded-back Louis XVI chaise à L'anglaise. French. c1780.

Georges Jacob side chair with openwork back. French. c1780.

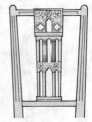

Square-framed beechwood dining chair with pierced splat. Dutch. Late C18.

Biedermeier inlaid maple chair with concave crest-rail and reeded crossbar. German. c1820.

Savonarola walnut armchair, double "X" shape. Italian. Mid C19.

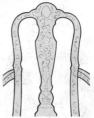

Marquetry dining chair with vase-shaped splat. Dutch. Late C19.

American chair backs

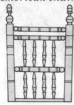

Pilgrim Brewster chair, c1700. New England. Note heavy back posts and turned finials and spindles.

Pilgrim slat-back armchair, c1685–1720. New England. Firm shapings and turnings are typical.

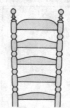

Pilgrim slat-back side chair, c1680–1720. New England. Often painted with delicate decoration.

Wavy slat-backed side chair, c1700–1730. Delaware. Shows strong vertical emphasis of William and Mary period.

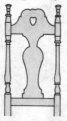

Fiddleback side chair, c1720. New England. With acorn finials and splat resembling outline shape of fiddle.

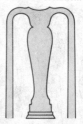

Queen Anne period walnut side chair, c1740–1760. New England. The better examples had finely shaped splats as here.

Queen Anne period balloon-back side chair, c1740–1760. Philadelphia. Note carving on crest rail and splat.

Banister-back side chair, c1750–1780. Massachusetts. Shows yoke-shaped crest rail in Queen Anne style.

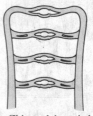

Chippendale period ladder-back chair, c1750–1780. Philadelphia. Many examples of this pattern survive.

Chippendale period carved mahogany corner chair, c1760–1780. New York.

Chippendale period side chair, 1760–1780. Philadelphia. Stiles are stop-fluted and splat carved.

Chippendale period armchair, c1760–1780. Philadelphia. Strap-work splat is typical.

Comb- or high-back Windsor armchair, c1760–1800. Connecticut.

Bow-back Windsor side chair, c1760–1800. Rhode Island. Brace-back examples, as here, are sought after.

New England side chair, c1775–1800. Boston. Richly coloured leather back with brass studs.

Federal shield-back mahogany side chair, c1790–1810. Massachusetts. Shield sharply cornered and splats with tassel carvings.

Federal square back mahogany side chair, c1790–1810. New York. Based on a Sheraton design.

Federal oval-back maple side chair, c1790–1800. Masschusetts. With painted decoration. Based on a Hepplewhite design.

Federal painted and stencilled armchair, c1800–1820. New York.

Federal square-back mahogany dining chair, c1800–1810. New York. Often with gilt decoration.

Hitchcock painted and fancy chair, c1830–1840. Connecticut. With stencilled decoration.

Rococo revival balloon-back side chair, c1865–1875. Well-distributed.

Renaissance revival-style armchair, c1880–1890. Michigan. With incised designs.

Lattice-back side chair, c1880–1890. Well-distributed. Shows Eastlake influence.

Legs and Feet

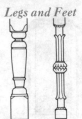

Above left: Turned
Tudor Gothic, C16
Above right: Carved
Tudor Gothic, C16

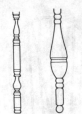

Above left: Turned
oak, end C16
Above right: Jacobean
baluster, early C17

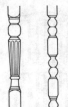

Above left: Fluted,
early C17
Above right: Bobbin
turning, mid C17

Above left: Walnut part
twist, mid C17
Above right: Walnut
scroll, c1675

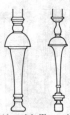

Above left: Turned
inverted cup, late C17
Above right: Turned
inverted cup, late C17

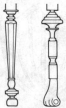

Above left: Octagonal,
late C17
Above right: Walnut
with paw foot, c1695

Above left: Carved
scroll, late C17
Above right: Double
scroll, late C17

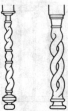

Above left: Twist
turned, late C17
Above right: Double
open twist, late C17

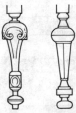

Above left: Scroll top,
late C17
Above right:
Portuguese bulb,
early C18

Feet: *a.* Spanish; *b.*
Paw, late C17; *c.* Paw,
c1720; *d.* Claw-and-
ball

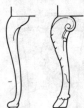

Above, left and right:
Queen Anne cabriole
legs, early C18

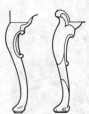

Cabriole legs, *left:*
carving on inside of
knee; *right:* hipping at
seat level

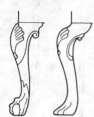
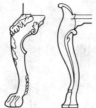
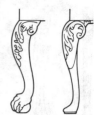

Above left: Cabriole
with shell motif
Above right: Cabriole
with pad foot

Above left: Early
Georgian cabriole
Above right: Cabriole,
mid C18

Above left: Cabriole
with claw-and-ball
foot
Above right:
Cabriole with paw
foot

Above left: Carved
hoof foot, early C18
Above right: Plain hoof
foot, c1720

Above left: Hoof foot
with pad, Mid C18
Above right: Stylized
hoof foot early C18

Above left: Plain club
foot, Mid C18
Above right: Knurl
foot, Mid C18

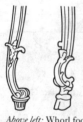
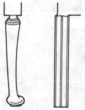
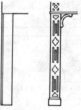

Above left: Whorl foot,
Mid C18
Above right: Cloven
hoof foot, mid C18

Above left: Club foot
with pad, mid C18
Above right: Straight
moulded leg, mid
C18

Above left: Plain
straight, mid C18
Above right:
Fretted, mid C18

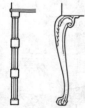
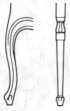

Above left: Straight
moulded, mid C18
Above right:
Cabriole,
mid C18

Above left: French
cabriole, late C18
Above right:
Square turned,
late C18

Above left: Adam
tapered, late C18
Above right:
Adam carved,
late C18

Above left:
Adam fluted,
late C18
Above right:
Sheraton painted,
c1770

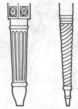

Above left:
Turned and fluted,
c1785
Above right:
Tapered scroll,
late C18

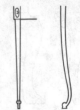

Above left:
Sheraton tapered,
late C18
Above right:
Sheraton shaped,
late C18

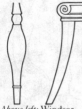

Above left: Windsor
turned, early C19
Above right:
Purplewood, early
C19

Above left: "Lion"
leg, early C19
Above right:
Victorian "Tudor", c1845

Above left: Victorian
"Elizabethan", mid
C19
Above right: Reeded,
mid C19

Bracket feet, bun feet and casters

Plain bracket foot,
c1725–1780

Ogee bracket foot,
mid C18

Splay foot, late C18

William and Mary
bun foot, late C17

Flattened bun foot,
late C17

Turnip foot, early
C18

Leather wheel caster,
c1750 (left) and
square cup caster,
c1760

Tapered cup caster.
c1785 (left), and
simple brass caster,
late C18

a. Plain toe caster; *b.*
Lion's paw caster; *c.*
Late Regency gilt
metal caster.

Sofas and settees

Many of the general pointers for Chairs (page 25) apply.
However, shape and style often provide useful clues to dating
and authenticity, as does the wood used. Walnut is seldom
found after 1760, rosewood and satinwood not until the C19.

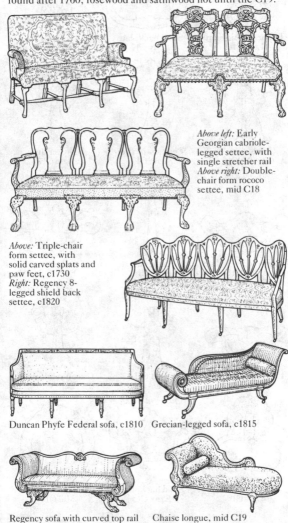

Above left: Early
Georgian cabriole-
legged settee, with
single stretcher rail
Above right: Double-
chair form rococo
settee, mid C18

Above: Triple-chair
form settee, with
solid carved splats and
paw feet, c1730
Right: Regency 8-
legged shield back
settee, c1820

Duncan Phyfe Federal sofa, c1810   Grecian-legged sofa, c1815

Regency sofa with curved top rail   Chaise longue, mid C19

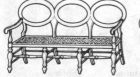

Cane-seated balloon back, c1870

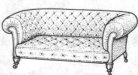

Chesterfield settee, late C19

Handles

Tudor Gothic loop
Late C16

Solid backplate
Early C17

Acorn drop
c1660–1710

Axe drop
c1660–1710

Pear shape drop
Late C17

Baluster drop
Late C17

Engraved backplate
Early C18

Split tail
Early C18

Brass
Early C18

Pierced backplate
Early C18

Split tail
c1690–1715

Queen Anne drop
Early C18

Stirrup
Early C18

Solid backplate
Early C18

Brass ring
Mid C18

Rococo
Mid C18

Rococo mount
Mid C18

Simple swan neck
Mid C18

Pierced backplate
Mid C18

Pierced backplate
Mid C18

Brass swan neck
c1770–1780

Stamped
Late C18

Oval with patera
Late C18

Octagonal
Late C18

Round brass
End C18

Lion's head
Late C18

Plain curved
Late C18

Oval
Late C18

Plain squared
Late C18

Plain ring drop
Early C19

Plain squared
Early C19

Regency lion
c1820–1830

Campaign
Mid C19

Porcelain
Mid C19

Wood with inset
Mid C19

Loop with solid plate
Late C19

Types of pediment

Swelled frieze, late C17

Double domed, end C17

Double arch, early C18

Triple arch, early C18

Broken arch, early Georgian

Cavetto flat top, early Georgian

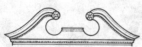

Early swan's neck, mid C18

Broken architectural, with dentil and cornice, mid C18

Swan neck bonnet top, late C18

Moulded dentil, late C18

Scrolled with carved finial, late C18

Rococo scrolled, mid C18

Sheraton domed, early C19

Early Victorian domed, c1850

Mid-Victorian triangular, c1880

Late Victorian carved, c1880

Types of moulding

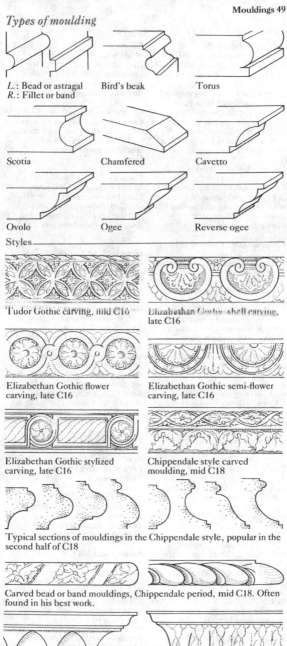

L.: Bead or astragal
R.: Fillet or band

Bird's beak

Torus

Scotia

Chamfered

Cavetto

Ovolo

Ogee

Reverse ogee

Styles

Tudor Gothic carving, mid C16

Elizabethan Gothic shell carving, late C16

Elizabethan Gothic flower carving, late C16

Elizabethan Gothic semi-flower carving, late C16

Elizabethan Gothic stylized carving, late C16

Chippendale style carved moulding, mid C18

Typical sections of mouldings in the Chippendale style, popular in the second half of C18

Carved bead or band mouldings, Chippendale period, mid C18. Often found in his best work.

Typically delicate Hepplewhite-style carved mouldings dating from c1760 to the end of the century.

Furniture Makers and Designers

Adam, Robert 1728–1792
Scottish architect who, with his
brother James, greatly influenced
furniture design in the late C18.
The brothers were largely
responsible for reviving classical
ornamentation and design.
Possibly the first to make
sideboards, they mainly worked in
mahogany and satinwood,
decorated with rich inlay. Their
designs were published in 1775.

Boulle, André-Charles 1642–
1732
Chief cabinetmaker to Louis XIV
of France, and famous for Boulle
work: brass and tortoise-shell inlay
in dense, scrolling patterns
dominating the design.

Chippendale, Thomas 1718–
1779
Son of a Worcestershire carver, in
1749 Chippendale set up business
as a cabinetmaker in London. A
master of proportion with a rococo
style embellished with delicate
and intricate carving, the quality
of his designs and workmanship
set new standards in furniture
making. His seminal book *The
Gentleman and Cabinet Maker's
Directory* was published in 1754.
He made a wide variety of articles
from bureau-bookcases to tea-
caddies – but no sideboards as
such. Many pieces attributed to
Chippendale are thought to have
been made by his contemporaries,
esp. "Chinese Chippendale",
though it is likely he contracted
work out when his workshops
were extra busy.

Cobb, John d.1778
English cabinetmaker and
upholsterer in partnership with
John Vile (*q.v.*).

Eastlake, Charles Locke 1836–
1906
Designer and exponent of
"modern Gothic", involving a
return to old values and simpler
shapes. His book *Hints on
Household Taste* (1868) was
influential both in Britain and
America, giving rise to the so-
called "Eastlake style". No pieces
actually made from his original
designs have been found.

Elfe, Thomas 1719–1775
English-born cabinetmaker in
Charleston, S. Carolina,
producing high quality furniture
in Chippendale style, with
distinctive use of fret.

Gillow's
Manufacturers founded in
Lancaster in 1695, moving to
London in 1761. They retained
their name for tasteful, well-made
furniture throughout C19.

Gibbons, Grinling 1648–1721
Famous for his naturalistic wood-
carving adorning house interiors as
well as furniture, Gibbon was
appointed master-carver to
George I in 1714.

Gimson, Ernest 1864–1919
Leading disciple of William
Morris and exponent of the Arts
and Crafts Movement, Gimson
practised as a cabinetmaker and
designer in the early years of the
C20.

Hepplewhite, George d.1786
English cabinetmaker particularly
identified with the post-
Chippendale period. None of his
furniture has survived, his
reputation being firmly based on
the detailed designs, styles and
patterns he produced, notably in
*The Cabinet Maker's and
Upholsterer's Guide* (1788). These
were widely circulated, copied
and adapted both in Europe and
North America. His style reflects a
more homely, simpler version of
the Neoclassicism of the Adam
Bros. for whom it is likely he
worked. Best known for his chairs,
(esp. shield back) and sideboards
(with concave corners).

Hope, Thomas 1770–1831
The apostle in England of an
equivalent of the Empire style in
France – a rich and pompous
Neoclassicism.

Ince, William 1759–1803
With his partner John Mayhew,
Ince produced *The Universal
System of Household Furniture*,
containing over 300 designs.

Jacob, Georges 1739–1814
The leading French *ébéniste* or
cabinetmaker of the years
immediately before the French
Revolution (1793). He worked in
a Neoclassical style, not without
some influence from England,
e.g. in use of mahogany.

**Jacob-Desmalter, François
Honoré** 1770–1841
Son of Georges Jacob, one of the
leading cabinetmakers of the
French Empire style. Apart from
its numerous classical motifs, his

work is notable for its bronze and other inserts such as mother-of-pearl and porcelain.

Jones, Inigo 1573–1652
Renowned English Renaissance architect, who also designed some pieces of furniture.

Kent, William 1686–1748
English architect and furniture designer, using classical forms.

Marot, Daniel 1663–1752
Huguenot architect and designer, Master of Works to William III of England.

Martin Brothers mid C18
French furniture makers, who in 1730 developed *vernis Martin*, a substitute for Oriental lacquer.

Morris, William 1834–1896
Rejecting Victorian machine-age standards, the "Apostle" of the Arts and Crafts Movement advocated a return to craftsman-made furniture of simple design, unspoiled by stains or similar preparations. His influence was stronger in Europe, esp. Scandinavia, than in Britain or America.

Phyfe, Duncan 1768–1854
Probably most famous of American makers. Worked in New York producing designs with roots in both English Regency (Sheraton) and French Empire styles.

Pugin, Augustus Welby 1812–1852
English architect of French descent, the leading champion of the C19 Gothic revival. He also designed Gothic furniture and interiors, using late Gothic architectural motifs.

Riesenburgh, Bernard van d.1767
French cabinetmaker, producing some of the most highly prized work of the Louis XV style. His rococo designs involve exquisite marquetry and Boulle work.

Riesener, Jean-Henri 1734–1806
The master *ébéniste* to Louis XVI of France. His furniture is rich and ornate, but has clear lines and an exceedingly solid look.

Ruhlmann, Jacques-Emile 1879–1933
Possibly the most prominent Parisian furniture designer of the 1920s. Typically his furniture is of very simple form executed in exotic and expensive woods, often with ivory inlays.

Schinkel, Karl Friedrich 1727–1801
Berlin architect, whose furniture and interior designs were a major influence on the Biedermeier style of C19 Germany. He simplified the predominant Empire taste and made furniture more comfortable.

Seddon, George 1727–1801
One of the leading London cabinetmakers of later C18.

Shearer, Thomas fl. end C18
Author of *The Cabinetmaker's London Book of Prices* (1788), which is comparable to Hepplewhite, but generally crisper and more elegant.

Sheraton, Thomas 1751–1806
English designer and author of practical and influential books on furniture linking Neoclassical and Regency styles. He used inlay work extensively, with marquetry taking the place of much of the carving employed by previous makers. Sheraton produced a variety of lightly framed pieces, his favoured wood being satinwood. Said to have invented the kidney-shaped table, and particularly famous for his sideboards (often with convex corners).

Smith, George active until 1836
London cabinetmaker, whose publications between 1805 and 1836 had great influence on the Regency style.

Van der Rohe, Mies 1886–1969
Generally accepted as one of the greatest designers of modern furniture, he succeeded Gropius as director of the Bauhaus in 1936. In 1938 he emigrated to the U.S.A. His Art Deco designs from the 1920s are keenly sought.

Vile, William d.1767
One of the leading C18 cabinetmakers and upholsterers, working in partnership with John Cobb.

Voysey, Charles F.A. 1857–1941
Pioneer of modern movement in industrial design. His furniture was plain, functional and simply decorated.

PORCELAIN and POTTERY
The Crucial Questions

The Chinese discovered the art of making porcelain in the Tang Dynasty (618–906). By the end of C17 it had become a European obsession to discover the secret, since Chinese porcelain was being exported to Europe in ever increasing quantities. Johann Böttger at Meissen discovered the formula for *hard paste* porcelain in the early years of the C18. By 1770 the secret had spread to Vienna, Strasbourg, Frankenthal and Nymphenburg. In France, Vincennes and Sèvres first produced *soft paste* porcelain in 1745–72. Soft paste porcelain was produced at most of the C18 English and Welsh factories. Only Plymouth, Bristol and Newhall used hard paste.

There are three essential lessons to be learnt.
1. The distinction between pottery and porcelain.
2. The distinction between hard and soft paste porcelain.
3. The distinction between hand-painted and printed wares.

1. With C18 pottery the earthenware body was often coarse and heavy especially in comparison with the delicate translucency of the Chinese porcelain. Towards the end of the C17, in Staffordshire, after much research the potteries discovered that salt added to the glaze led to a near white salt-glazed stoneware. It is important to realise that the production of porcelain was totally reliant on the discovery of china clay and china stone. The potteries were producing various types of bodies due to the different clays used.

In 1745 William Cookworthy from Plymouth finally discovered china clay and china stone (petuntse) in England. This was the beginning of English hard paste porcelain. Soon Lund's factory at Bristol and factories at Bow and Chelsea were to produce *soft paste* porcelain using frit or soapstone in place of china stone.

Now the distinction:
Pottery includes anything made from baked clay. It embraces a large number of quite different materials: with earthenwares and stonewares covered in many distinct glazes.
Porcelain is a hard translucent white substance made from china clay and china stone; it has a clear ringing sound when struck.

The most common distinction between pottery and its sub-classification porcelain is that pottery is not translucent and porcelain is. While as a simple rule this has some truth, a number of porcelains have little translucency.

2. Porcelain itself can be sub-divided into *hard* and *soft* paste. While it is possible to give some indication as to how to distinguish these, the best advice one can profer is to obtain a damaged example of each type and study the difference. These damaged pieces should certainly be chipped and are even more helpful if broken!

* *Hard paste:* fired at a higher temperature than soft paste; cold feel to the touch; chip is flint- or glass-like; hard, glittery glaze which is fused to the paste.

* *Soft paste:* a file will cut easily into soft paste (not a test to be recommended!); chip is granular; warmer feeling to the touch; less stable in the kiln – figures in particular were difficult to fire (*note:* no English soft paste figures can compare with Meissen and other German factories); the glaze was soft as it tended not to fuse into the body as much as glaze on hard paste and was liable both to pooling and crazing; early soft paste was prone to discoloration.

3. It is vital to learn the difference between hand-painted and printed decoration. Easy and quick identification comes with constantly looking at comparative pieces. However a few points may help:
* A painted pattern is achieved by brush stroke and hence has a fluidity that is impossible with a print.

* Brush work is most obvious where there is shading of colour.
* The brush tends to be less precise than an engraving – note the hatch marks evident on a print.
* A printed pattern results from an etched or engraved copper plate.
* The decoration on English porcelain can be divided into four main types: underglaze, overglaze, painted and printed.
* Most underglaze work was effected in blue. A point to bear in mind is that when this "blue" was actually applied to the unglazed porcelain it in fact appeared black to the painter, since the true colour only appeared after firing. The painter had, therefore, to use his skill and experience to estimate how tones and shading would appear on the piece.
* Overglaze printing was introduced in the mid 1750s. This was at least five years before underglaze printing.

Museums and Collections

The best, and perhaps the only reliable way to learn about the various types of porcelain and pottery, is to look at and to *study*, to touch and to *feel*, as many different pieces as possible. For most of us, the chance to touch is obviously limited (though remember that broken and damaged pieces can tell us a great deal about texture, opacity and decoration). Looking, however, is available to all, wherever we happen to be, either in internationally famous museums and exhibitions, or in quite small, but often extremely informative, local or private collections. Make a point of seeking out such riches, and returning again and again. A good tip is to concentrate on just one factory or style per visit: otherwise you won't see the "wood" for the "trees"! In that way you will begin to recognize period, style and quality, and be able to apply such knowledge to your own collecting.

Here, to start you off, is a list of recommended museums and collections.

Great Britain
Art Gallery & Museum, Glasgow
Bethnall Green Museum, London
The British Museum, London
The Burrell Collection, Glasgow
The Glaisher Collection, Fitzwilliam Museum, Cambridge
Hastings Museum & Art Gallery, Cambridge Road, Hastings
Cecil Higgins Museum, Castle Close, Bedford
The Museum of London, London
Royal Scottish Museum, Edinburgh
The Schreiber Collection, Victoria & Albert Museum, London
Sir Percival David Foundation, University of London, London
Stoke-on-Trent Public Museum & Art Gallery, Hanley, Stoke-on-Trent
Temple Newsam House, Leeds
Victoria & Albert Museum, London
The Wallace Collection, Hertford House, London
Wedgwood Collection, Barlaston, Stoke-on-Trent, and Wigmore Street, London
The Willet Collection, Art Gallery & Museum, Brighton

USA
Boston Museum of Fine Arts, Boston, Massachusetts
Colonial Williamsburg, Williamsburg, Virginia
Cooper-Hewitt Museum of Decorative Art & Design, New York
Cooper Union Museum for the Arts of Decoration, New York
Frick Collection, New York
Metropolitan Museum of Art, New York
Van Cortland Mansion & Museum, Van Cortland Park, Bronx, New York

Europe
Musée Céramique, Sèvres, Paris, France
Musée des Beaux-Arts, Rouen, France.
Musée National de Céramique Adrien-Dubouché, Limoges, France
Musée Régional Dupuy-Mestreau, Saintes, Charente Maritime, France
Museum für Kunst und Gewerbe, Hamburg, W. Germany
National Museum, Copenhagen, Denmark
National Museum, Stockholm, Sweden
Rijksmuseum, Amsterdam, Holland

What to look for

When we start to develop an interest in pottery and porcelain it is difficult to work out how a dealer can look at a piece and say "it speaks Derby to me" or "certainly early Meissen of *circa* 1723". (It is important to note that when the dates we use are approximate we use "c" or "*circa*".) In the following pages we will deal with marks and the major factories, discussing points about the body, paste, glaze and decoration which give us clues to factory and date. First, the question of marks. A mark on a piece of porcelain or pottery should be regarded with some suspicion or at best as part of the overall discovery process.

One also has to distinguish between different types of marks. There are factory marks which are treated separately, and also workmen's marks which were individual. A workman's mark is difficult to trace. Don't fall into the trap of thinking an unmarked piece is old. Many 19th century and 20th century wares from small factories are unmarked.

We have collated some hints and tips on dating that may be useful:
* Royal Arms in a mark would be no earlier than 1800 but could be much later.
* Pattern numbers don't denote a specific factory but tend to date from after 1815 and are USUALLY much later.
* "Limited" or "Ltd." tends to denote a date after 1861 – but became much more common after 1885.
* An impressed "Trade Mark" can be assumed to be after 1862.
* The word "Royal" in a firm's name tends to be late C19.
* From 1891 wares started to state country of origin: "France", "England" etc., to comply with the McKinley Tariff Act of America.
* From c1910 wares often had the full "Made in Japan", "Made in Germany".
* "Bone China" and "English bone China" are C20 marks.

One of the most useful marks for later porcelain is the *Design registration mark*. Registration began in 1839 following the Copyright of Design Act but the insignia was used from 1842.

1842–67	1868–83
a – class	a – class
b – year	b – day
c – month	c – bundle
d – day	d – year
e – bundle	e – month

The letters were not used in sequence as the table below shows:

1842–67				1868–83		
A – 1845	I – 1846	Q – 1866	Y – 1853	A – 1871	K – 1883
B – 1858	J – 1854	R – 1861	Z – 1860	C – 1870	L – 1882
C – 1844	K – 1857	S – 1849		D – 1878	P – 1877
D – 1852	L – 1856	T – 1867		E – 1881	S – 1875
E – 1855	M – 1859	U – 1848		F – 1873	U – 1874
F – 1847	N – 1864	V – 1850		H – 1869	V – 1876
G – 1863	O – 1862	W – 1865		I – 1872	X – 1868
H – 1843	P – 1851	X – 1842		J – 1880	Y – 1879

The months from both periods:

A – December	D – September	H – April	M – June
B – October	E – May	I – July	R – August
C/O – January	G – February	K – November	W – March

From 1884 consecutive numbers were used, nearly always prefixed by Rd or Rd No. A guide to the year from the number is given below:

Rd No			
1 – 1884	163767 – 1891	311658 – 1898	447000 – 1905*
19754 – 1885	185713 – 1892	331707 – 1899	471000 – 1906*
40480 – 1886	205240 – 1893	351202 – 1900	494000 – 1907*
64520 – 1887	224720 – 1894	368154 – 1901	519000 – 1908*
90483 – 1888	246975 – 1895	385500 – 1902*	550000 – 1909*
116648 – 1889	268393 – 1896	402500 – 1903*	*Approximate
141273 – 1890	291241 – 1897	420000 – 1904*	only

The numbering system is still in use today and in 1980 was around one million.

Some Useful Year Cyphers
DERBY

1882	1883	1884	1885
1886	1887	1888	1889
1890	1891	1892	1893
1894	1895	1896	1897
1898	1899	1900	1901

MINTON

1842	1843	1844	1845
1846	1847	1848	1849
1850	1851	1852	1853
1854	1855	1856	1857
1858	1859	1860	1861
1862	1863	1864	1865
1866	1867	1868	1869
1870	1871	1872	1873
1874	1875	1876	1877
1878	1879	1880	1881

WEDGWOOD

WEDGWOOD

* Impressed mark. c1759 – on. From 1891 "ENGLAND" was added.
* Impressed year letters: where there is a group of 3 letters, the 3rd denotes year.

Letter	Year		Letter	Year
O	1860		H	1879
P	1861		I	1880
Q	1862		J	1881
R	1863		K	1882
S	1864		L	1883
T	1865		M	1884
U	1866		N	1885
V	1867		O	1886
W	1868		P	1887
X	1869		Q	1888
Y	1870		R	1889
Z	1871		S	1890
A	1872		T	1891
B	1873		U	1892
C	1874		V	1893
D	1875		W	1894
E	1876		X	1895
F	1877		Y	1896
G	1878		Z	1897

PATTERN NUMBERS
Pattern numbers can indicate a particular porcelain factory although few are unique to one factory. Examples are:

Chamberlain-Worcester
Pattern nos. started c1790.
reached 100 by 1797
400 by 1807
610 by 1812
790 by 1817
1000 by 1822
numbers then go to 1752; 2000–2624; 3000–3099; 4000–4099; 5000–5019.

Coalport: John Rose & Co
Pattern nos. started c1805.
1–999 used to c1825
2/1; 2/2 – 2/999 to c1832
3/1; 3/2 – 3/999 used c1832–38
4/1; 4/2 – 4/1000 used c1838–43
5/1; 5/2 – 5/1000 used c1843–50

albarello Waisted drug jar.
applied Attached, rather than modelled in the body.
baluster vase Vase which swells first out and then in to create a shape like a baluster (see p. 10).
bellarmine Type of stoneware flagon, made in Germany from C16.
bat printed Transfer printed.
bianco-sopra-bianco C18 Delft or C16 majolica decorated in white over a whitish-greyish ground.
biscuit Porcelain or pottery fired, but unglazed, made first in France in C18.
bisque French for **biscuit**.
blue-dash Blue dabs round the rim of a plate, found on C17 and C18 delftware.
bocage The bush, shrub or foliage surrounding or supporting a pottery or porcelain figure.
body The shaped clay itself, as distinct from its subsequent surface glaze or decoration.
bone china Pearlware with bone ash in the formula: almost entirely porcellanous. Produced from just before 1800.
Castleford ware Shiny white porcellanous stoneware made in Castleford and elsewhere from c1790.
cow creamer Silver or china jug or boat for pouring cream, modelled as a cow.

crazing Cracks in a glaze.
creamware Earthenware glazed in a cream or butter colour with a porcelain effect, developed by Wedgwood in the 1760s and soon widely made elsewhere.
crenellated Crinkly or wavy.
crested china Ware decorated with heraldic crests, made first by **Goss** and then, after 1880, by many different Staffordshire and other English and also German potteries.

delft or delftware Tin-glazed earthenware, often decorated in styles deriving either from Chinese porcelain or from C17 Dutch painting. "Delftware" acceptably embraces not only ware with a Delft mark but any C17 or C18 pottery of the same type and style. If actually made in Delft, it is written "Delft ware" with a capital D.
Deutsche Blumen "German flowers". Loose flowers or bouquets painted on ware (e.g. from Meissen) of mid C18.
dry-edge With edges clear or bare of glaze.
earthenware Pottery made with porous clay which therefore requires a sealant glaze (unlike stoneware or porcelain).
écuelle French soup bowl with two handles; usually made with a cover and stand (e.g. Sèvres).
enamel Second, coloured glaze over the first glaze.
Enghalskrüge Large German tin-glazed jug with a cylindrical neck.
everted Turned or curled over, e.g. a rim.
faience Tin-glazed earthenware (after Faenza in Italy, a majolica centre).
fairings Porcelain figures of C19 and C20 made in the mould, especially in Germany. They depict genre or situation comedy, or animal figures, and usually carry descriptive captions.
famille verte or **rose** Type of oriental porcelain (see page 90).
flatware Flat pottery or porcelain, e.g. plates.
frit Glassy dross, an ingredient of soft-paste porcelain; also sometimes applied with or over pottery glaze.
garniture Set of ornamental pieces of pottery or porcelain.
Goss china Range of porcelain and parian ware produced from 1858 at Stoke-on-Trent, but particularly heraldic china.
hard-paste porcelain Porcelain made with kaolin and petuntse, as the Chinese produce it. First made in Europe in early C18 at Meissen. See pages 52–3.
Imari Type of oriental porcelain (see page 90).
Indianische Blumen "Indian flowers". European imitation of the Japanese Kakiemon style, found in mid C18 e.g. on Meissen or Höchst.
ironstone Type of stoneware patented in 1813 by Mason, in

which slag from iron furnaces was mixed into the clay, toughening the ware.

istoriato Italian for "with a story on it", said of majolica.

jardinière A stand for flowers, rather wider than a vase.

jasper ware Variety of coloured stoneware developed by Wedgwood.

lead-glazed The type of glaze first used in Western pottery, taken over perhaps from glass-making. In C17 refined to "liquid lead glaze" and in C18 to "colourless lead glaze". Lead (lead sulphide) continued as an ingredient in other glazes (e.g. tin glaze, salt glaze).

lustre Ware of any kind decorated with a metallic coating (which changes colour when fired: e.g. gold becomes ruby-red).

majolica Tin-glazed earthenware, usually decorated, made in Renaissance Italy; or C19 ware using the same technique, made by Minton and others.

overglaze A second glaze laid over the first; the pot is then fired again. May also be called "enamel".

parian Porcelain formula developed in mid C19 by Copeland, named after "Parian" white marble: the figures are typically uncoloured, resembling biscuit.

pearlware A type of earthenware, whiter and shinier than creamware, produced from late C18 by Wedgwood, Spode and others and commonly print decorated.

petuntse See **porcelain**.

porcelain Porcelain is made from a clay (or paste) called kaolin (after the place in China where it is found) combined with petuntse, the Chinese term for the feldspathic rock that produces a glaze. Similar clay and rock were first found in Europe at Meissen about 1700, making direct imitation of Chinese ware possible (hard-paste porcelain); elswhere, notably in England, there were increasingly successful attempts to reproduce the strength and translucency of oriental porcelain with substitute ingredients (soft-paste porcelain). See pages 52–3.

porcellanous Having some (but not all) of the ingredients or characteristics of true porcelain.

Prattware A type of earthenware made in Staffordshire in late C18 and early C19, decorated in distinctive colours on a buff ground.

print decoration Decoration not hand-painted.

redware Primitive C18 American clay pottery which turned red-brown when fired.

reserved Kept clear, e.g. from painted decoration applied after glazing.

resist An area reserved from the overall decoration (usually silver or gilt).

saltglaze Type of stoneware. Salt added into the hot kiln fuses with the body to create a glassy surface approximating true porcelain. Either brown or almost white, depending on the composition of the body, saltglaze is found from c1720.

scratch blue Decoration incised or scratched, then painted blue. Found on C18 saltglaze ware.

sgraffito Scratched or incised, said of older pieces.

shoulder Outward projection of a vase under the neck or mouth.

slipware Slip is clay mixed with water. Slipware is earthenware to which slip is applied as decoration.

soft-paste porcelain Porcelain in which frit or soapstone is used (instead of the petuntse of hard-paste porcelain). Developed by English potters in mid C18.

spill vase Vase for holding spills (lighting tapers).

sponged Blurred decorative dabs, representing e.g. foliage. Typical of C17 and early C18 delft.

sprig Applied or relief ornament, not necessarily consisting of sprigs or foliage.

stoneware Any earthenware that is not porous after firing (usually due to the presence of sand or flint in the clay).

tazza Italian for "plate".

tin-glazed Earthenware with a lead glaze to which tin is added. Used for fine ware in Europe in C16 and C17 (e.g. majolica).

transfer Type of print decoration perfected in the 1820s, using colours held in oil.

underglaze Colour or design painted under or before the glaze.

well The hollow or interior of a bowl or plate.

Wemyss ware Distinctive lead-glazed ware produced from the 1880s originally in Fife, Scotland. Typically features flowers and animals, painted by hand underglaze.

Porcelain and Pottery Marks

When examining a mark it is important to remember that only comparatively modern marks exhibit the uniformity that goes with mass-production. Previously marks were applied by hand, often by young unskilled workers; as a result no two marks were identical. To complicate matters even more, some factories blatantly copied the marks of their more successful competitors. A mark should therefore be regarded as just one clue – and not the most important – in establishing the factory responsible. The marks that follow are representative of those most likely to be met. Arranged 'like with like' for easy reference, they exclude all marks containing a factory name.

Index to marks

Letter Marks
A Individual letters **58**
B Letters in combination **62**
C Letters in combination with dates and/or numbers **70**

Graphic Marks
D Anchors **71**

E Animals, birds, fishes and insects **72**
F Arrows **73**
G Crescents **74**
H Crosses **74**
I Combination crosses **74**
J Cross swords **75**
K Crowns **76**
L Curves **77**
M Fleur de lys **78**

N Flowers **78**
O Geometric: circles, squares and triangles **78**
P Oriental copies **79**
Q Ornamental **80**
R Pictorial **80**
S Shields **80**
T Symbols **80**
U Miscellaneous **81**

A

Bow, (E) c1745-75	Paris, (F) c1793-97	Bow, (E) c1745	Bow, (E) c1745-75	Bow, (E) c1745-75
St. Cloud, (F) c1670-1766	Paris, (F) c1770-80	Ansbach, (G) c1760-65	Amstel, (H) c1780	Bow, (E) 1745-75
Amstel, (H) c1780-1800	Copenhagen, (D) c1903-05	Paris, (F) c1778-97	Paris, (F) c1775-1870	Alcora, (SP) c1785
Arnhem, (H) c1780	Copenhagen, (D) c1903	Moscow, (R) c1750	Paris, (F) c1773	St. Petersburg (R) c1800
Arnoldi, Elgersburg, (G) c1910-60	Weesp, (H) c1765-70	Ansbach, (G) c1760	Bow, (E) c1745-75	Sèvres, (F) 1753
Aprey, (F) c1750	Ansbach, (G) c1758-65	Ansbach, (G) c1700-10	Ansbach, (G) c1770	Sèvres, (F) 1778

Arras,
(F) *c1770-90*

Angelo Minghetti,
Bologna, (I) *c1850*

Ansbach,
(G) *c1758*

Arabia Porcelain,
Helsinki, (FIN) *1874-present*

Worcester,
(Flight & Barr),
(E) *1793-1807*

Marseilles,
(F) *c1769*

Kiel,
(G) *c1770*

Worcester,
(Flight & Barr),
(E) *1793-1807*

Bow,
(E) *c1745-75*

Worcester
(Flight & Barr),
(E) *1793-1807*

J. Brouwer,
Delft, (H)
c1760

Moustiers,
(F) *c1650-1750*

Lille,
(F) *c1720-80*

Frankenthal,
(G) *c1755-1799*

Bristol,
(E) *c1773-81*

Sèvres,
(F) *1754*

Bristol,
(E) *c1773-81*

Bristol,
(E) *c1773-81*

Hohenstein,
(G) *c1850*

Boch & Buschmann,
Mettlach, (G)
c1813-28

WM. C. Brouwer,
Gouda &
Leierdorp, (H)
c1898-1902

Nantes,
(F) *c1780*

Caughley,
(E) *1775-99*

Caughley,
(E) *1775-99*

Caughley,
(E) *1775-99*

Caughley,
(E) *1775-99*

Caughley,
(E) *c1775-99*

Carstens-Uffrecht,
Haldensleben,
(G) *c1930–45*

Orleans,
(F) *c1753-1783*

C.H. Levy,
Charenton, (F)
c1876-78

Davenport,
Longport, (E)
c1795-1810

Derby,
(E) *c1770-84*

Caughley,
(E) *1775-99*

Derby,
(E) *c1749-55*

Worcester,
(John Donaldson),
(E) *c1770*

Derby
(Chelsea), (E)
c1770-84

Derby
(Chelsea), (E)
c1770-84

Coalport
Coalbrookdale,
(E) *c1828-50*

Denby Tableware,
Derby, (E) *Current*

D & Cº
FRANCE
R. Delinieres,
Limoges, (F)
c1879-1901

Elton Pottery,
Somerset, (E)
c1880-90

Rouen,
(F) *c1673-96*

Furstenberg,
(G) *c1760-70*

Furstenberg,
(G) *c1760-70*

Furstenberg,
(G) *c1760-70*

Copenhagen, (D) *c1755-60*

Longton Hall, Newcastle. Staffs., (E) *c1749-60*

Bow, (E) *c1750-59*

Bow, (E) *c1750-59*

Bow, (E) *c1750-59*

Furstenberg, (G) *c1753-60*

Rouen, (F) *c1673-96*

Bow, (E) *c1750-59*

Buen Retiro, Madrid, (SP) *1759-1808*

Tavernes, (F) *c1760-80*

Gotha, (G) *c1805-30*

Gotha, (G) *c1775-1800*

Tavernes, (F) *c1760-80*

Bow, (E) *c1750-59*

Faenza, (I) *Late 15C*

Tavernes, (F) *c1760-80*

Unger, Schneider, Thuringia, (G) *1861-1972*

Unger, Schneider, Thuringia, (G) *c1861-1887*

Paris (Hannong), (F) *c1773-79*

Paris (Hannong), (F) *c1773-79*

Strasbourg, (G) *c1750-80*

Nevers, (F) *Late 17C.*

Haviland, Limoges, (F) *c1878-80*

Haviland, Limoges, (F) *c1878-80*

Heinrich Selb, Bavaria, (G) *c1910-14*

Bow, (E) *c1750-59*

St. Cloud, (F) *c1670-1766*

Longton Hall, Newcastle, Staffs., (E) *c1749-60*

Ilmenau, Thuringia, (G) *c1900-40*

Copenhagen, (D), *c1750-1760*

Paris, (F) *c1774-84*

Valenciennes, Nord, (F) *c1735-85*

Sèvres, (F) *1764*

Lille, (F) *Late 18C.*

Paris, (F) *c1774-84*

Paris, (F) *c1774-84*

Tours, (F) *c1750*

Rouen, (F) *c1720-30*

Minton, Stoke, Staffs., (E) *c1800-30*

Longton Hall, Newcastle, Staffs., (E) *1750-60*

Voigt & Holland, Thuringia, (G) *c1884-87*

Rouen, (F) *c1720-30*

Derby, (E) *c1770-80*

New Hall, Shelton, Staffs., (E), *c1782-1810*

Baroni Giovanni, Nove, (I) *c1800-25*

New Hall, Shelton, Staffs, (E), *c1782-1810*

 Limbach, (G) *Late 18C*

Bow, (E) *c1750*

Liverpool, (Seth Pennington), (E) *Late 18C*

 St. Cloud, (F) *c1670-1776*

Liverpool, (Seth Pennington), (E) *Late 18C.*

Liverpool, (James & John Pennington), (E) *Mid-18C*

Pinxton, Derbyshire, (E) *c1795-1812*

Pinxton, Derbyshire, (E) *c1795-1812*

Liverpool, (James & John Pennington), (E) *Mid-18C*

Liverpool, (James & John Pennington), (E) *Mid-18C*

Pinxton, Derbyshire, (E) *c1795-1801*

Liverpool, (James & John Pennington), (E) *Mid-18C*

Pinxton, Derbyshire, (E) *c1795-1801*

 Nymphenburg, (G) *Mid 18C*

 Lille, (F) *c1778*

 Chantilly, (Pigory), (F) *Late 18C.*

Pilkington's Lancs. (E) *c1897-1905*

Eloury-Porquier, Quimper, (F) *c1840-45*

 Pilkington's Lancs. (E) *c1905-14*

 Dagobert Peche, Vienna, (A) *c1909-*

 Pilkington's Lancs. (E) *c1905-14*

 Pearl Pottery Co. Hanley, Staffs. (E) *1894-1912*

Faiencerie de la Grande Maison, Quimper (F) *c1810-20*

Marseilles (Robert), (F) *c1773-93*

Marseilles (Robert), (F) *c1773-93*

Bristol Ware (Ring), (E) *Mid-*

Marseilles (Robert), (F) *1773-93*

Chelsea (Derby), (E) *c1769-75*

Gotha, (G) *1805-30*

Rouen, (F) *Mid 17C*

Sèvres, (F) *1793-1804*

Bow, (E) *1750-59*

J. H. Koch, Regensburg, (G) *c1805-15*

Faiencerie de la Grande Maison, Quimper (F) *c1920-30*

Rheinsberg Porc. Rheinsberg, Prussia, (G) *c1954*

Greiner & Holzapfel, Thuringia, (G) *c1805-20*

 Rorstrand, Lidköping, (SWE) *c1938*

 Rosenthal, Selb, Bavaria (G) *1961+*

R & Cᵒ LIMOGES FRANCE **Raynaud,** Limoges, (F) *c1928-40*

Caughley, (E) *1775-99*

Nymphenberg, (G) *Mid-18C*

Caughley, (E) *1775-99*

Caughley, (E) *1775-99*

Caughley, (E) *1775-99*

62 Porcelain & Pottery Marks

Caughley,
(E) c1775–99

Rouen,
(F) c1760–70

G. Greiner,
Schauberg,
Bavaria, (G)
c1890–1930

Slama,
Vienna (A)
c1955–present

St. Cloud,
(F) c1670–1766

Sèvres,
(F) 1912

**Silesian
Porcelain,** (G)
c1895–1920

**Kister
Porcelain,**
Thuringia, (G)
c1900–70

**Scheibe-
Alsbach Porc.**
Thuringia,
(G) c1970

Kister,
Thuringia,
(G) c1900–70

Caughley,
(E) c1775–99

**Schmidt
& Greiner,**
Tettau, Bavaria,
(G) c1794–1880

Bristol,
(E) c1773–75

Bow
(Thos. Frye),
(E) c1745–60

Bow
(Thos. Frye),
(E) c1745–60

Bow
(Thos. Frye),
(E) c1745–60

Utzchneider,
Sarreguemines,
(F) Mid 19C

Venice,
(I) c1755–65

W. Goebel,
Rodenthal,
Bavaria, (G)
c1950–55

W. Goebel,
Rodenthal,
Bavaria, (G)
c1957

W. Goebel,
Rodenthal,
Bavaria, (G)
c1960–72

**Nicolas
Villeroy,**
Wallerfangen,
Saar, (G)
c1789–1835

Worcester,
(E) c1775–83

Worcester,
(E) c1775–83

Faenza,
(I) 16C

Berlin
(Wegeli),
(G) c1751–60

Plymouth,
(E) c1768–70

Bordeaux
(Vanier),
(F) 1787

Berlin
(Wegeli),
(G) c1751–60

Plymouth,
(E) c1768–70

Berlin
(Wegeli),
(G) c1751–60

Worcester,
(E) c1775–83

Worcester,
(E) c1775–83

Worcester,
(E) c1775–83

Rouen,
(F) Early 18C

M.W. Reutter,
Denkendorf,
Wurtemberg, (G)
1948–present

**Wiener
Werkstätte,**
Vienna, (A)
c1912–25

H.M. Williamson,
Longton, Staffs.
(E) c1900–1905

Rouen,
(F) c1760–70

Worcester,
(E) c1775–83

B

Moustiers,
(F) 18C

Le Nove,
(I) Mid 18C

Lille, (F)
c1720–80

Moustiers,
(F) 18C.

Fontainebleau,
(F) 17C.

Ashby Potters, Burton-on-Trent, (E) *Mid 19C*

Bauscher Bros., Weiden, Bavaria, (G) *c1881–1900*

Nymphenberg, Bavaria, (G) *Mid 18C.*

Paris (Advenir Lamarr), (F) *c1773–84*

Paris (Advenir Lamarr), (F) *c1773–84*

Paris (Advenir Lamarr), (F) *c1773–84*

Amstel, Amsterdam, (H) *late 18C.*

Andennes, (B) *Early 19C.*

Limoges, (F) *c1840–1900*

Bow, (E) *c1745–75*

Venice, (I) *Mid 18C*

Delft, (H) *c1750–60*

Delft, (H) *c1750–60*

Delft, (H) *c1750–60*

Delft, (H) *c1750–60*

Delft, (H) *c1750–60*

Delft, (H) *c1750–60*

Delft, (H) *Mid 17C*

Delft, (H) *Late 17C.*

Delft, (H) *c1750–60*

Delft, (H) *Late 17C*

Delft, (H) *late 17C.*

Alcora, (SP) *c1785*

Aich, Bavaria, (G) *Mid 19C.*

Moustiers, (F) *18C.*

Moscow, (R) *c1805–70*

Delft, (H) *c1750–60*

Aprey, (F) *Mid 18C*

Wm. Ault, Staffs., (E) *1887–1923, 1937–c1965*

Aylesford Priory, Kent, (E) *c1955–62*

P&F France **Pillivuyt,** Foecy, (F) *c1900–20*

Aprey, (F) *Mid 18C.*

Delft, (H) *Mid 17C*

Aprey, (F) *Mid 18C*

Arras, (F) *c1770–90*

Paris, (F) *Mid 17C.*

Meillonas, Ain, (F) *Late 18C*

Delft, (H) *Mid 17C.*

Arras, (F) *c1770–90*

Meissen (Augustus Rex), (G) *c1720–50*

Meissen (H. Wolfsohn), (G) *Mid 19C*

Meissen (H. Wolfsohn), (G) *Mid 19C.*

Meissen (H. Wolfsohn), (G) *Mid 19C*

Meissen (Augustus Rex), (G) *c1720–50*

St. Amandles-Eaux, (F) *Early 19C.*

August Saeltzer, Eisenach, (G) *Mid 19C.*

Alan Caiger-Smith, Aldermaston, Berks., (E) *c1955–65*

Delft, (H) *Mid 17C.*

Wedgwood, (Thos. Allen), (E) *c1875–1905*

Delft, (H) *Mid 18C.*

Don Pottery, Yorks., (E) *19C.*

Aprey, (F) *Mid 18C.*

Aich, Bavaria, (G) *Mid 19C.*

Samson, Edme, Paris, (F) *Late 19C.*

Auguste Delaherche, Armentieres, (F) *End 19C.*

Moustiers, (F) *Late 18C.*

Niderviller, (F) *c1744–80*

Britannia China, Longton, Staffs., (E) *Early 20C.*

Rouen (Duprey), (F) *End 18C*

Rouen (Duprey), (F) *End 18C*

St. Amand-les-Eaux, (F) *Mid 18C.*

Brussels, (B) *Late 18C.*

Bayreuth, Bavaria, (G) *Mid 18C.*

Lille, (F) *c1720–80*

Copenhagen, (D) *Mid 19C.*

Bayreuth, Bavaria, (G) *Early 18C.*

Bayreuth, Bavaria, (G) *End 18C.*

Katharine Pleydell-Bouverie, Kilmington, Wilts., (E) *c1945–50*

Bayreuth, Bavaria, (G) *Mid 18C.*

Bayreuth, Bavaria, (G) *Mid 18C.*

C.J.C. Bailey, Fulham, London, (E) *Mid 19C.*

Limbach, (G) *19C.*

Orleans, (F) *Early 19C*

Limbach, (G) *Late 18C*

Limbach, (G) *Late 18C.*

Niderviller, (F) *c1744–80*

Niderviller, (F) *c1744–80*

Burgess & Leigh, Burslem, Staffs., (E) *Mid 19C.*

Bernard Moore, Stoke, Staffs., (E) *1905–15*

Bayreuth, Bavaria, (G) *Mid 18C.*

Bayreuth, Bavaria, (G) *Mid 18C.*

Limbach, (G) *Late 18C.*

Limbach, (G) *Late 18C*

Barker, Sutton & Till, Burslem, Staffs., (E) *c1830–50*

Limbach, (G) *Late 18C.*

Doccia, (I) *Mid 18C.*

Bayreuth, Bavaria, (G) *c1740–50*

Charles Bone, Brighton, (E) *1952–c1965*

Bayreuth, Bavaria, (G) *c1740–50*

Coalport, Coalbrookdale, (E) *c1828–50*

C·B·S.

Delft (Strale),
(H) *Mid 18C.*

C·D

Limoges,
(F) *c1783*

C·D

Limoges,
(F) *c1783*

C·D·

Coalport,
Coalbrookdale,
(E) *Early 19C.*

Coalport,
Coalbrookdale
(E) *Early 19C.*

C:d

Limoges,
(F) *c1783*

C & F

Glasgow
(Cochran
& Fleming),
(S) *Mid 19C.*

Charles Ford,
Hanley, Staffs. (E)
1874–1904

C F H
G D M
FRANCE

C. F. Haviland,
Limoges, (F)
1870–82

C G

Leeds,
(E) *Late, 18C*

C & G

Copeland
& Garrett,
Stroke-on-Trent,
(E) *1833–47*

C G
W

Leeds,
(E) *Late 18C.*

CH

Ceramics
Hispania,
Manises, (SP)
c1941–45

C M +

St. Cloud,
(F) *c1722–40*

CM

M. Casson,
Prestwood,
Bucks. (E)
1952–55

CM

M. A, Cardew,
Wenford Bridge,
Cornwall, (E)
1926–

NC

Camille
Naudot,
Paris, (F)
c1905–20

C° S

Marseilles,
(F) *Late 18C.*

CSA

Carter,
Stabler & Adams,
Poole, Dorset,
(E) *1921–*

DB

Dora Barrett,
Harpenden,
Hertfordshire
(E) *1938–*

DB

Dora May
Billington,
London,
(E) *c1920*

BD

Coalport,
Coalbrookdale,
(E) *Early 19C.*

DL

Longton Hall,
Newcastle,
Staffs, (E)
c1749–60

MD

Green Dene,
East Horsley,
Surrey, (E)
1953–c1965

N

N. Dickinson,
Worthing,
Sussex, (E)
1948–

P

Deacon Pottery,
London, (E)
1952–58

D

Taxile Doat,
Sèvres, (F)
*Late 19C.
early 20C.*

E. I. B.

Hanley,
(E.I. Birch)
Staffs. (E)
Late 18thC.

EBD

E.J.D. Bodley,
Burslem,
Staffs. (E)
1875–92

ET

Ernst Teichert,
Meissen, (G)
Late 19C.

EMB

Blensdorf,
Bruton,
Somerset, (E)
1950–

E J

E. Jacquemin,
Fontainebleau,
(F) *1862–66*

B

Lille,
(F) *c1750–1780*

F B

Lille,
(F) *c1750–1780*

FBB

Worcester
(Flight,
Barr & Barr),
(E) *c1808–40*

FBB

Worcester
(Flight,
Barr & Barr),
(E) *c1808–40*

f.c

F. G. Cooper,
Sheffield, Yorks.
(E) *1945*

F. F. D.

Dallwitz,
Bohemia, (CZ)
Early 19C.

HFK

Hugo
F. Kirsch,
Vienna, (A)
c1908–1912

F & R

Pirkenhammer,
(G) *Early 19C.*

 F & R

Pirkenhammer,
(G) *Early 19C.*

Bordeaux,
(F) *c1781–87*

F Z H

Buen Retiro,
Madrid, (SP)
Mid 18C.

G D M

Limoges,
(F) *c1840–1900*

G.H. & CO.

Swansea,
(W) *Mid 19C.*

Champion,
Rustington,
Sussex. (E)
1947–

Emile Gallé,
Nancy. (F)
Early 20C.

Agnes Benson,
Ruislip, Middx.,
(E) *c1958–64*

Pfeffer,
Gotha, (G)
c1900–05

Limoges,
(F) *19C.*

Amstelhoek,
Omwal, (H)
Early 20C

**Faiencerie
de la Grande
Maison,**
Quimper, (F)
c1882–90

**Les Faienceries
de Quimper,**
Quimper, (F)
c1970–85

**Faiencerie
de la Grande
Maison,**
Quimper. (F)
c1898–1902

Turin,
(I) *18C.*

Delft,
(H) *17C.*

Vincennes,
(F) *Mid 18C.*

Vincennes,
(F) *Mid 18C.*

Palmer,
Hanley, Staffs.,
(E) *Mid 18C.*

Henriot,
Quimper, (F)
Early 19C.

Derby,
(Keys), (E)
c1815–20

Vincennes,
(F) *Late 18C.*

Prague,
(CZ) *Early 19C.*

Bristol,
(E) *c1770–81*

**Friedrich
Carl Muller,**
Thuringia, (G)
c1885–1920

I.W
Wrotham,
(E) *17/18 C.*

J.A
Aprey,
(F) *Mid 18C.*

Josef Boch,
Vienna, (A)
c1890–1930

J. Dimmock,
Hanley, Staffs.,
(E) *Late 19C.*

J. Dimmock,
Hanley, Staffs.,
(E) *Late 19C.*

G. Jones,
Stoke, Staffs.,
(E) *Late 19C.
early 20C.*

G. Jones,
Stoke, Staffs.,
(E) *Mid 19C.*

Jas. Hadley,
Worcester, (E)
Late 19C.

Jas. Hadley,
Worcester, (E)
Late 19C.

St. Cloud,
(F) *c1670–1766*

Fontainebleau,
(F) *End 18C.*

Jacob Petit,
Fontainebleau,
(F) *c1830–60*

Limoges
(Pouyat), (F)
Mid 19C.

Marseilles,
(F) *c1773–93*

Longport,
Staffs., (E)
c1793

Ashby Potters,
Burton-
on-Trent, (E)
Early 20C

**Katherine
Pleydell-
Bouverie,**
Kilmington, Wilts.,
(E) *1925–?*

William Kirkby,
Fenton, Staffs.,
(E) *1879–85*

Meissen,
(G) *c1720–60*

Meissen,
(G) *c1720–60*

Kandern Pottery,
Kandern, (G)
Early 20C.

C. Krister,
Waldenburg, (G)
Early 20C.

Berlin,
(G) *Mid 18C.*

Meissen,
(G) *c1720–60*

Krister Porc.
Waldenburg,
(G) *Late 19C.*

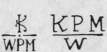

Krister Porcelain, Waldenburg, (G) *Early 20C.*

Krister Porcelain, Waldenburg, (G) *Early 20C.*

Keystone Pottery, Hanley, Staffs., (E) *1964–*

Limbach, Thuringia, (G) *Late 18C.*

Limbach, Thuringia, (G) *Late 18C.*

Limbach, Thuringia, (G) *Late 18C.*

Luxembourg, (LUX) *Late 18C.*

Limbach, Thuringia, (G) *Late 18C.*

Limbach, Thuringia, (G) *Late 18C.*

Limbach, Thuringia, (G) *Late 18C.*

Limbach, Thuringia, (G) *Late 18C.*

Limbach, Thuringia, (G) *Late 18C.*

L.C.

Brussels, (B) *End 18C.*

David Leach, Bovey Tracey, Devon, (E) *1956–*

Lesme, Limoges, (F) *Mid 19C.*

LJ

John Leach, Langport, Somerset, (E) *1950–57*

L.L.

Lille, (F) *Late 18C.*

St. Cloud, (F) *c1670–1766*

L.P.

Leeds, (E) *Late 18C.*

Lubtheen Porcelain, Mecklenburg, (G) *1933–45*

L.P.&Cᴵᴱ

L. Parant, Limoges, (F) *Mid 19C.*

Bordeaux, (F) *c1825–30*

Moreau Aîné, Limoges, (F) *Late 19C.*

MB

Marieburg, (SWE) *Mid 18C.*

Villeroy & Boch, Mettlach, (G) *Mid 19C.*

C.E. & F. Arnoldi, Elgersburg, (G) *Early 20C.*

Fortuné de Monestrol, Rungis, (F) *Mid 19C.*

M.E. Bulmer, Burill, Yorks., (E) *1956–60*

M&E

Mayer & Elliot, Longport, Staffs., (E) *Mid 19C.*

MGH

Buckfast Abbey, Devon (E) *1952–*

MO

Mennecy, (F) *Late 18C.*

M:oL

Oude Loosdrecht, (H) *c1770–90*

Rouen, (F) *Mid 18C.*

Etoilles (Monier & Pellevé), (F) *1768–c1780*

Herculaneum, Liverpool, (E) *c1833–41*

Dresden, (G) *Early 18C.*

Paris, (F) *c1784–86*

M.J.J.

Amund, (G) *Mid 18C.*

MV

Rouen, (F) *Mid 18C.*

Schmidt Bros., (G) *Mid 19C.*

N.H

Wrotham, (E) *Late 17C.*

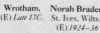

Norah Braden, St. Ives, Wilts., (E) *1924–36*

Norah Braden, St. Ives, Wilts., (E) *1924–36*

N.V

N. Vergette, London (E) *1946–*

o B

Menecy-Villeroy, (F) *1734–c1748*

Menney
(F) *Late 18C.*

Ansbach,
(G) *Early 18C.*

Oscar Schlegelmilch,
Thuringia, (G)
Late 19C.

Rouen,
(F) *Late 17C.*

Moustiers,
(F) *18C.*

Peggy Cherniavsky,
London, (E)
1951–54

Arno Fischer,
Thuringia,
(G) *Early 20C.*

Rouen, (F)
Early 18C.

Paris,
(Potter Blancheron),
(F) *Late 18C.*

Percy Brown,
Middlesex,
(E) *Mid 20C.*

Rouen,
(F) *Early 18C.*

Rouen,
(F) *Late 18C.*

Triebner, Ens & Eckert,
Thuringia, (G)
Late 19C.

Strasbourg,
(F) *Mid 18C.*

Strasbourg,
(F) *Mid 18C.*

Frankenthal,
(G) *Mid 18C.*

Peter Holdsworth,
Ramsburg, Wilts.,
(E) *1945–*

Ashby Potters Guild,
Derbyshire, (E)
Early 20C.

Hutschen-reuther,
Thuringia, (G)
c1886–1950

Rouen,
(F) *Early 18C.*

Carl Thieme,
Potschappel,
Saxony (G)
Early 20C.

Stadtlengsfeld
Thuringia, (G)
1909–45

Michael Powolny,
Vienna, (A)
Late 19C.

Michael Powolny,
Vienna, (A)
Late 19C.

Mosa,
Maastricht, (H)
End 19C/early 20C.

Pauline Thompson,
E. Hendred,
Berks., (E)
Mid 20C.

Pinxton,
Derbyshire, (E)
1795–1801

Porc. Factory,
Neumunster,
(G) *End 19C.*

Portland Pottery,
Cobridge, Staffs.,
(E) *Mid 20C.*

Rouen,
(F) *Early 18C.*

Hutschen-reuther,
Hohenberg, (G)
Late 19C.

Yellowsands,
Bembridge,
I.O.W., (E)
Mid 20C.

Paul Rauschert,
Huttengrund,
Thuringia, (G)
1898–1945

Nevers,
(F) *Mid 17C.*

Steinwiessen,
Bavaria, (G)
1910–65

Stadtlengsfeld,
Thuringia,
(G) *Early 20C.*

Tirschenreuth,
(G) *1969–*

Ashby Potters Guild,
Derbyshire, (E)
Early 20C.

Powell & Bishop,
Hanley, (E)
Late 19C.

Ram,
Arnhem, (H)
c1923–30

Bow,
(E) *1750–59*

Risler,
Freiberg, (G)
Late 19C.

Marseilles,
(F) *c1773–93*

Meissen
(Augustus Rex),
(G) *c1720–50*

Sèvres,
(F) *1793–1804*

R. F.
Sèvres,
(F) *1793–1804*

R
Lowe, Ratcliffe,
Longton,
Staffs., (E)
Late 19C.

RM (in star)
Reinhold
Merkelbach,
Hohr-
Grenshausen,
(G) *Mid 20C.*

RMG
Reinhold
Merkelbach,
Hohr-
Grenshausen,
(G) *End 19C.*

R VEB
Earthenware
Factory,
Rheinsberg, (G)
Mid 20C.

·R·X·
Marseilles,
(F) *c1773–93*

LA
Porcelaine
Limousine,
Limoges, (F)
c1931–

S.A. & CO.
Smith
Ambrose,
Burslem, Staffs.,
(E) *Early 19C.*

St C / T
St. Cloud,
(F) *Early 18C.*

S+C / T
St Cloud,
(F) *Early 18C.*

So
Caughley,
(E) *1775–99*

Fasold & Stauch,
Bock-Wallendorf,
Thuringia, (G)
c1914–70

S:t
St. Eriks,
Upsala, (SWE)
1929–37

**Schutzmeister
& Quendt**,
Gotha,
Thuringia, (G)
Early 20C.

Samson, Edme,
Paris,
(F) *Mid 20C.*

U&C
M. Utzschneider,
Sarreguemines,
(F) *Mid 19C.*

·S
Caughley,
(E) *1775–99*

Sx
Sceaux,
Seine, (F)
c1763–84

S X
Sceaux,
Seine, (F)
c1763–84

S·X
Sceaux,
Seine, (F)
c1763–84

S X
Sceaux,
Seine, (F)
c1763–84

S·X· ʒh
Sceaux,
Seine, (F)
c1763–84

Frankenthal,
(G) *Mid 18C.*

TC
Torquay
Terra-cotta,
Devon, (E)
1875–1909

Kenneth Quick,
St. Ives,
Cornwall, (E)
Mid 20C.

Ruskin,
Birmingham, (E)
Late 19C.

R
Nevers,
(F) *Mid 19C.*

R
Villeroy & Boch,
Wurttemberg, (G)
Early 20C.

U. & C.
J. Uffrecht,
Haldensleben
(G) *Late 19C.*

V&B / M
Villeroy & Boch,
Mettlach,
Saar (G)
c1890–1910

V&B / M / geft
Villeroy & Boch,
Mettlach,
Saar (G)
c1885–1900

CHELSEA
Charles Vyse,
Chelsea, (E)
1928–

V
Kloster
Veilsdorf,
Thuringia, (G)
First half 20C.

Vf
Moustiers,
(F) *18C.*

Valenciennes,
(F) *Late 18C.*

**V. L.
B. X.**
Veuve Langlois,
Bayeux, (F)
Mid 19C.

VR
Van Recum,
Grunstadt, (G)
Early 19C.

VR / F
Frankenthal,
(G) *Mid 18C.*

W
Barnhouse,
Brockwei, (W)
Mid 20C.

W. B.
Wm.
Brownfield,
Cobridge,
Staffs., (E)
Mid 19C.

WB
F. Thomin,
Bavaria (G)
Early 19C.

WB
William Barnes,
Manchester, (E)
Mid 20C.

WB
W. B. Dalton,
London, (E)
Early 20C.

W B / & S (in box)
W.B. Simpson,
London, (E)
Late 19C.

W.B & S.
Wm. Brownfield,
Cobridge, Staffs.,
(E) *Late 19C.*

Wiesbaden,
(G) *Late 18C.*

W. F.
Bristol,
(E) *Mid 19C.*

**Fasold
& Stauch,**
Bock-Wallendorg,
(G) *Mid 20C.*

W. G
Wilhelm Gerike,
Althaldensleben,
(G) *End 19C/
early 20C.*

William Gill,
Castleford,
Yorks., (E)
Late 19C.

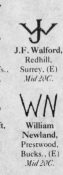

**Hawley,
Webberly,**
Longton, Staffs..
(E) *End 19C.*

J.F. Walford,
Redhill,
Surrey, (E)
Mid 20C.

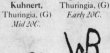

P. Wolfinger,
Weingarten
(G) *Early 20C.*

**Weiss,
Kuhnert,**
Thuringia, (G)
Mid 20C.

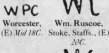

Wagner & Apel
Thuringia, (G)
Early 20C.

W. Moorcroft,
Burslem,
Staffs., (E)
Mid 20C.

**William
Newland,**
Prestwood,
Bucks., (E)
Mid 20C.

**Wm. Fishley
Holland,**
Clevedon,
Somerset, (E)
1921–

W PC
Worcester,
(E) *Mid 18C.*

Wm. Ruscoe,
Stoke, Staffs., (E)
20C.

**Eduard Josef
Wimmer,**
Vienna (A)
Early 20C.

W.VDB
Delft,
(H) *Early 17C.*

**Wenck &
Zitzmann,**
Kups, Bavaria,
(G) *Late 19C.*

Y.M.P
**Ynyamedw
Pottery,**
Ynyamedw, (W)
Mid 19C.

Reginald Wells,
Storrington,
Sussex, (E)
c1910

Delft
(H) *Mid 18C.*

Delft,
Rotterdam, (H)
Early 18C.

Bristol,
(E) *Late 18C.*

Delft,
(H) *Late 18C.*

B 2
Bristol,
(E) *c1773–81*

Bristol,
(E) *c1773–81*

B4 + 5
Bristol,
(E) *c1773–81*

Bristol,
(E) *c1773–81*

B 7
Bristol,
(E) *c1773–81*

Pinxton,
(E) *c1795–1801*

B
Tournai,
(F) *Mid 18C.*

12
B B
St. Cloud,
(F) *Early 18C.*

B 2
Rouen,
(F) *End 18C.*

D2
Lille,
(F) *c1720–80*

Derby,
(E) *1779*

E·L
1754
Bow,
(E) *1754*

**E
M+B
J760**
Bristol,
(E) *1760*

Copenhagen,
(D) *Mid 18C.*

·F.R.1734
Nevers,
(F) *1734*

**G.L
1728
30 Dec:**
Meissen,
(G) *1728*

Wrotham,
(E) *1651*

H I 1669
Wrotham,
(E) *1669*

Wrotham,
(E) *1697*

Worcester,
(E) *1764*

Delft,
(H) *1731*

M8.
Shelton,
Staffs., (E)
Late 17C.

Bristol,
(E) *c1773–81*

Pinxton,
(E) *c1795–1801*

New Hall,
Shelton, Staffs.,
(E) *1782–1810*

S 97
Sèvres,
(F) *End 19C.*

Bristol,
(E) *Mid 18C.*

Plymouth,
(E) *c1768–70*

Bristol,
(E) *c1773–81*

Bristol,
(E) *c1773–81*

Bow,
(E) *c1770–80*

Plymouth,
(E) *c1768–8*

Bristol,
(E) *c1773–81*

Bristol,
(E) *c1773–81*

1776
Bristol,
(E) *c1773–81*

W1
Chelsea
(E) *1743–83*

Chelsea,
(E) *1753–69*

Chelsea,
(E) *c1753–69*

Chelsea,
(E) *1753–69*

Chelsea,
(E) *1753–69*

Chelsea,
(E) *1753–69*

Chelsea,
(E) *1753–69*

Worcester,
(E) *1751–83*

Derby,
(E) *c1770–80*

Chelsea,
(E) *c1770–80*

Chelsea,
(E) *1753–69*

Chelsea,
(E) *1753–69*

Leeds,
(E) *Late 18C.*

Chelsea,
(E) *1753–69*

Samson, Edme,
Paris
(F) *Late 19C.*

Chelsea
(E) *1753–69*

Chelsea,
(E) *1753–69*

Chelsea,
(E) *c1753–69*

Chelsea
(E) *c1753–56*

Bow,
(E) *c1758–70*

Anchor Porc.
Longton, Staffs.
(E) *Early 19C*

Chelsea,
(E) *c1747–53*

Chelsea-Derby
(E) *c1770–84*

Chelsea,
(E) *1753–69*

A|M
Armand
Marseille
Thuringia,
(G) *Early 20C.*

Ernst. Bohne
Rudolfstadt,
Thuringia, (G)
1878–1920

British Anchor
Longton, Staffs.,
(E) *1884–1913*

F.G.
Wien
Goldscheider,
Vienna, (A)
Late 19C.

G|H
Hubbe Bros.
Prussia, (G)
Late 19C.

Moller & Dippe,
Thuringia, (G)
1883–1931

P|P
Prosgrund,
Prosgrunn, (N)
Mid 20C.

72 Porcelain & Pottery Marks

Fr. Bohme, Sorau, Brandenburg, (G) *1894–1918*

Worcester (Richard Holdship), (E) *Mid 18C.*

Chelsea, (E) *c1758–69*

Chelsea, (E) *c1753–69*

Chelsea, (E) *c1753–69*

Chelsea, (E) *c1758–69*

Chelsea, (E) *c1758–69*

Chelsea, (E) *c1753–69*

Chelsea, (E) *c1753–69*

Bow, (E) *Mid 18C.*

Bow, (E) *Mid 18C.*

Bow, (E) *Mid 18C.*

Bow, (E) *Mid 18C.*

Bow, (E) *Mid 18C.*

Bow, (E) *Mid 18C.*

Derby-Chelsea, (E) *c1770–83*

Derby-Chelsea, (E) *c1770–83*

Chelsea, (E) *1753–56*

Newcastle (Thos. Fell), (E) *Early 19C.*

Longton, (E) *Mid 19C.*

Bow, (E) *Mid 18C.*

Bow, (E) *Mid 18C.*

Bow, (E) *Mid 18C.*

Bow, (E) *Mid 18C.*

Bow, (E) *Mid 18C.*

Ludwigsburg, (G) *Mid 18C.*

De Klaauw, Delft, (H) *Mid 18C.*

De Klaauw, Delft, (H) *Mid 18C.*

Edgem Malkin, Burslem, Staffs., (E) *Late 19C.*

Williamson, Longton, Staffs., (E) *Early 20C.*

Frankenthal, (G) *Mid 18C.*

Amsterdam, (H) *Mid 18C.*

W.F. Murray, Glasgow, (S) *Late 19C.*

Thomas Morris, Longton, Staffs., (E) *End 19C.*

Furstenberg, (G) *18C.*

Ansbach, (G) *c1760–65*

Ansbach (G) *1760–65*

De Klaauw, Delft, (H) *Mid 18C.*

Amsterdam, (H) *Late 18C.*

Liverpool, (E) *c1830–40*

Liverpool, (E) *Late 18C.*

Ansbach (G) *c1760–65*

Charles Ford, Hanley, Staffs., (E) *Early 20C.*

Boulton, Machin, Tunstall, Staffs., (E) *End 19C.*

T. Rathbone, Tunstall, Staffs., (E) *Early 20C.*

Lille,
(F) *Late 18C.*

Lille,
(F) *Late 18C.*

Nyon,
(SW) Late 18C.

Slama & Co.,
Vienna, (A)
Mid 20C.

Pfluger Brothers,
Nyon,
(SW) Early 19C.

Horn Brothers,
Hornberg, (G)
Late 19C.

Faïencerie
de la Grande
Maison, Quimper,
(F) *1939*

Julius Hering,
Koppelsdorf,
Thuringia,
(G) *1908-45*

Limoges,
(F) *19C.*

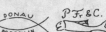
Ford & Riley,
Burslem Staffs.,
(E) *Late 19C.*

Alfred Bruno
Schwartz,
Berlin, (G)
Late 19C.

Derby,
(E) *Early 19C.*

Bow,
(E) *Mid 18C.*

Leeds,
(E) *Late 18C.*

Yarmouth
(Absolon) (E)
Early 19C.

Bristol,
(E) *Mid 18C.*

Caughley,
(E) *c1776-99*

Bow,
(E) *Mid 18C.*

Plymouth,
(E) *c1768-70*

Bow,
(E) *Mid 18C.*

Derby,
(E) *Mid 18C.*

Bow,
(E) *Mid 18C.*

Bristol
(E) *c1748-52*

Bow,
(E) *Mid 18C.*

Leeds,
(E) *Late 18C.*

Bow,
(E) *Mid 18C.*

Caughley,
(E) *c1775-99*

Rue de la
Roquette,
Paris, (F)
Late 18C.

Kalk Porcelain,
Eisenberg,
Thuringia, (G)
Early 20C.

R. Bloch,
Paris,
Mid 20C.

Christian Fischer,
Zwickau,
Saxony, (G)
c1875-1930

Bow,
(E) *Mid 18C.*

Rue de la
Roquette,
Paris, (F)
Late 18C.

Rue de la
Roquette,
Paris, (F)
Late 18C.

Nymphenberg,
(G) *Mid 18C.*

Bow,
(E) *Mid 18C.*

Lowestoft,
(E) *c1757-80*

Caughley,
(E) *c1775-99*

Bow,
(E) *Mid 18C.*

Delft,
(H) *Mid 18C.*

Caughley,
(E) *c1775-99*

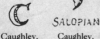
Caughley,
(E) *c1775-99*

Worcester,
(E) *c1751-83*

Worcester,
(E) *c1751-83*

Caughley,
(E) *c1775-99*

Worcester,
(E) *1751–83*

Bow,
(E) *Mid 18C.*

Caughley,
(E) *c1775–99*

Worcester,
(E) *1751–83*

Caughley,
(E) *c1775–99*

Pinxton,
(E) *c1795–1801*

Caughley,
(E) *c1775–99*

Bow,
(E) *Mid 18C.*

Worcester,
(E) *1751–83*

Nymphenberg,
(G) *Mid 18C.*

Lowestoft,
(E) *Late 18C.*

Worcester,
(E) *1751–83*

Caughley,
(E) *c1775–99*

Worcester,
(E) *1751–83*

W. Goebel,
Oeslau, (G)
End 19C.

Fulda,
(G) *c1764–89*

Varages,
(F) *Early 18C.*

Bristol,
(E) *Mid 18C.*

Bristol,
(E) *Mid 18C.*

Goult,
(F) *Mid 18C.*

Bristol,
(E) *Mid 18C.*

Vinovo,
(I) *c1776–1820*

Varages,
(F) *Late 18C.*

Chelsea,
(E) *Mid 18C.*

Leeds,
(E) *Late 18C.*

Bow,
(E) *Mid 18C.*

Nymphenberg,
(G) *Mid 18C.*

Copenhagen,
(D) *c1770*

Samson, Edme
Paris, (F)
Mid 20C.

Swansea,
(E) *c1814*

Samson, Edme
Paris, (F)
c1940

Ernst Teichert,
Meissen,
Saxony, (G)
Late 19C.

Schoenau Bros,
Huttensteinach,
Thuringia, (G)
Late 18C/early 19C.

Carl Thieme,
Pottschappel,
Saxony, (G)
Late 19C.

Karl Ens,
Volkstedt,
Thuringia, (G)
1919–1972

Sorau Porcelain,
Brandenburg, (G)
Early 20C.

Bow,
(E) *Mid 18C.*

Bow,
(E) *Mid 18C.*

Bow,
(E) *Mid 18C.*

Bow,
(E) *Mid 18C.*

Bow,
(E) *Mid 18C.*

Bow,
(E) *Mid 18C.*

Bow,
(E) *Mid 18C.*

Longton Hall,
Staffs., (E)
c1749-60

Longton Hall,
Staffs., (E)
c1749-60

Plymouth,
(E) *c1768–70*

Bow,
(E) *Mid 18C.*

Limbach,
Thuringia, (G)
Late 18C.

Limbach,
Thuringia, (G)
Late 18C.

Bristol,
(E) *c1773–81*

Bristol,
(E) *c1773–81*

Meissen,
(G) *c1725–40*

Meissen,
(G) *19C.*

Meissen,
(G) *19C.*

Caughley,
(E) *c1775–99*

Worcester,
(E) *Late 18C.*

Bristol,
(E) *Mid 18C.*

Meissen,
(G) *Mid 18C.*

Meissen,
(G) *Early 18C.*

Meissen,
(G) *19C.*

Bristol,
(E) *1770–1780*

Meissen,
(G) *Mid 18C.*

Meissen,
(G) *Mid 18C.*

Meissen,
(G) *c1763–74*

Meissen,
(G) *c1774*

Derby,
(E) *Mid 18C.*

Meissen,
(G) *c1725–63*

Worcester,
(E) *Mid 18C.*

Meissen,
(G) *c1730*

Bristol
(Champion),
(E) *c1773–81*

Coalport,
Coalbrookdale,
(E) *Early 19C.*

Meissen,
(G) *c1766*

Meissen,
(G) *Mid 18C.*

Meissen,
(G) *c1750*

Meissen,
(G) *c1750*

Meissen,
(G) *c1750*

Bristol,
(E) *c1773–81*

Samson, Edme,
Paris, (F)
Mid 20C.

Meissen,
(G) *c1730*

Meissen,
(G) *Late 18C.*

Meissen,
(G) *Mid 18C.*

Meissen,
(G) *Early 19C.*

Meissen,
(G) *Early 19C.*

Bristol,
(E) *c1773–81*

Meissen,
(G) *Mid 18C.*

Worcester,
(E) *Mid 18C.*

Meissen,
(G) *Early 19C.*

Samson, Edme.,
Paris, (F)
End 19C/early 20C.

Coalport,
Coalbrookdale,
(E) *Early 19C.*

Meissen,
(G) *Mid 18C.*

Caughley, (E) *c1775–99*

Caughley, (E) *c1775–99*

Meissen, (G) *Mid 18C.*

Meissen, (G) *Mid 18C.*

Meissen, (G) *Mid 18C.*

Meissen, (G) *Mid 18C.*

Meissen, (G) *Mid 18C.*

Worcester, (E) *Mid 18C.*

Jacob Petit, Fontainbleau, (F) *c1830–40*

Bristol, (E) *1773–81*

Bristol, (E) *1773–81*

Achille Bloch, Paris, (F) *c1926–30*

Bristol, (E) *1773–81*

Bristol, (E) *1773–81*

Bristol, (E) *1773–81*

Meissen, (G) *c1723*

Ruskin Pottery, Birmingham, (E) *End 19C.*

Paris, (F) *c1820*

Tournai, (B) *Mid 18C.*

Meissen, (G) *Mid 18C.*

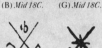

Meissen, (G) *c1723*

Meissen, (G) *c1723*

Bristol, (E) *c1773–81*

Worcester, (E) *Mid 18C.*

Meissen, (G) *c1725*

Bristol, (E) *c1773–81*

Bristol, (E) *c1773–81*

Bristol, (E) *c1773–81*

Bristol, (E) *c1773–81*

Bristol, (E) *c1773–81*

Derby, (E) *c1755–1770*

Derby, (E) *c1755–1770*

Derby (Bloor), (E) *c1820–50*

Vincennes, (F) *Mid 18C.*

Derby, (Duesbury), (E) *c1784–1815*

Derby, (E) *c1780–84*

Belleek, Co. Fermanagh, (IR) *Late 19C.*

Derby, (E) *c1784–1815*

Worcester, (E) *c1813–40*

Derby, (E) *1784–1815*

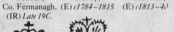

Royal Crown Derby, (E) *1877–89*

Leeds, (E) *Mid 18C.*

Derby, (E) *c1784–1815*

Sèvres, (F) *1781*

Sèvres, (F) *1773*

K

Derby,
(E) *Late 18C.*

Limoges,
(F) *c1783*

Sèvres,
(F) *c1824–30*

Stevenson
& Hancock,
Derby, (E)
Mid 19C.

Sèvres,
(F) *c1830–48*

Derby,
(Duesbury
& Kean),
(E) *End 18C.*

Meissen,
(G) *Mid 18C.*

Derby,
(E) *c1815–48*

Derby,
(Duesbury
& Kean),
(E) *End 18C.*

Buen Retiro,
Madrid, (Sp)
c1760–1808

Frankenthal,
(G) *c1755–99*

Hochst,
(G) *Mid 18C.*

Ludwigsberg,
(G) *c1758–93*

Derby,
(E) *c1815–1848*

Hilditch,
Longton,
Staffs., (E)
Early 19C.

Meissen,
(G) *c1720–50*

Sèvres,
(F) *1814–48*

R.H. Plant,
Longton,
Staffs., (E)
Late 19C.

Tournai,
(B) *Mid 18C.*

Meissen,
(G) *Late 19C*

Vincennes,
(F) *Mid 18C.*

Clignancourt,
(F) *c1780–98*

Chelsea,
(E) *Mid 18C.*

Vincennes,
(F) *Mid 18C.*

Vincennes,
(F) *Mid 18C.*

Samson, Edme,
Paris, (F)
20C.

Sèvres,
(F) *c1745–53*

Sèvres,
(F) *c1745–53*

Sèvres,
(F) *c1745–53*

Sèvres,
(F) *c1745–53*

Sèvres,
(F) *c1745–53*

Coalport,
Coalbrookdale,
(E) *Early 19C.*

Sèvres,
(F) *1745–53*

Worcester,
(E) *Mid 18C.*

Sèvres,
(F) *c1745–53*

Sèvres,
(F) *1745–53*

Buen Retiro,
Madrid, (Sp)
c1759–1808

Minton,
Stoke, Staffs.,
(E) *End 18C.*

Royal
Copenhagen,
Copenhagen, (D)
Late 19C.

Buen Retiro,
Madrid, (Sp)
c1759–1808

Ludwigsburg,
(G) *c1758–93*

Niderviller,
(F) *Late 18C.*

Nuremburg,
(G) *Early 18C.*

Niderviller,
(F) *Late 18C.*

Niderviller,
(F) *Late 18C.*

78 Porcelain & Pottery Marks

Ludwigsburg, (G) *c1758–93*

Moustiers, (F) *c1650–1750*

Bruges, (B) *18C.*

Tournai, (B) *Mid 18C.*

Nymphenberg, (G) *Est 1747*

Saint Cloud, (F) *c1670–1766*

Marseilles, (F) *Late 18C.*

Ginori, (I) *After 1820*

Buen Retiro, Madrid, (Sp) *c1759–1808*

Ginori, (I) *Mid 19C.*

Marseilles, (F) *Late 18C.*

Buen Retiro, Madrid, (SP) *c1759–1808*

Buen Retiro, Madrid, (Sp) *c1759–1808*

Minton, Stoke, Staffs., (E) *After 1850*

Bow, (E) *Mid 18C.*

Rouen, (F) *Late 16C.*

Capo-di-Monte, Naples, (I) *c1730–40*

Marseilles, (F) *Late 18C.*

Marseilles, (F) *Late 18C.*

Orleans, (F) *Late 18C.*

Delft, (H) *Late 17C.*

Delft, (H) *Late 17C.*

Delft, (H) *Late 17C.*

Delft, (H) *Late 17C.*

Coalport, Coalbrookdale, (E) *Early 19C.*

Caughley (Rose), (E) *c1799–1814*

Longport, Staffs., (E) *Early 19C.*

Delft, (H) *Mid 18C.*

Volkstedt, Thuringia, (G) *Late 18C.*

Grosbreitenbach, (G) *Late 18C.*

Faenza, (I) *Late 17C.*

Walton Pottery, Derbyshire, (E) *Mid 20C.*

I H

Shelton, Staffs., (E) *Late 18C.*

Spode, Stoke, Staffs., (E) *Late 18C.*

Hochst, (G) *Mid 18C.*

D

Hochst, (G) *Mid 18C.*

Hochst, (G) *Mid 18C.*

Hochst, (G) *Mid 18C.*

Hochst, (G) *Mid 18C.*

Copenhagen, (D) *Early 20C.*

Kerr & Binns, Worcester, (E) *Mid 19C.*

Worcester, (E) *Late 18C.*

Worcester, (E) *Late 18C.*

Bow, (E) *Mid 18C.*

Pendley Pottery, Tring, Herts., (E) *Mid 20C.*

Worcester, (E) *Late 18C.* | **Meissen,** (G) *Early 18C.* | **Worcester,** (E) *Late 18C.* | **Worcester,** (E) *Late 18C.* | **Worcester,** (E) *Late 18C.*

Worcester, (E) *Late 18C.* | **Meissen,** (G) *Early 18C.* | **Longton,** (Mayer & Newbold), Staffs., (E) *19C.* | **Meissen,** (G) *Early 18C.* | **Meissen,** (G) *Early 18C.*

Derby, (E) *Late 18C.* | **Chelsea,** (E) *c1758–69* | **Baden,** (G) *Mid 18C* | **Bow,** (E) *Mid 18C.* | **Bow,** (E) *Mid 18C.*

Derby, (E) *Mid 18C.* | **Chelsea,** (E) *c1743–47* | **Bevington,** (F) *c1872–92* | **Chelsea,** (E) *c1743–47* | **Bow,** (E) *Mid 18C.*

Bristol, (E) *c1763–73* | **Hanley,** Staffs., (E) *19C.* | **Newcastle,** (E) *Mid 19C.* | **Adolf Bauer,** Prussia, (G) *End 19C.* | **Kahla,** Thuringia, (G) *20C.*

Worcester, (E) *c1751–83* | **Worcester,** (E) *c1751–83* | **Worcester,** (E) *c1751–83* | **Worcester,** (E) *c1751–83* | **Worcester,** (E) *c1751–83*

Worcester, (E) *c1751–83* | **Worcester,** (E) *c1751–83* | **Worcester,** (E) *c1751–83* | **Burslem,** Staffs., (E) *Early 18C* | **Caughley,** (E) *c1775–99*

Caughley, (E) *c1775–99* | **Worcester,** (E) *c1751–81* | **Meissen,** (G) *Early 18C.* | **Meissen,** (G) *Early 18C.* | **Samson, Edme,** Paris, (F) *Late 19C.*

Coalport, Coalbrookdale, (E) *c1828–50* | **Meissen,** (G) *Early 18C.* | **Meissen,** (G) *Early 18C.* | **Meissen,** (G) *Early 18C.* | **Delft,** (H) *Mid 18C.*

Q

Gustafsberg,
(SWE) *Mid 19C.*

Minton,
Stoke, Staffs.,
(E) *Mid 19C.*

Burgess & Leigh,
Burslem, Staffs.,
(E) *Early 20C.*

Rockingham,
Swinton, Yorks.
(E) *Early 19C.*

Robert Heron,
Kirkcaldy, (S)
c1880–1929

Minton,
Stoke, Staffs.,
(E) *c1836–41*

Swansea,
(W) *Early 19C.*

J. Dimmock,
Hanley,
Staffs., (E)
Late 19C.

Read &
Clementson,
Hanley, Staffs.,
(E) *1833–35*

Wm. Ridgway,
Hanley,
Staffs., (E)
c1830–50

R

Derby,
(E) *Mid 18C.*

Derby,
(E) *Mid 18C.*

Tournai,
(B) *Mid 18C.*

Savona,
(I) *18C.*

Barn Pottery,
(E) *1964–*

Limoges,
(F) *Late 18C.*

J. & M.P. Bell,
Glasgow, (S)
Late 19C.

Worcester,
(E) *c1751–83*

Chantilly,
(F) *c1725–93*

Chantilly,
(F) *c1725–93*

Royal Factory,
Vienna, (A)
Mid 19C.

W.T. Copeland,
Stoke, Staffs.,
(E) *Early 20C.*

A.E. Gray,
Stoke, Staffs., (E)
Early/mid 20C.

Ridgways,
Hanley, Staffs.,
(E) *Late 19C./*
early 20C.

Hackwood,
Shelton, Staffs.,
(E) *Early/*
mid 19C.

S

Meissen,
(G) *Early 18C.*

Nymphenberg,
(G) *Mid 18C.*

Nymphenberg,
(G) *Late 18C.*

Royal
Factory,
Vienna, (A)
Mid 18C.

Royal
Factory,
Vienna (A)
Mid 18C.

Hutschendreuther,
Bavaria, (G)
Mid 19C.

Royal
Factory,
Vienna, (A)
Late 18C.

Royal
Factory,
Vienna, (A)
Late 18C.

Hutschendreuther,
Bavaria, (G)
Early 19C.

Ansbach,
(G) *Mid/late 18C.*

Vienna,
(A) *Mid 18C.*

Ansbach,
(G) *Mid 18C.*

Marieberg,
(SWE) *Mid 18C.*

Ludwigsburg,
(G) *Mid/late 18C.*

Plaue,
(G) *After 1817*

T

Liverpool,
(E) *Mid 18C.*

Paris,
(Rue Popincourt),
(F) *Late 18C.*

Milan,
(I) *18C.*

Derby,
(I. Farnsworth),
(E) *Late 18C.*

Wallendorf,
Thuringia, (G)
Mid 18C.

Ginori,
Doccia, (I)
Mid 18C.

Caughley,
(E) *c1775–99*

Hochst,
(G) *Mid 18C.*

Nevers,
(F) *Late 17C.*

Nymphenberg,
(G) *Mid 18C.*

Derby (Bloor),
(E) *c1815–48*

Saint Cloud,
(F) *c1670–1766*

Saint Cloud,
(F) *c1670–1766*

Ginori,
Doccia, (I)
Early 18C.

Savona,
(I) *Late 17Cl
early 18C.*

Vincennes,
(F) *Mid 18C.*

Vincennes,
(F) *Mid 18C.*

Vincennes,
(F) *Mid 18C.*

Vincennes,
(F) *Mid 18C.*

Worcester,
(E) *Mid 18C.*

Baden,
(G) *Mid 18C.*

Ansbach,
(G) *c1760–65*

Bow,
(E) *Mid 18C.*

Caughley,
(F) *c1775–99*

Bow,
(F) *Mid 18C.*

Bristol,
(E) *Late 18C.*

Orleans,
(F) *Mid/late 18C.*

Ludwigsburg,
(G) *Mid 18C.*

Frankenthal,
(G) *c1755–59*

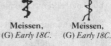

Royal
Factory,
Berlin, (G)
Mid 18C.

Royal
Factory,
Berlin, (G)
Mid 18C.

Royal
Factory,
Berlin, (G)
Mid 18C.

Royal
Factory,
Berlin, (G)
Mid 18C.

Meissen,
(G) *Early 18C.*

Meissen,
(G) *Early 18C.*

Worcester,
(E) *Mid 18C.*

Royal
Factory,
Berlin, (G)
Late 18C.

Meissen,
(G) *Early 18C.*

Chelsea,
(E) *c1747–53*

Caughley,
(E) *c1775–99*

Derby,
(E) *Late 18C.*

Chelsea/Derby,
(E) *Late 18C.*

Meissen,
(G) *Early 18C.*

Meissen,
(G) *Early 18C.*

Faenza,
(I) *16C.*

Kloster-Veilsdorf,
Thuringia (G)
Late 18C.

Hispano-
Moresque,
(Sp) *17C.*

Gubbio,
Umbria (I)
17C.

Castel Durante,
Urbino (I)
Late 16Clearly 17C.

Castelli,
Abruzzi (I)
17C.

The Major Factories

BOW

Bow shares with Chelsea the distinction of being one of the first two porcelain factories in England, but its early history is obscure. It was founded by Thomas Frye, an Irish painter, and Edward Heylyn, a glass merchant, at Stratford Langthorne in the East End of London. In 1775 the factory was acquired by W. Duesbury, owner of the Derby porcelain factory, who removed all the moulds and tools to Derby. There they were joined by those of the Chelsea factory in 1786.

Bow Blue and White Wares

* Blue and white wares are divided into three periods which coincide roughly with changes in the appearance of the wares.
* *Early period 1749–54:* Wares often thickly potted, glaze can be blue/green in pools. Many wares painted in a pale clear royal blue which sometimes blurs. Some very well potted wares, often marked with an incised R also produced.
* "In the white"' wares with applied decoration also produced.
* *Middle period 1755–65:* Darker underglaze blue. Wares more thinly potted but relatively heavy. Body more porous and prone to staining. Painter's numerals used on base and occasionally inside footrings as with Lowestoft.
* *Late period 1765–76:* Translucency poor. Marked deterioration in quality. Can resemble earthenware.

Bow Polychrome Wares

* Early period wares are decorated in vivid "famille rose" colours.
* The patterns used usually include chrysanthemum and peony.
* Earliest wares have a greyish body but by 1754 a good ivory tone was often achieved.
* On wares after 1760 the colours can appear dull and dirty with an adverse effect on value.
* In the late 1750's some attractive botanical plates were produced.
* After 1760 Meissen influenced floral decoration most commonly found.

BRISTOL

The first porcelain to be produced at Bristol was a soft paste first discovered by Benjamin Lund c1749. The formula included soaprock from Cornwall.

Bristol c1749–52

* These porcelains are very rare but examples sometimes show the relief moulded marks "Bristol" or "Bristoll".
* Mostly underglaze blue ware with chinoiserie decoration.
* The glaze was tight fitting although it had a tendency to pool and bubble.
* The blue often looks watery where it has run in the firing.
* In 1752 Bristol moulds were sold to Worcester.
* It is extremely difficult to differentiate late Lund's Bristol from early Worcester.

Bristol c.1770–81

* William Cookworthy transferred his Plymouth factory to Bristol in 1770.
* The body had a tendency to slight tears and firing cracks.
* Early wares extremely difficult to differentiate from Plymouth – both show same firing imperfections, such as smoky ivory glaze and wreathing in the body.
* Champion took over in 1773.
* Towards mid and late 1770's the dominant decorative style was neo-classical with particular reliance on delicate swags and scattered flowers.
* Later pieces showed small imperfections in enamel and potting.
* Later Bristol colours are sharp and gilding is of an excellent quality.

CAUGHLEY

A pottery was established at Caughley near Broseley in Shropshire soon after 1750. It began producing porcelain after it was taken over by Thomas Turner in 1772. In 1775 Robert Hancock, formerly of the Worcester Porcelain factory, joined the factory and introduced transfer printing in blue underglaze.

* Painted wares tend to be earlier than printed ones.
* Caughley body of the soapstone type often shows orange to transmitted light, but in some cases can even show slightly greenish which adds to the confusion with Worcester.

* Glaze is good and close fitting, although when gathered in pools may have greeny-blue tint.
* From 1780's many pieces heightened in gilding; some blue and white Chinese export wares were similarly gilded in England.
* Caughley is often confused with Worcester; they have many patterns in common, eg. "The Cormorant and Fisherman" and "Fence" patterns. Hatched crescents never appear on Caughley; they were purely a Worcester mark.

CHANTILLY

Founded in 1725 under the patronage of Louis-Henri de Bourbon, Prince de Condé and managed by Ciquaire Cirou until his death in 1751. Only soft paste porcelain was made, covered until c1735 (and sometimes later though much less frequently after 1751) with an opaque tin glaze. The products of the factory have been extensively copied and faked since C19. So be sure before buying.

* Up to 1750's, milk white opaque tin-glaze.
* Beautiful white finish, inspired by Japanese porcelain.
* In the mid C18. European floral styles introduced.
* In 1750's transparent lead glaze introduced to compete with Vincennes.
* Tended then to copy Meissen and Vincennes designs.
* From 1755–1780 many floral designs produced often in one colour, like the "Chantilly sprig" which was then copied by other factories e.g. Caughley.
* The factory had basically ceased by the end of the century.

CHELSEA

The factory's early history is very vague but it may have acquired the vital secret of porcelain manufacture from Thomas Briand who demonstrated a fine white porcelain to the Royal Society in 1742.

Chelsea Triangle Period 1745–49
* Wares scarce and costly.
* Many based on silver prototypes and "Blanc de Chine" ware.
* Mainly left undecorated.
* Body comparatively thick, slightly chalky with "glassy" glaze.

Chelsea raised anchor period 1749–1752
* Paste now improved.
* Shapes still derived from silver, although Meissen influence noticeable.
* Mostly restrained decoration, either Kakiemon or sparse floral work (often to cover flaws).
* Often difficult to distinguish from rare "Girl in a Swing" factory wares.
* The most collectable ware of this and the Red Anchor period was fable decoration by J.H. O'Neale.
* The creamy almost waxy appearance of glaze is virtually indistinguishable from red anchor glaze, apart from the higher content of earlier body.

Red Anchor Period 1752–1756
* This period mainly influenced by Meissen.
* Glaze now slightly opaque.
* Paste smoother with few flaws.
* The figures unsurpassed by any other English factory.
* On useful wares, fine flower and botanical painting.
* Chelsea "toys" are rare and very expensive.

Gold Anchor Period 1757–1769
* Chelsea's rococo period, with rich gilding and mazarine blue.
* Quite florid in style, in comparison to earlier more restrained painting.
* Influenced by Sèvres.
* Elaborate bocage greatly favoured on figures.
* Has thick glaze which tends to craze.

COALPORT
(Rose & Co.)

Founded by John Rose in the early 1790's at Coalbrookdale. He purchased the Caughley works in 1799 but had them demolished in 1814. In around 1811 the firm was taken over by John Rose, William Clarke and Charles Maddison. The Coalport factory is still in existence today.

* Early blue and white wares very close in style and feeling to Caughley products.
* Note particularly the somewhat clear royal blue tone of the cobalt.
* Produced hard paste porcelain certainly after 1800, before then produced soapstone porcelain; this was quite similar to Caughley but does not have the yellow-brown translucency.

* Early wares heavy, with greyish appearance.
* In this period quite similar to Newhall and Chamberlains.
* The highly decorated Japan wares were of exceptional quality as are some of the flower painted examples.
* In 1820 a new leadless glaze was invented and they also began to use Billingsley's frit paste. Whereas original Welsh plates were thinly potted, Coalport were heavier and less crisp.
* In 1820 Rose also bought moulds from Nantgarw and Swansea and Billingsley came to work at Coalport.
* Best period for the Coalport factory began in 1820 when the factory produced a brilliantly white hard felspar porcelain, with a high translucency.
* The rococo wares of the late 1820's and 30's are often confused with Rockingham.
* After 1820, CD, CD monogram, C. Dale, Coalbrookdale and Coalport were all used; before this date the marks tend to vary and much was unmarked.
* In 1840's and 1850's Coalport perfected many fine ground colours: maroon, green and pink.
* These often rivalled Sèvres especially in 1850's and 1860's and are close to the Minton examples of this period.
* Coalport also at this time produced Chelsea copies, with fake marks – these are rare.

DAVENPORT

A factory making earthenware was started by John Davenport at Longport, Staffordshire in 1793 and a porcelain factory was added in 1820. The porcelain produced often imitated Derby porcelain as some of the painters were employed at both factories.

* Early porcelain of a hard-paste variety.
* Any Davenport marked "Longport" is quite rare.
* High quality wares produced, particularly in mid C19.
* On botanical wares if the flowers are named it can add 50% to the value.
* High quality Davenport often wrongly classified as Rockingham.
* Davenport produced the Imari styles better known on Royal Crown Derby; this is rarer than Derby but not as collectable.
* The factory closed in 1887.

DERBY

The first Derby porcelain factory was functioning in an experimental way by 1750, and was, possibly, started by Thomas Briand of the Chelsea factory with James Marchand. In 1756 William Duesbury from Chelsea joined John Heath and André Planche in an agreement to start a factory and this presumably became the first Derby Porcelain Factory.

18th-Century Derby

* Some early white jugs incised with the letter D have been attributed to the early Derby factory.
* Early Derby is soft paste and is generally lighter than Bow and Chelsea.
* Very rare to find crazing on early Derby; the glaze was tight fitting and thinner than Chelsea.
* Glaze often kept away from the bottom edge or edge was trimmed, hence the term "dry-edge" (particularly applied to figures).
* c1755, three (or more) pieces of clay put on bottom of figure to keep it clear of kiln furniture, giving "patch" or "pad" marks – which now have darker appearance.
* Duesbury's early works display quite restrained decoration, with much of the body left plain, in the Meissen style.
* Derby can be regarded as the English Meissen.
* The porcelain of this period has an excellent body, sometimes with faintly bluish appearance.
* 1770–84 known as the Chelsea-Derby period.
* Chelsea-Derby figures almost always made at Derby.
* 1770's saw the introduction of unglazed white biscuit Derby figures.
* This points to the move away from the academic Meissen style towards the more fashionable French taste.
* In 1770's leading exponent of the neo-classical style, and comparable to contemporary wares of Champion's Bristol.
* Body of 1770's is frequently of silky appearance and of bluish-white tone.
* 1780's Derby body very smooth and glaze white. The painting on such pieces was superb, especially landscapes of Jockey Hill and Zachariah Boreman.
* 1780's and 1790's noted for exceptional botanical painting

by "Quaker" Pegg and John Brewer.
* Around 1800 the body degenerated, was somewhat thicker, and the glaze tended to crackle and allow discolouration.

LIVERPOOL

The attribution of Liverpool porcelains to their various factories has, for the most part, taken place within the last thirty years. Previously, Liverpool wares were grouped together and largely disregarded. This attitude has now changed completely and porcelain from the Liverpool factories is eagerly collected.

Samuel Gilbody's Factory c1754–1761
* Samuel Gilbody purchased his father's factory from his mother in 1754.
* The Gilbody group is the rarest of all Liverpool groups.
* An attractive, sometimes blurred greyish underglaze blue.
* Some blurred blue designs were then enamelled in iron red.
* Heavily potted early wares in blue and overglaze iron red can be confused with Bow wares.
* The typical Gilbody glaze is smooth and silky.

Richard Chaffers & Partners c1754–1765
* Richard Chaffers & Partners conducted an earthenware manufactory in Liverpool during the 1740's.
* In 1755 Chaffers engaged Robert Podmore as manager in return for the secret "of making earthenware in imitation of or to resemble china ware".
* Early phosphatic wares have a greyish body.
* Later steatitic wares are noticeably whiter.
* Potting based on Worcester shapes.

William Ball c1755–1769
* The factory produced a large variety of shapes including teawares.
* Decoration often resembled delft.
* Paste often shows small turning tears. These show up as lighter flecks when held up to the light.
* Polychrome wares are rare and collectable.
* Elaborate rococo sauceboats were a factory speciality.

William Reid c1755–1761
* Often a crude and semi opaque body.
* Glaze opacified by the use of tin outside.
* Mainly blue and white.
* Reid became bankrupt in 1761 and his factory was occupied by William Ball.

Philip Christian c1765–1776
* Philip Christian took over Richard Chaffers factory upon his death.
* In 1772 Christian renewed his licence to mine steatite at Predannak, Cornwall.
* In 1776 Philip Christian and Son sold their interest and ceased manufacturing.

James, John and Seth Pennington c1769–1799
* The majority of the output was blue and white.
* Some highly collectable ship painted dated jugs and bowls produced in 1770's and 1780's.
* A very dark underglaze blue was used in 1770's and 1780's.
* The glaze is sometimes tinted blue/grey.
* Transfer prints often smudgy in appearance.

Wolfe & Co c1795 to 1800
* In 1795 Thomas Wolfe and partners took over one of the Pennington family's factories.
* Unlike the other Liverpool factories the vast majority of their output was decorated in polychrome.
* Some of the wares are well potted and attractively painted.

LONGTON HALL

The Longton Hall porcelain factory was the first porcelain factory in Staffordshire. Founded in 1749 by William Jenkinson, it was run by William Littler and William Nicklin. The factory closed in 1760 and all the wares are now rare.
* Earliest pieces are the "Snowman" figures and some blue and white wares.
* There has been a re-attribution of some Longton wares to the West Pans factory started by Wm. Littler in the early 1760's.
* West Pans wares are usually decorated in a crude tone of blue, polychrome decoration is often badly rubbed.
* Some West Pans wares are marked with two crossed L's with a tail of dots below.
* The figures, in particular, tend

to have a stiff, lumpy appearance.
* The porcelain is of the glassy soft-paste type.
* The glaze can tend to have a greenish-grey appearance.
* Pieces often thickly potted.
* Duesbury worked at Longton Hall before going to Derby.
* The "middle period" of the factory from c1754–57 saw the best quality porcelain produced.
* Specialized in wares of vegetable form, some of ungainly appearance, unlike the more sophisticated wares of Chelsea.
* Much of the output of the middle period was moulded.
* Two famous painters from the period are the "Castle painter" and the "trembly rose" painter.
* Sadler's black printed wares are extremely rare and sought after.
* The porcelain is generally unmarked.
* Some Longton moulds purchased by Cookworthy for use at Plymouth.

LOWESTOFT

The Lowestoft porcelain factory was founded in 1757 and produced soft-paste porcelain similar in quality to Bow. The factory closed c1800 but its manager, Robert Allen, continued to work as a porcelain painter, using a muffle kiln.
* Soft paste porcelain using bone ash.
* Damage tends to stain brown.
* Decoration of early wares is well detailed and less stylized than post 1765.
* Collectors are interested in unusual shapes.
* Coloured wares presently undervalued.
* No factory mark but many pieces pre-1775 numbered inside footrim or on base if no footrim.
* Numbers are usually between 1 and 11.
* Late period blue and white teabowls and saucers and other common teawares in painted or printed patterns should still be found at reasonable prices, particularly if damaged.
* Coloured wares have been undervalued in recent years and it is still possible to form a collection of extremely interesting pieces without spending a fortune.
* Many collectors are interested in unusual shapes – bottles,

inkwells, eggcups, salts, eye baths and so on. Even damaged items can be very collectable but tend to be expensive.
* Lowestoft produced quite a large number of inscribed and dated pieces. These are highly collectable even if damaged. Beware of fakes produced by French factories earlier this century which are hard, rather than soft paste.
* Early blue and white wares are of great interest to collectors. It is worth consulting a specialist book in order to help identify these pieces correctly as there is a growing tendency to give pieces an optimistically inaccurate early date.

MEISSEN

The Meissen porcelain factory was founded in 1710, but from an artistic point of view the factory's great period began in 1720 with the appointment of J. C. Herold as chief painter.
* In 1709 J F Böttger produced a white hard paste porcelain.
* Wares often decorated by outside decorators (Hausmaler).
* In 1720 kilnmaster Stozel came back to Meissen bringing with him J G Herold.
* From 1720–50 the enamelling on Meissen was unsurpassed – starting with the wares of *Lowenfinck* – bold, flamboyant chinoiserie or Japonnaise subjects, often derived from the engravings of Petruschenk, particularly on Augustus Rex wares. *J G Herold* specialized in elaborate miniature chinoiserie figure subjects. *C F Herold* noted for European and Levantine quay scenes.
* Crossed swords factory mark started in 1723.
* Marks, shapes and styles much copied.
* Underside of wares on later body has somewhat greyish chalky appearance.
* In late 1720's a somewhat glassier, harder looking paste was introduced, different from the early ivory tones of the Böttger period.
* Finest Meissen figures modelled by J J Kändler from 1731.
* Best figures late 1730's and early 1740's – especially the great Commedia dell'Arte figures and groups.
* Other distinguished modellers who often worked in association with Kändler were Paul

Reinicke and J F Eberlein.
* Cut-flower decoration
  (Schnittblumen) often
  associated with J G Klinger.
  The naturalistic flower subjects
  of the 1740's, epitomized by
  Klinger, gradually became less
  realistic and moved towards the
  so-called "manier Blumen" of
  the 1750's and 1760's.
* Early models had been
  mounted on simple flat pad
  bases, whereas from 1750's
  bases were lightly moulded
  rococo scrolls.

MINTON

Minton's pottery and porcelain
factory was founded at Stoke-on-
Trent, Staffordshire. The site was
bought in 1793 by Thomas
Minton who had worked at
Caughley and Spode. The factory
first produced earthenware and
started to make porcelain c1798.
* Factory mainly famous for its
  bone china.
* Early patterns tend to be very
  similar to Newhall, Pinxton and
  Spode.
* Early wares not marked but did
  often have a pattern number,
  sometimes with N. or No. in
  front.
* Minton palette is closest to
  Pinxton.
* Much pre-1850 Minton is
  wrongly ascribed to other
  factories, espec. Pinxton,
  Rockingham and Coalport.
* The early figures are prone to
  damage – watch for restoration.
* Very few heavily flower
  encrusted wares have escaped
  without damage.
* Some beautiful ground colours
  with excellent gilding, Minton
  had particular success with a
  turquoise ground.
* As with other factories, signed
  pieces are most desirable.
* Artists of note include:- G.
  Hancock, J. Bancroft, T.
  Kirkby, T. Allen, R. Pilsbury,
  Jesse Smith and A. Boullemier.
* Note on marks: – MINTON
  became MINTONS from
  c1873.

NEWHALL

The usual date given for
commencement of the factory is
1782; however it was then known
as Hollins, Warburton & Co.
* Newhall was the second
  Staffordshire pottery to make
  porcelain successfully, Longton
  Hall being the first.
* Newhall used the Cookworthy
  method of making a class of

porcelain known as hybrid hard-
paste.
* Porcelain is a greyish colour to
  transmitted light and is seldom
  crazed.
* Duvivier, who had worked at
  Derby and Worcester, also
  painted at Newhall from 1782–
  1790 – because of the rarity of
  attributable pieces one wonders
  if some of his work at Newhall
  has been wrongly attributed to
  another factory.
* Very few pre-1790 wares had a
  pattern number.
* Around 1812 a new bone-china
  body was introduced and the
  factory was by this time known
  as Newhall.
* After 1820 the bone-china wares
  seemed to lose some quality
  and the factory closed in 1835.

PINXTON

Established in Derbyshire by
William Billingsley under the
patronage of a local land owner,
John Coke. It produced soft-paste
porcelain wares from 1796 to 1801.
From 1804–1831 factory was
under management of John Cutts.
* In the early stages the
  porcelain, glaze and even
  designs are similar to Derby.
* The body has good
  translucency.
* In comparison with other
  factories the palette has a
  yellow/brown look.
* The glaze is of a fine "creamy"
  white with the occasional slight
  suggestion of blue.
* The enamels tend to have
  subdued or pastel tones.
* Well known for its excellent
  flower painting (some no doubt
  by Billingsley).
* The factory closed in 1812/13
  but it is not certain how much
  porcelain was produced from
  1805 to the closure.
* Pinxton is a rare factory and the
  yellow ground wares, in
  particular, are sought after.

PLYMOUTH

The Plymouth porcelain factory
was the first to make hard-paste
porcelain in England. The factory
was founded by Cookworthy who
had discovered kaolin on the
estate of Lord Camelford. In 1768
he took out a patent for the use of
this material with Petuntse. In
1770 the factory moved to Bristol.
* Factory ran from c1768–70.
* High proportion of kiln
  wastage.
* Had a tendency to firing flaws
  and smokiness as a result of

improper technique in kiln and imperfections in glaze.
* Very black underglaze blue.
* Most recognized products are the bell-shaped tankards painted with dishevelled birds in the manner of the mysterious Monsieur Soqui.
* The shell salt, also known at Worcester, Derby and Bow, most commonly found piece.
* Cookworthy transferred the factory to Bristol c1770.

ROCKINGHAM
The Rockingham pottery and porcelain factory was established on the estate of the Marquis of Rockingham in Yorkshire c1745. Porcelain seems to have been manufactured from 1826 when Earl Fitzwilliam (heir to the Rockingham estates) helped to finance the factory and the griffin from his family crest was adopted as a mark. The porcelain factory closed in 1847.
* Potters of the Brameld family.
* Bone china appears softer than contemporaries.
* Of a smoky ivory/oatmeal colour.
* Glaze had a tendency to irregular fine crazing.
* Factory known for rococo style of decoration, frequently with excellent quality flower painting.
* Tended to use green, grey and puce.
* Larger numbers of erroneous attributions made to the Rockingham factory, especially pieces actually made at Minton and Coalport.
* Pattern numbers over 2,000 are *not* Rockingham.

ST CLOUD
The St Cloud factory produced wares from the late 17th Century to the 1770s.
* Pieces heavily potted.
* Glaze thick and clear, frequently showing pitting.
* Body has a yellowish tone.
* Until mid 1730's pieces mainly decorated in underglaze blue.
* Also specialized in pieces influenced by the blanc-de-Chine wares.
* After mid 1730's polychrome wares produced.

SAMSON, EDME ET CIE
Opened in Paris in 1845 and reproduced copies not only of Chinese, German and English porcelain but also French faience and Dutch Delft, together with some wares of the Strasbourg factory.
* Their fakes of Meissen and Chinese porcelain are excellent.
* Their English soft-paste porcelain fakes are easier to detect, as they used a Continental hard-paste body.
* Samson claims that all wares have an S contained within the mark. However this can be easily removed by the unscrupulous.
* More pieces are attributed to Samson than they could possibly have made.

SÈVRES
The Sèvres porcelain factory led European ceramics fashions from 1760 to 1815. Founded in 1738 in the Château de Vincennes with workmen from Chantilly, in 1745 it was granted a 20 year monopoly for the production of "porcelain in the style of the Saxon". The products of the early period were all soft-paste. The factory moved to Sèvres from Vincennes in 1756.
* In early days copied Meissen and influenced by Kakiemon.
* Most decoration of these early years has a somewhat tentative appearance and few pieces show the sharpness of German contemporaries.
* The vases and other hollow wares including ice pails and flower holders epitomized the rococo style popular at court.
* Sèvres managed to discover the secret of hard paste porcelain at the same time as Cookworthy at Plymouth in 1768.
* "Jewelled porcelain" was introduced in 1773, using a technique of fusing enamels over gilt or silver foil.
* Most sought after ground colour is the yellow (jaune jonquille).
* Factory also noted for clock cases, small sets for tea, coffee and chocolate, and boxes.

SWANSEA PORCELAIN
Swansea potteries and porcelain factories were active from 1765, under the banner of The Cambrian Pottery, but the factory owes its reputation to the fine soft-paste porcelain made from 1814 in the factory started by Dillwyn, Billingsley and Walker. The Glamorgan Pottery was active at Swansea from 1813 to 1839.
* Superb translucent body, excellent glaze.
* In many ways one of the best porcelain bodies produced in the British Isles.

* Also noted for delicacy of flower painting, usually attributed to Billingsley although much was done by other decorators including Pollard and Morris.
* A close study of marked pieces will give one an idea of Billingsley's work but unless actually signed by him pieces should be marked "possibly by Billingsley".
* On pieces moulded with the floral cartouches the moulding can be detected on the other side of the rim, unlike the heavier Coalport wares which later utilized same moulds.
* Especially notable are figure and bird paintings by T Baxter.
* The Swansea mark often faked, particularly on French porcelain at the end of the C19 and beginning of the C20.
* In 1816 Billingsley left to start up again at Nantgarw.
* Many pieces decorated in London.

VIENNA

Founded in 1719 by a court official of Dutch origin, Claudius Innocentius Du Paquier with the assistance of the arcanist C.C. Hunger and the kiln master Samuel Stolzel, both from Meissen. In 1744 Du Paquier relinquished the factory to the state which had been helping him with loans for some years. In 1784 the ailing factory was unsuccessfully offered for sale but taken under the direction of Konrad von Sorgenthal, who quickly transformed it into a prosperous concern. The factory closed in 1864.

* The body of Du Paquier wares has a distinctive smoky tone.
* Decoration tends to cover much of the body and can be more elaborate than Meissen.
* Extensive use of trellis work or "gitterwerk".
* The style of this period was "baroque", with scrollwork and lattice-like gilding.
* Plain bases were used from mid-1760's.
* Excellent figure modelling was undertaken by J J Niedermayer from 1747–84.

VINCENNES

Founded in 1738. The French National manufactury of soft-paste porcelain was established at Vincennes before it moved in 1756 to Sèvres.

* Early production was generally of indifferent quality.
* Inferior to the contemporary productions of St. Cloud and Mennecy.
* Towards end of 1740's, probably influenced by Meissen, introduced coloured grounds.
* 1750's lightly tooled gilding used to heighten reserve panels.
* Coloured grounds: "bleu" from the late 1740's. "Bleu celeste" from 1752. "Jaune jonquille" from 1753. "Rose pompadour" from 1757.

WORCESTER

Founded in 1751. The first porcelain was a soft paste; the formula for this included soaprock (steatite).

* c1751–53 a short experimental period. Sometimes difficult to differentiate between Lund's Bristol and Worcester.
* Both blue and white and "famille verte" polychrome wares produced.
* c1752–54 some wares marked with an incised cross or line.
* c1755–60 some finely painted and potted wares produced.
* Painters' marks, resembling Chinese letters, appear on base of wares.
* The underglaze blue is well controlled and of a good pale colour.
* Polychrome decoration is crisp and clean.
* Almost all patterns are based on Chinese prototypes.
* Transfer printed wares appear c1754.
* From 1760–76 a consistently high standard of potting and decorating though lacking spontaneity of earlier wares.
* Most blue and white pieces now marked with a crescent.
* Often difficult to differentiate from Caughley where open crescent mark also used.

Worcester Porcelain Dates

1751–1783	First Period.
1751–1774	"Dr Wall" Period.
1776–1792	Davis/Flight Period.
1783–1792	Flight Period.
1792–1804	Flight and Barr Period.
1804–1813	Barr, Flight
1813–1840	Flight, Barr
1788–1840	Chamberlain – Worcester.
1840–1852	Chamberlain and Company.
1852–1862	Kerr and Binns (W.H. Kerr & Co.).
1862–	Worcester Royal Porcelain Company.

an hua "Secret" decoration of Chinese ware, lightly incised and visible only when held up to the light.

Ao Kutani "Green" **Kutani** ware.

Arita Capital of a district in Japan known for its kilns; famous in particular for a type of ware known as Imari after the port from which it was shipped.

blanc-de-chine European term for the clear-glazed white porcelain made in China at Dehua (Tē Hua) in Fukien province, imported to Europe from C17 and widely imitated in C18. It is remarkable for its sharp modelling and famous for its figures with swirling drapery.

bulb bowl Smallish bowl, about 12in (30cm) across for growing bulbs in, typically with three feet.

celadon European name for a Chinese ware famous for its greyish or olive green glaze (though other colours occur), usually laid over a relief or incised pattern. While celadon from the southern province of Chekiang, the original celadon, has a distinctive deep red body, Northern and other celadon has body of a brown or other colour. First developed under the Sung dynasty; but Sung pieces are priceless.

Chinese export porcelain Porcelain made in China for the European (and later American) market. The Chinese copied both the forms and the decoration of European ware, though usually either the one or the other; they copied the shapes as early as the late C16, and later even copied European *chinoiserie* decoration.

Chinese Imari Chinese imitations of Japanese **Imari**, made from early C18, almost as early as the true Imari.

clair-de-lune A translucent blue glaze introduced in Chinese porcelain in the early C18.

clobber To enamel over original blue-and-white ware with glazes of different colour.

dog of Fo Mythical Chinese lion-spaniel, a guardian spirit of the temple of the Buddha (Fo).

doucai (tou-ts'ai) In Chinese, "contrasting colours", a type of enamel decoration introduced in the reign of the Ming emperor Chenghua (1465–87).

famille jaune Variety of **famille verte**, with a yellow ("jaune") ground.

famille noire Variety of **famille verte** with a black ground.

famille rose C19 European term for a Ming style of porcelain introduced at the end of the reign of Kangxi (died 1722) – a little later than "famille verte". It is polychrome, but features a rose-pink of European origin.

famille verte C19 European term for a Ming style of porcelain (reign of Kangxi, 1662–1722). It is polychrome, but features a brilliant copper-green.

Fukugawa Japanese ceramic company, based in Arita. Said to have been founded in 1689, but only C19 ware is common.

gorgelet Drinking vessel with spouts or jets, made in China and Japan for export from C17.

Guanyin Chinese Buddhist goddess of mercy, a favourite subject e.g. of **blanc-de-chine**.

Guan yao Chinese term meaning "imperial ware". Sung dynasty. Glazed thickly but more smoothly and regularly than other Sung dynasty ware, often with a crackle, blue or grey. Now found only in C18 copies.

Hirado Blue-and-white ware made exclusively for the Lords of Hirado, near Arita (Japan), from mid C18 to mid C19. Renowned for its milk-white body, its velvety glaze, and its exquisite figure and landscape decoration.

Imari Japanese porcelain made in or around Arita from early C18 and shipped to Europe from the port of Imari. It has distinctive colours of blue, red and gold (often with others); commonly it is decorated in a flower-basket pattern.

imperial yellow A distinctive yellow enamel developed in the Chinese imperial kilns in C15.

Jian yao Ware from Jian (Chien) in Fukien province, known for its mottled brown or "hare's fur" glaze. Sung and later.

Jizhou yao Ware resembling **ting**, from Jizhou (Chi Chou). Sung dynasty.

Jun yao Ware from Jun (Chün) in Honan province, with an opalescent glaze typically thick at the foot and thin at the rim. Sung dynasty and later.

Kaga The district in which **Kutani** ware was made.

Kakiemon Name of a succession of Japanese potters, of whom the first, Kakiemon I Sakaida, died in 1666. The name stands for ware of distinctive colours and pattern, imported to Europe and widely imitated there after 1650: a brilliant azure, a soft red, yellow (and others) over a white body; delicate figures brush-drawn in asymmetrical compositions.

Ko Kutani See **Kutani**.

Kraak porselain Dutch term meaning porcelain raided from Portuguese ships called carracks. It describes the earliest kind of Chinese export porcelain (late C16 to early C17), in blue and white.

Kutani Japanese ware made at Kutani in the province of Kaga in C17 (Ko or "old" Kutani), and revived in C19. It is difficult to tell from Imari ware, though the Japanese value it more highly. Ao or green Kutani is a distinct stoneware, painted in green, yellow and purple.

kylin See **qilin**.

Kyoto Capital of Shogunate Japan, and a centre of porcelain production in C19.

lang yao See **sang-de-boeuf**.

Li shui Chinese term for ware of celadon type. Sung dynasty.

lingzhi A floral motif, found on Chinese porcelain from the reign of Jijing (C16).

meiping (mei p'ing) Chinese for "prunus", describing a common type of Ming flower-vase, of baluster shape, with a high shoulder, small neck and narrow mouth.

mon Japanese crest or coat of arms.

potiche French name for an oriental vase-shaped jar, usually with a cover.

Pu-Tai Chinese luohan or disciple of the Buddha, known as "the laughing Buddha"; he has a bag of happiness.

qilin Mythical Chinese creature (also ch'ilin, kylin) with the head of a dragon, limbs and body of a deer and the tail of a lion: symbol of good.

raku Pottery bowl associated with the Japanese tea-ceremony, prized for its almost rough simplicity.

sang-de-boeuf Brilliant red glaze developed in the reign of Kangxi (early C18), characteristic of a ware called "lang" in Chinese.

Satsuma Leading Japanese port, known also for its ware, commonly with a crackle glaze.

shishi Chinese or "Buddhist" mythical lion (also called **dog of Fo**).

six-character mark Six Chinese characters naming the reigning emperor, found on the base of imperial ware from the early C15 (Xuande) to the early C18 (Kangxi). Thereafter an archaic script is often found instead of characters.

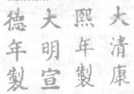

Xuande	**Kangxi**
1426–35	1662–1722

See page 92 for Chinese dynasties and marks.

sleeve vase Vase of long thin tubular shape.

ting yao Variety of Sung porcelain. The glaze, commonly white, called gummy or fatty by the Chinese, is rich and oily, with an ivory tone.

tokkuri Bottle for sake.

Transitional Wares produced between the end of the Ming, and the establishment of the Qing, dynasties.

wucai (wu ts'ai) Ware of "five colours" or, in practice, more than five, either enamelled (overglazed) or single-fired. Ming and Transitional.

yao Kiln or ware: e.g. Jian yao, ware from Jian.

yen yen European term (perhaps from Chinese "yen", beautiful) for a baluster vase with a long, broad flaring neck.

Yue yao Ware from Yue (Yüeh) in Chekiang province, mostly undecorated, a forerunner of Sung celadon.

Chinese Porcelain, Dynasties and their marks

Chinese porcelain dates back to about C10 AD. From then until C14, different regions produced their own characteristic wares, such as Dingyao and Xingyao in the north and Shufu and Yingqing in the south. The Ming period (1368–1644) then saw a remarkable growth both in quality and quantity throughout the country, many thousands of pieces being exported to an eager Europe. The demand resulted in a falling off in quality towards the end of the period. However, this trend was halted in the Transitional period (from the fall of the Ming Dynasty until the final consolidation of the Qing (Manchu) Dynasty). With stability at the end of the C17 came a flourishing porcelain industry, with a large part of the output produced specifically for the European market. Standards tended to decline again during the late C18 and C19, but fine quality non-export "Chinese taste" pieces continued to be produced and are much sought after.

Chinese Dynasties

Shang Yin c1532–1027BC
Western Zhou (Chou) 1027–770BC
Spring and Autumn Annals 770–480BC
Warring States 484–221BC
Qin (Ch'in) 221–206BC
Western Han 206BC-24AD
Eastern Han 25–220
Three Kingdoms 221–265
Six Dynasties 265–589
Wei 386–557
Sui 589–617
Tang (T'ang) 618–906
Five Dynasties 907–960
Liao 907–1125
Sung 960–1280
Chin 1115–1260
Yüan 1280–1368
Ming 1368–1644
Qing (Ch'ing) 1644–1916

The Marks

The "reign" marks found on porcelain (and on other works of art) record the dynasty and the emperor's name. However, they should be regarded with some caution since the Chinese often added early Ming marks to pieces made in the later Qing period – not to deceive but as a mark of veneration for their ancestors. These pieces could be "in the style of" the earlier period, but not always!

The square seal marks are sometimes used instead of the more usual character marks.

The characters read from the top right down. In a six character mark, the characters therefore read:

1. Character for "Great" 大

2. Dynasty 明

3. Emperor's first name 弘

4. Emperor's second name 治

5. } Period made 年 製
6. }

Ming Dynasty

Hongwu
(Hung Wu)
1368–1398

Yongle
(Yung Lo)
1403–1424

Xuande
(Hsüan Té)
1426–1435

Chenghua
(Ch'éng Hua)
1465–1487

Hongzhi
(Hung Chih)
1488–1505

Zhengde
(Chéng Té)
1506–1521

大明嘉靖年製
Jiajing
(Chia Ching)
1522–1566

大明隆慶年製
Longqing
(Lung Ching)
1567–1572

大明萬曆年製
Wanli
(Wan Li)
1573–1620

大明天啟年製
Tianqi
(Tien Chi)
1621–1627

崇禎年製
Chongzhen
(Ch'ung Chéng)
1628–1644

Qing (Ch'ing) Dynasty

大清順治年製
Shunzhi
(Shun Chih)
1644–1661

大清康熙年製
Kangxi
(K'ang Hsi)
1662–1722

大清雍正年製
Yongzheng
(Yung Chêng)
1723–1735

大清乾隆年製
Qianlong
(Ch'ien Lung)
1736–1795

大清嘉慶年製
Jiaqing
(Chiä Ch'ing)
1796–1820

大清道光年製
Daoguang
(Tao Kuang)
1821–1850

大清咸豐年製
Xianfeng
(Hsien Féng)
1851–1861

大清同治年製
Tongzhi
(T'ung Chih)
1862–1874

大清光緒年製
Guangxu
(Kuang Hsu)
1875–1908

大清宣統年製
Xuantong
(Hsuan T'ung)
1909–1911

洪憲年製
Hongxian
(Hung Hsien)
1916

Pronunciation

Standard (Mandarin) Chinese was until recently transcribed into western script (romanized) according to the Wade-Giles system devised early this century. This system is now being superseded by the Pinyin system which tends to give more easily understood phonetic values to the Chinese words being represented. Since many books still follow the Wade-Giles system, the comparison given below should help in developing a pronunciation of Chinese terms that is acceptable and can be used with reasonable confidence.

The sounds _____

Wade-Giles		Pinyin	Approx. only
ch	pronounced	*zh* or *j*	as in *jeans*
ch'		*ch* or *q*	as in *cheap* or *cringe*
hs		*x*	as in *shell*
j		*r*	as in *rage*
k		*g* or *k*	as in *gorse* or *core*
p		*b*	as in *born*
p'		*p*	as in *pour*
t		*d*	as in *door*
t'		*t*	as in *torn*
ts, tz		*z*	as in *roads*
ts', tz'		*c*	as in *tsetse*

The words _____

Wade-Giles	Pinyin		
		Chien yao	Jianyao
		Ching-tê Chên	Jingdezhen
an hua	anhua	*Chi chou*	Jizhou
Pa Hsien	Baxian	*chüeh*	jue
pi	bi	*Chun yao*	Junyao
Pu Tai	Budai	*ling chih*	lingzhi
ch'ih lung	chilong	*Lung-ch'üan*	Longquan
Tz'ŭ chou	Cizhou	*mei-p'ing*	meiping
Tê Hua	Dehua	*nien tsao*	nianzao
ting	ding	*ch'i-lin*	qilin
Ting yao	Dingyao	*Ju yao*	Ruyao
tou ts'ai	doucai	*ju-i*	ruyi
Fukien	Fujian	*san ts'ai*	sancai
Kuan Ti	Guandi	*t'ao-t'ieh*	taotie
kuang	guang	*wu ts'ai*	wucai
Kuangtung	Guangdong	*yen-yen*	yanyan
Kuan yao	Guanyao	*ying ch'ing*	Yingqing
Kuan yin	Guanyin	*I Hsing*	Yixing
Honan	Henan	*Yüeh yao*	Yueyao
chia	jia	*chung*	zhong

Japanese periods _____

Prehistory and protohistory
c7,000 BC. Jomon culture; first recorded pottery with simple design.
c300 BC. Yayoi culture; bronzes and more sophisticated pottery.
C1 to C4 AD. Haniwa culture bronzes and distinctive red pottery. 220 AD. first influence from Korea.
ASUKA: 552–645
HAHUKO: 672–685
NARA: 710–794
HEIAN: 794–1185
KAMAKURA: 1185–1333
MUROMACHI (AHIKAGA): 1338–1573
MOMOYAMA: 1573–1615
1598: Immigrant Korean potters

begin kilns at Kyushu, producing the first glazed pottery to be seen in Japan.
EDO (TOKUGAWA): 1615–1867
1616: First porcelain made by Ninsei (1596–1666)
1661–1673: Great age of porcelain; Arita, Nabeshima, Kutani and Kakiemon.
1716–1736: Popularity of lacquering and netsuke as art forms.
MEIJI: (1868–1912) Strong influence of Western cultures developing and growing. Japanese art appears to decline in many respects. Much trading with the West.

What you should know about:
Oriental porcelain

The Chinese had perfected the techniques of porcelain making during the T'ang dynasty (AD 618–906). The potters of the Sung dynasty (960–1279) made exquisite pieces for the Imperial Court, and in the Yuan dynasty (1280–1368) underglaze painting was developed.

General pointers

* When buying Chinese porcelain there are certain facts you should consider. Firstly the condition of the piece as this affects the price considerably – a very good piece with a hairline crack or small chip can be reduced in value by up to two thirds.

* The rarity of the item is also important; rare items fetch considerably more than their common counterparts. Most of the high prices for Chinese porcelain come from the Hong Kong salerooms. The Far eastern buyer tends to collect the pieces made by the Chinese potters for their own internal market rather than exportware made for the European trade.

* It is sometimes difficult to determine the age of oriental porcelain because the patterns were repeated throughout the ages. In order to distinguish Ming porcelain from the later Qing wares it is necessary to appreciate the technical rather than the decorative differences between the two. The Qing decorators frequently copied ancestral designs with great accuracy, therefore making it difficult to attribute certain pieces.

* With certain exceptions, Ming porcelain is more heavily glazed and the depth of glaze effects a bluish or greenish tint. Rarely is the glaze evenly applied, and if carefully examined one can detect runs and dribbles of excess glaze. Most Qing wares are covered in a glaze of uniform thickness.

* Particularly characteristic is the pure white appearance achieved by the Kangxi potters by only coating the vessel in a thin and even wash.

* The reigns of Yongzheng and Qianlong did, however, witness some pieces which were deliberately covered in a thick glaze in order to emulate the early C15 porcelains.

* Other signs of age include footrims: the footrims on Ming wares are generally knife-pared and little effort was made to remove the facets left by the blade. Most, if not all, Qing pieces are smoothed after the trimming.

* The feet on Ming dishes or bowls are for the most part higher than Qing examples. The footrim on Ming wares will generally manifest a narrow orange zone abutting the edge of the glaze. This is due to the presence of iron in the body of the porcelain which appears to oxidize more strongly in the kiln in the area most closely in contact with the glaze.

* The later Chinese wares tended to be mass-produced for export, often to specific demands from traders. It is on these mass-produced items that the potters frequently used the marks of earlier dynasties. This was not the work of a faker, since the Chinese believed they should venerate the skills of previous generations. Accordingly, they marked the piece with the mark of the Emperor reigning at the time they wished to honour.

DINGYAO

* This is a northern type of Chinese porcelain produced during the Sung and Yuan periods. The glaze is a rich ivory colour which appears either a pale green or brown where it has pooled. The decoration is mainly floral.

JUNYAO

* A northern Chinese stoneware made from the Sung Dynasty through to the Yuan and Ming periods. The coarse granular body is thickly applied with a blue glaze, sometimes varying from lavender to deep purple.

YINGQING

* This is a type of porcelain produced during the Sung and Yuan dynasties in various regions of central and southern China. The dominant characteristic being the pale blue-green translucent glaze. Yingqing translates as misty blue. Like Dingyao, the designs are either moulded or carved floral subjects.

METALWARE

Glossary

andiron Iron support for wooden logs burning in a fire, used until C18 instead of a grate; in C17 they were often just decorative.

apostle spoon Spoon of type common till early C17, with figure of an apostle as finial.

argyle Spouted pots, made from c1750 to c1830, with two layers or skins, to keep contents hot.

biggin Small teapot or coffee-pot, sometimes with a stand and spirit-lamp, named after inventor George Biggin.

brandy saucepan Small bulbous or baluster-shaped saucepan, usually with handle at right angles to the pouring spout.

bright-cut Silver effect popular in the last years of C18, achieved by an engraving technique which made the design stand out more brilliantly than usual.

Britannia metal Cheap substitute for silver, actually a form of pewter, employed in the first half of C19.

British plate Substitute for silver employed in 2nd quarter of C19, until superseded by electroplating. Often carries marks resembling silver hallmarks.

caddy Container for tea.

caddy spoon Spoon for taking tea out of the caddy, with a short handle and a large bowl, often decorated. Introduced late C18.

canteen Either a large urn with a tap at the bottom; or a case containing a silver service.

card case Case for visiting cards, popular in silver from c1820 to end of C19.

cartouche Frame or surround as decoration round e.g. a coat-of-arms engraved on a piece.

caster or **castor** Vessel for sprinkling, usually pepper or sugar.

caudle cup Covered cup with a warm drink, whether caudle (spiced gruel laced with wine or ale) or some other.

centrepiece Ornament designed to occupy centre of dining table.

chafing dish Stand for dishes and plates, incorporating a spirit lamp to keep them warm. From mid C17.

chased Decorated and worked, usually with hammer and punches, but not carved, cut away or engraved. Flat chasing is chasing in very low relief.

chenet French andiron, of a type common in C17, often elaborately decorated.

claret jug Ewer or jug used for serving claret in C19, but not easy to distinguish from ewers made for other purposes.

coaster Saucer or small tray for a bottle, on which it was passed or slid round the table (some have wheels).

counter box Box, usually round, for storing counters or tokens used in gambling. From C17.

cow creamer Jug for pouring cream modelled in the shape of a cow, popular in C18.

cruet Frame holding salt cellars and other vessels containing condiments, or for casters.

cut-card work Silver decoration achieved by applying or overlaying the silver body with a second, patterned piece or sheet (often fretted) of silver. Common in C17, particularly with Huguenot craftsmen.

damascene Inlay of precious metal (gold, silver) on to another metal (steel), a craft in which Syrian Muslims excelled (in and around Damascus: hence the name).

dinanderie Vessel or other object of brass, made in the factories in Dinant near Liège in C15.

douter Implement resembling scissors, for snuffing out a candle flame.

dram cup Small cup with two handles, common in C17 and half of C17. Also called **porringers**.

electroplate To cover one metal with a thin layer of another — usually silver plated over an alloy body. Process was patented in the 1830s, and gradually superseded Sheffield plate.

embossed Having a **relief** ornament, achieved by hammering the metal into shape from its reverse side.

épergne Type of **centrepiece** featuring a large central bowl and several smaller ones.

étuis Small box for holding oddments, from pins to pencils. C18.

everted Outward-turned or flaring, e.g. a rim.

finial Endpiece, e.g. at the top of a spoon handle.

freedom box Silver box bestowed with the "freedom" of a city, in late C18 and early C19.

jardinière Ornamental pot or vase for flowers or plants.

latten The old English word for what is now called brass.

mazarine Strainer, typically oval, fitting over a dish into which meat or fish drained. From mid C18.

mount Metal fitment or adjunct.

nutmeg grater Box containing nutmeg and a grater, usually for sprinkling nutmeg on ale. C18.

obverse Of a coin or medal; the front side, opposite to the reverse.

patch-box Box, often round, for ladies' "beauty spots" or patches. C17.

pepperette Vessel for sprinkling pepper.

copper, to which it is fused. The process was invented in Sheffield and recognised by the Sheffield assay-office in 1784, though Sheffield plate was being made at Sheffield and elsewhere (e.g. Birmingham) by the 1760s.

sparrow-beak jug Jug with a simple, triangular spout.

standish An inkstand.

stirrup cup Cup used for drinking prior to making a journey or going hunting. Usually shaped as the head of an animal, e.g. a fox. From 2nd half C18.

pewter Alloy of tin and lead (and usually a variety of other metals), used for table utensils and other vessels until into C19.

porringer Cup, usually quite large, with two handles and a cover, originally for holding porridge or gruel.

pounce box Cylinder or bottle with sprinkler for "pounce", a powder used before blotting paper was invented. C18.

punch bowl Large bowl on a stepped or moulded foot, usually with two ring handles. End of C17.

relief Proudness from the surface; or the apparent volume of a figure modelled on a surface.

repoussé Meaning "pushed out", this is another term for **embossed**. More exactly, it is the secondary process of **chasing** the metal that has been embossed, to refine the design further.

salt A bowl for salt may be called simply "a salt".

salver Flat dish or tray on which to place other dishes.

scalloped With a series of circular edges like those of a scallop shell.

sconce Plate for attachment to wall, bearing one or more candle-holders. From C17.

scroll Anything that winds or unwinds, creating a loop.

Sheffield plate Rolled sheet silver sandwiching an internal layer of

swagged With applied strips formed in a mould, but not necessarily in a swag or hanging garland shape.

tankard Large mug with a hinged lid and thumbpiece, for drinking beer.

thumbpiece Flange attached to a hinged lid, which, when pressed by the thumb, raises the lid.

tine Prong of a fork.

tôle peinte Sheet iron subjected to a varnish developed in France in mid C18, allowing it to be painted on.

touch mark Maker's individual mark stamped on much, but not all, early English pewter.

trefid C17 spoon of which the handle terminates in the shape of a bud, typically cleft or grooved into a central stem and two lobes.

trembleuse Stand with feet on which to place a cup.

tureen Large bowl (e.g. for soup), usually on a foot, often with handles. Popular early C18.

uniface Medal modelled only on one side.

vesta case Silver matchbox for early vesta matches, which were easily flammable and needed such protection. Popular 2nd half C19, in many shapes and designs.

vinaigrette Small box to hold a sponge soaked in vinegar; C18 equivalent of smelling salts.

Silver marks

Because gold and silver were of such commercial importance it became necessary by the end of the 13th Century to establish and maintain reliable standards which everyone dealing in the metals must follow. In England the first mark guaranteeing such a standard was stamped on silver in 1300, by the the Goldsmiths' Company based at Goldsmiths' Hall in London. From then on such marks were known as "Hall" or "Town" marks. In Britain all silver wares, with a few minor exceptions, carry such marks, which provide precise information on place of origin, quality and date. On the Continent and in North America marking has never been systematized in this way and is therefore not always a reliable method of identification and dating. Town and manufacturer's marks can, however, often provide useful clues.

British silver marks

These are usually four, but sometimes five or more.

1. *The specific "Hall" or "Town" mark:* Different for each assay office. Variations to the basic mark occur over the years.
2. *"Standard" or quality mark:* All English assay offices show a lion walking to left *(passant)* to indicate "Sterling" quality, though with variations from time to time. When, between 1697–1719, the silver standard was raised, the existing hall mark was replaced by

"Britannia", and the *Lion passant* by a Lion's Head in profile *(erased)*. When the lower standard was restored in 1719, the original marks were revived. However, the "Britannia" marks were, and are, still permitted on silver that reaches the higher standard.

In Scotland the Edinburgh standard mark is a thistle (used since 1759); in Glasgow a *Lion Rampant* (with a thistle since 1914).
The Irish Republic has no standard mark, the Dublin Town mark (crowned harp) doubling for it on Irish silver.
Note: The "Standard" mark is frequently placed first, before the Hall Mark.
3. *Annual Date Letter:* Each assay office allocates its own specific letter for each year. This letter and the shield enclosing it are distinctive in form, enabling the piece to be dated precisely. An alphabetical sequence is normally followed (though "J" is often omitted).
4. *Maker's mark or initial (See pages 112–113).*

Other marks

5. *Sovereign's Head:* Between 1784 and 1890 a duty was levied on items of silver or gold. The "Sovereign's Head" mark indicated that this duty had been paid.

6. *Jubilee Mark:* A special mark, commemorating King George V's Silver Jubilee, on articles assayed between 1933 and 1936.
7. *Leopard's Head:* London's hall mark, the Leopard's Head, was also sometimes used as an *additional* mark by provincial assay offices except Birmingham and Sheffield.
8. *Foreign silver:* From 1843 imported silver articles of the required standard were marked with letter "F". Each assay office now has its own symbol that is applied to all silver articles of foreign origin.
9 *Coronation mark:* A special mark, showing the crowned head of Queen Elizabeth II facing towards the right was authorized at the time of the Coronation in 1953. Its use was voluntary and restricted to letters for 1952, 1953 and 1954.

Beware

* Early silver marks are far from uniform, because the punches were hand-made. Often there is considerable variation even for the same year.
* Hallmarks should never be used as a sole guarantee of authenticity. They are easily – and frequently – faked.

British Assay Offices

Town	Operating	Date letter changed		Hall Mark
London	1300–present	29 May		Leopard's Head
Birmingham	1773–present	1 July		Anchor
Chester	1686–present	1 July		Wheatsheaves & Dagger (some variation)
Exeter	1701–1883	–		Three-towered Castle
Newcastle	1423–1884	–		Three Castles
Norwich	1423–1697	–		Castles & Lion and/or Crowned Rose
Sheffield	1773–present	1 July		Crown
York	1423–1857	–		Fleur-de-Lys & Leopard's Head (to 1700); then Cross with 5 Lions
Edinburgh	1485–present	Mid-Oct.		Castle on Rock
Glasgow	1819–present	1 July		Oak, Bird, Salmon & Bell and (from 1914) Thistle
Dublin	1837–present	1 Jan.		Crowned Harp with (from 1730) Hibernia

Note: for brief periods, usually in the 16th and 17th Centuries, other towns had their own assay offices and hallmarks, normally based on the town's coat-of-arms. Examples are: Leeds (1650–1702/Three Crowns), Lincoln (1560–1706/Fleur-de-Lys) and Greenock (1758–1830/Anchor). Marks vary greatly and articles carrying them are very rare.

British Hall Marks

The marks that follow are those of all the important British assay offices from late C17 to 1939, the period of most interest for collectors and dealers.

London		1687	1698	1710	1721
		1688	1699	1711	1722
1678		1689	1700	1712	1723
1679		1690	1701	1713	1724
1680		1691	1702	1714	1725
1681		1692	1703	1715	1726
1682		1693	1704	1716	1727
1683		1694	1705	1717	1728
1684		1695	1706	1718	1729
1685		1696	1707	1719	
1686		1697	1708		1730
			1709	1720	

Year	Mark	Year	Mark	Year	Mark	Year	Mark	Year	Mark
1731	Q	1764	J	1798	C	1833	S	1867	m
1732	R	1765	K	1799	D	—	[marks]	1868	n
1733	S	1766	L	1800	E	1834	t	1869	o
1734	T	1767	M	1801	F	1835	u	1870	p
1735	V	1768	N	1802	G	1836	A	1871	q
1736	a	1769	O	1803	H	1837	B	1872	r
1737	b	1770	P	1804	I	—	[marks]	1873	S
1738	C	1771	Q	1805	K	1838	C	1874	t
1739	d	1772	R	1806	L	1839	D	1875	u
—	[marks]	1773	S	1807	M	1840	E	1876	A
1739	d	1774	T	1808	N	1841	F	1877	B
1740	e	1775	U	1809	O	1842	G	1878	C
1741	f	1776	a	1810	P	1843	H	1879	D
1742	g	1777	b	1811	Q	1844	J	1880	E
1743	h	1778	c	1812	R	1845	K	1881	F
1744	i	1779	d	1813	S	1846	L	1882	G
1745	k	1780	e	1814	T	1847	M	1883	H
1746	l	1781	f	1815	U	1848	N	1884	I
1747	m	1782	g	1816	a	1849	O	1885	K
1748	n	1783	h	1817	b	1850	P	1886	L
1749	o	—	[marks]	1818	C	1851	Q	1887	M
1750	p	1784	i	1819	d	1852	R	1888	N
1751	q	1785	k	1820	e	1853	S	1889	O
1752	r	—	[marks]	1821	f	1854	T	1890	P
1753	s	1786	l	—	[marks]	1855	U	—	[marks]
1754	t	1787	m	1822	g	1856	a	1891	Q
1755	u	1788	n	1823	h	1857	b	1892	R
—	[marks]	1789	O	1824	i	1858	C	1893	S
1756	A	1790	P	1825	k	1859	D	1894	T
1757	B	1791	q	1826	l	1860	E	1895	U
1758	C	1792	r	1827	m	1861	f	—	[marks]
1759	D	1793	S	1828	n	1862	g	1896	a
1760	E	1794	t	1829	o	1863	h	1897	b
1761	F	1795	u	1830	p	1864	i	1898	C
1762	G	1796	A	1831	q	1865	k	1899	d
1763	H	1797	B	1832	r	1866	l	1900	e

Year	Mark	Year	Mark	Year	Mark	Year	Mark	Year	Mark
1901	f	1935	u	1798	a	1833	k	1866	R
1902	g (town marks, lion)	1936	A	1799	b (town marks)	1834	l	1867	S
1903	h	1937	B	1800	c	1835	M	1868	T
1904	i	1938	C	1801	d	1836	N	1869	U
1905	k	1939	D	1802	e	1837	O	1870	V
1906	l	**Birmingham**		1803	f	1838	p	1871	W
1907	m	1773	A	1804	g (town marks)	1839	Q	1872	X
1908	n (town marks, anchor)	1774	B	1805	h	1840	R	1873	Y
1909	o	1775	C	1806	i	1841	S	1874	Z
1910	p	1776	D	1807	J	1842	T	1875	a (town marks)
1911	q	1777	E	1808	k	1843	U	1876	b
1912	r	1778	F	1809	l	1844	V	1877	c
1913	s	1779	G	1810	m	1845	W	1878	d
1914	t	1780	H	1811	n	1846	X	1879	e
1915	u	1781	I	1812	O	1847	Y	1880	f
1916	a (town marks)	1782	K	1813	P	1848	Z	1881	g
1917	b	1783	L	1814	q	1849	A (town marks)	1882	h
1918	c	1784	M (town marks)	1815	r	1850	B	1883	i
1919	d	1785	N	1816	s (town marks, anchor)	1851	C	1884	k
1920	e	1786	O (town marks, anchor)	1817	t	1852	D	1885	l
1921	f	1787	P	1818	u	1853	E	1886	m
1922	g	1788	Q	1819	V	1854	F	1887	n
1923	h (town marks)	1789	R	1820	W	1855	G	1888	o
1924	i	1790	S	1821	X	1856	H	1889	p
1925	k	1791	T	1822	y	1857	I	1890	q
1926	l	1792	U	1823	Z	1858	J	1891	(town marks)
1927	m	1793	V	1824	a	1859	K	1891	r
1928	n	1794	W	1825	b	1860	L	1892	s
1929	o	1795	X	1826	c	1861	M	1893	t
1930	p	1796	Y	1827	d	1862	N	1894	u
1931	q	1797	Z	1828	e	1863	O	1895	v
1932	r			1829	f	1864	P	1896	w
1933	s (town marks)			1830	g	1865	Q	1897	x
1934	t			1831	h			1898	y
				1832	J			1899	z

Date	Letter
1900	a
1901	b
1902	c
1903	d
1904	e
1905	f
1906	g
1907	h
1908	i
1909	k
1910	l
1911	m
1912	n
1913	o
1914	p
1915	q
1916	r
1917	s
1918	t
1919	u
1920	v
1921	w
1922	x
1923	y
1924	z
1925	A
1926	B
1927	C
1928	D
1929	E
1930	F
1931	G
1932	H
1933	J
1934	K
1935	L
1936	M
1937	N
1938	O
1939	P

Chester

Date	Letter
1701	A
1702	B
1703	C
1704	D
1705	E
1706	F
1707	G
1708	H
1709	I
1710	K
1711	L
1712	M
1713	N
1714	O
1715	P
1716	Q
1717	R
1718	S
1719	T
1720	U
1721	V
1722	W
1723	X
1724	Y
1725	Z
1726	A
1727	B
1728	C
1729	D
1730	E
1731	F
1732	G
1733	H
1734	I
1735	K
1736	L
1737	M
1738	N
1739	O
1740	P
1741	Q
1742	R
1743	S
1744	T
1745	U
1746	V
1747	W
1748	X
1749	Y Y
1750	Z
1751	a
1752	b
1753	c
1754	d
1755	e
1756	f
1757	G
1758	h
1759	i
1760	k
1761	l
1762	m
1763	n
1764	o
1765	p
1766	q
1767	r
1768	s
1769	t
1770	t
1771	u
1772	v
1773	w
1774	x
1775	y
1776	a
1777	b
1778	c
1779	d
1780	e
1781	f
1782	g
1783	h
1784	i
1785	k
1786	l
1787	m
1788	n
1789	o
1790	p
1791	q
1792	r
1793	s
1794	t
1795	u
1796	V
1797	A
1798	B
1799	C
1800	D
1801	E
1802	F
1803	G
1804	H
1805	I
1806	K
1807	L
1808	M
1809	N
1810	O
1811	P
1812	Q
1813	R
1814	S
1815	T
1816	U
1817	V
1818	A
1819	B
1820	C
1821	D
1822	D
1823	E
1824	F
1825	G
1826	H
1827	I
1828	K

Year	Mark	Year	Mark	Year	Mark	Year	Mark	Year	Mark
1829	L	1864	a	1897	O	1931	ff	1724	Z
1830	M	1865	b	1898	P	1932	g	1725	a
1831	N	1866	c	1899	Q	1933	h	1726	b
1832	O	1867	d	1900	R	1934	J	1727	c
1833	P	1868	e	1901	A	1935	K	1728	d
1834	Q	1869	f	1902	B	1936	k	1729	e
1835	R	1870	g	1903	C	1937	w	1730	f
1836	S	1871	h	1904	D	1938	A	1731	g
1837	T	1872	i	1905	E	1939	Q	1732	h
1838	U	1873	k	1906	F	**Exeter**		1733	U
1839	A	1874	l	1907	G	1701	A	1734	K
1840	B	1875	m	1908	H	1702	B	1735	I
1841	C	1876	n	1909	J	1703	C	1736	m
1842	D	1877	o	1910	K	1704	D	1737	n
1843	E	1878	p	1911	L	1705	E	1738	o
1844	F	1879	q	1912	M	1706	F	1739	p
1845	G	1880	r	1913	N	1707	G	1740	q
1846	H	1881	s	1914	O	1708	H	1741	r
1847	I	1882	t	1915	P	1709	I	1742	s
1848	K	1883	u	1916	Q	1710	K	1743	t
1849	L	1884	A	1917	R	1711	L	1744	u
1850	M	1885	B	1918	S	1712	M	1745	w
1851	N	1886	C	1919	T	1713	N	1746	x
1852	O	1887	D	1920	U	1714	O	1747	y
1853	P	1888	E	1921	V	1715	P	1748	z
1854	Q	1889	F	1922	W	1716	Q	1749	A
1855	R	1890	G	1923	X	1717	R	1750	B
1856	S	1891	H	1924	Y	1718	S	1751	C
1857	C	1892	I	1925	Z	1719	T	1752	D
1858	U	1893	K	1926	a	1720	V	1753	E
1859	V	1894	L	1927	b	1721	W	1754	F
1860	W	1895	M	1928	c	1722	X	1755	G
1861	X	1896	N	1929	d	1723	Y	1756	H
1862	Y			1930	e				
1863	Z								

Date	Mark	Date	Mark	Date	Mark	Date	Mark	Date	Mark
1757	I	1790	T	1822	f	1855	T	1707	F
1758	K	1791	P	1823	g	1856	u	1708	G
1759	L	1792	t	1824	h	1857	A	1709	H
1760	M	1793	u	1825	i	1858	B	1710	
1761	N	1794	W	1826	k	1859	C	1711	
1762	O	1795	X	1827	l	1860	D	1712	
1763	P	1796	y	1828	m	1861	E	1713	
1764	Q	1797	A	1829	n	1862	F	1714	D
1765	R	1798	B	1830	o	1863	G	1715	
1766	S	1799	C	1831	p	1864	H	1716	
1767	T	1800	D	1832	q	1865	I	1717	P
1768	U	1801	E	1833	r	1866	K	1718	G
1769	W	1802	F	1834	s	1867	L	1719	R
1770	X	1803	G	1835	t	1868	M	1720	C
1771	Y	1804	H	1836	u	1869	N	1721	a
1772	Z	1805	I	1837	A	1870	O	1722	B
1773	A	1806	K	1838	B	1871	P	1723	C
1774	B	1807	L	1839	C	1872	Q	1724	D
1775	C	1808	M	1840	D	1873	R	1725	E
1776	D	1809	N	1841	E	1874	S	1726	f
1777	E	1810	O	1842	f	1875	T	1727	G
1778	F	1811	P	1843	G	1876	U	1728	B
1779	G	1812	Q	1844	h	1877	A	1729	J
1780	H	1813	R	1845	j	1878	B	1730	K
1781-2	I	1814	S	1846	k	1879	C	1731	L
1783	K	1815	T	1847	l	1880	D	1732	M
1784	L	1816	U	1848	m	1881	E	1733	N
1785	M	1817	a	1849	n	1882	F	1734	O
1786	N	1818	b	1850	o			1735	P
1787	O	1819	c	1851	p	1702	A	1736	Q
1788	P	1820	d	1852	q	1703	B	1737	R
1789	Q	1821	e	1853	r	1704	C		
				1854	s	1705	D		
						1706	E		

Leopard's head not used after 1777

Newcastle

Between 1721 and 1728. Shapes of shields and lion passant vary, and lion sometimes faces left.

1738	Ⓢ	1780	Ⓞ	1813	Ⓨ
1739	Ⓣ	1781	Ⓟ	1814	Ⓩ

Year	Letter	Year	Letter	Year	Letter	Year	Letter	Year	Letter
1738	S	1780	O	1813	Y	1847	I	1882	t
1739	T	1781	P	1814	Z	1848	J	1883	u
1740	A	1782	Q	1815	A	1849	K		
1741	B	1783	R	1816	B	1850	L	1773	Œ
1742	C	1784	S	1817	C	1851	M	1774	F
1743	D	1785	T	1818	D	1852	N	1775	H
1744	E	1786	U	1819	E	1853	O	1776	R
1745	F	1787	W	1820	F	1854	P	1777	h
1746	G	1788	X	1821	G	1855	Q	1778	S
1747	H	1789	Y	1822	H	1856	R	1779	A
1748	I	1790	Z	1823	I	1857	S	1780	C
1749	K	1791	A	1824	K	1858	T	1781	D
1750	L	1792	B	1825	L	1859	U	1782	G
1751	M	1793	C	1826	M	1860	W	1783	B
1752	N	1794	D	1827	N	1861	X		
1753	O	1795	E	1828	O	1862	Y	1784	U
1754	P	1796	F	1829	P	1863	Z	1785	V
1755	Q	1797	G	1830	Q	1864	a	1786	K
1756	R	1798	H	1831	R	1865	b	1787	U
1757	S	1799	I	1832	S	1866	c	1788	m
1758		1800	K	1833	T	1867	d	1789	
1759	A	1801	L	1834	U	1868	e	1790	L
1760-8	B	1802	M	1835	W	1869	f	1791	P
1769	C	1803	N	1836	X	1870	g	1792	U
1770	D	1804	O	1837	Y	1871	h	1793	Q
1771	E	1805	P	1838	Z	1872	i	1794	m
1772	F	1806	Q	1839	A	1873	k	1795	q
1773	G	1807	R	1840	B	1874	l	1796	Z
1774	H	1808	S	1841	C	1875	m	1797	X
1775	I	1809	T	1842	D	1876	n	1798	V
1776	K	1810	U	1843	E	1877	o	1799	E
1777	L	1811	W	1844	F	1878	p	1800	N
1778	M	1812	X	1845	G	1879	q	1801	H
1779	N			1846	H	1880	r	1802	M
						1881	s	1803	F

Year	Mark	Year	Mark	Year	Mark	Year	Mark	Year	Mark
1804	G	1839	t	1873	F	1908	q		York
1805	B	1840	u	1874	G	1909	r	1700	A
1806	A	1841	v	1875	H	1910	s	1701	B
1807	S	1842	X	1876	J	1911	t	1702	C
1808	P	1843	Z	1877	K	1912	u	1703	D
1809	K	1844	A	1878	L	1913	v	1705	F
1810	L	1845	B	1879	M	1914	w	1706	G
1811	C	1846	C	1880	N	1915	x	1708	(I)
1812	D	1847	D	1881	O	1916	y	1711	(m)
1813	R	1848	E	1882	P	1917	z	1713	(O)
1814	W	1849	F	1883	Q	1918	a		
1815	O	1850	G	1884	R	1919	b	No piece yet found bearing date letter between 1713 to 1778.	
1816	T	1851	H	1885	S	1920	c	1778	C
1817	X	1852	I	1886	T	1921	d	1779	D
1818	I	1853	K	1887	U	1922	e	1780	E
1819	V	1854	L	1888	V	1923	f	1781	F
1820	Q	1855	M	1889	W	1924	g	1782	G
1821	Y	1856	N	1890	X	1925	h	1783	H
1822	Z	1857	O	1891	Y	1926	i	1784	J
1823	U	1858	P	1892	Z	1927	k	1785	K
1824	a	1859	R	1893	a	1928	l	1786	L
1825	b	1860	S	1894	b	1929	m	1787	A
1826	c	1861	T	1895	c	1930	n	1788	B
1827	d	1862	U	1896	d	1931	o	1789	C C
1828	e	1863	V	1897	e	1932	p	1790	d
1829	f	1864	W	1898	f	1933	q	1791	e
1830	g	1865	X	1899	g	1934	r	1792	f
1831	h	1866	Y	1900	h	1935	s	1793	g
1832	k	1867	Z	1901	i	1936	t	1794	h
1833	l	1868	A	1902	k	1937	u	1795	i
1834	m	1869	B	1903	l	1938	v	1796	k
1835	P	1870	C	1904	m	1939	w	1797	L
1836	q	1871	D	1905	n			1798	M
1837	r	1872	E	1906	o				
1838	S			1907	p				

Date	Letter	Date	Letter	Date	Letter	Date	Letter	Date	Letter
1799	N	1831	u	1711	G	1746	R	1781	B
1800	O	1832	v	1712	H	1747	S	1782	C
1801	P	1833	w	1713	I	1748	T	1783	D
1802	Q	1834	x	1714	K	1749	U	1784	[marks] E
1803	R	1835	y	1715	L	1750	U	1785	F
1804	S	1836	z	1716	M	1751	W	1786	[marks] G
1805	T	1837	[marks] A	1717	N	1752	X	1787	G
1806	U	1838	B	1718	O	1753	Y	1788	H
[mark] Lion found for 1803 and 1806 facing right.		1839	C	1719	P	1754	Z	1789	IJ
		1840	D	1720	Q	1755	A	1790	K
1807	V	1841	E	1721	R	1756	B	1791	L
1808	W	1842	F	1722	S	1757	C	1792	M
1809	X	1843	G	1723	T	1758	[marks] D	1793	N
1810	Y	1844	H	1724	U	1759	E	1794	O
1811	Z	1845	I	1725	V	1760	F	1795	P
[marks]		1846	[marks] K	1726	W	1761	G	1796	Q
1812	a	1847	L	1727	X	1762	H	1797	R
1813	b	1848	M	1728	Y	1763	I	1798	S
1814	c	1849	N	1729	Z	1764	K	1799	T
1815	d	1850	O	1730	A	1765	L	1800	U
1816	e	Leopard's head not used after 1850.		1731	B	1766	M	1801	V
1817	f	1851	P	1732	C	1767	N	1802	W
1818	g	1852	Q	1733	D	1768	O	1803	X
1819	h	1853	R	1734	E	1769	P	1804	Y
1820	i	1854	S	1735	F	1770	Q	1805	Z
1821	k	1855	T	1736	G	1771	R	1806	a
1822	l	1856	V	1737	H	1772	S	1807	b
1823	m	Edinburgh		1738	I	1773	T	1808	c
1824	n	[castle]		1739	K	1774	U	1809	d
1825	o	1705	A	1740	L	1775	V	1810	e
1826	p	1706	B	1741	M	1776	W	1811	f
1827	q	1707	C	1742	N	1777	X	1812	g
1828	r	1708	D	1743	O	1778	Z	1813	h
1829	s	1709	E	1744	P	1779	Y	1814	i
1830	t [mark]	1710	F	1745	Q	1780	A		

Year		Year		Year		Year		Year	
1815	j	1849	S	1884	c	1919	O	1828	J
1816	k	1850	T	1885	d	1920	P	1829	K
1817	l	1851	U	1886	e	1921	Q	1830	L
1818	m	1852	V	1887	f	1922	R	1831	M
1819	n	1853	W	1888	g	1923	S	1832	N
1820	⬛⬛⬛ O	1854	T	1889	h	1923	⬛⬛	1833	O
1821	P	1855	X	1890	i	1924	T	1834	P
1822	Q	1856	Z	1891	k	1925	U	1835	Q
1823	R	1857	A	1892	l	1926	V	1836	R
1824	S	1858	B	1893	m	1927	W	1836	⬛⬛⬛
1825	t	1859	C	1894	n	1928	X	1837	S
1826	u	1860	D	1895	o	1929	Y	1838	T
1827	V	1861	E	1896	p	1930	Z	1839	U
1828	W	1862	F	1897	q	1931	⬛⬛	1840	V
1829	X	1863	G	1898	r	1931	A	1841	W
1830	y	1864	H	1899	s	1932	B	1842	X
1831	Z	1865	I	1900	t	1932	⬛⬛⬛	1843	Y
1832	A	1866	K	1901	u	1933	C	1844	⬛⬛⬛
1833	B	1867	L	1902	w	1934	D	1845	A
1834	C	1868	M	1903	x	1935	E	1846	B
1835	D	1869	N	1904	y	1936	F	1847	C
1836	E	1870	O	1905	z	1937	G	1848	D
1837	F	1871	P	1906	A	1938	H	1849	E
1838	G	1872	Q	1907	B	1938	⬛⬛	1850	F
1839	H	1873	R	1908	C	1939	V	1851	G
1840	J	1874	S	1909	D	Glasgow		1852	H
1840	⬛⬛⬛	1875	T	1910	E	1819	⬛⬛ A	1852	⬛⬛⬛
1841	k	1876	U	1911	F	1819	⬛⬛ A	1853	I
1842	L	1877	V	1912	G	1820	B	1854	J
1843	M	1878	W	1913	H	1821	C	1855	K
1844	A	1879	X	1914	I	1822	D	1856	L
1845	O	1880	Y	1915	K	1823	E	1857	M
1846	P	1881	Z	1916	L	1824	F	1858	N
1847	Q	1882	a	1917	M	1825	G	1859	O
1848	R	1883	b	1918	N	1826	H	1860	P
						1827	I	1861	Q

Year	Mark	Year	Mark	Year	Mark	Year	Mark	Year	Mark
1862	[R]					1725	[F]	1762	[O]
1863	[S]	1897	[A]	1930	[h]	1726	[G]	1763	[P]
1864	[T]	1898	[B]	1931	[i]	1727	[H]	1764	[Q]
1865	[U]	1899	[C]	1932	[j]	1728	[J]	1765	[R]
1866	[W]	1900	[D]	1933	[k]	1729	[k]	1766	[S]
1867	[X]	1901	[E]	1934	[l]	1730	[L]	1767	[T]
1868	[Y]	1902	[F]	1935	[m]	1731	[L]	1768	[U]
1869	[U]	1903	[G]	1936	[n]	1732	[M]	1769	[W]
1870	[Z]	1904	[H]	1937	[o]	1733	[N]	1770	[X]
1871	[A]	1905	[J]	1938	[p]	1734	[O]	1771	[Y]
1872	[B]	1906	[I]	1939	[q]	1735	[P]	1772	[Z]
1873	[C]	1907	[K]			1736	[Q]	1773	[A]
1874	[D]	1908	[L]	**Dublin**		1737	[R]	1774	[B]
1875	[E]	1909	[M]	1700		1738	[S]	1775	[C]
1876	[F]	1910	[N]	1701	[O]	1739	[T]	1776	[D]
1877	[G]	1911	[O]	1702	[P]	1740	[U][U]	1777	[E]
1878	[H]	1912	[P]	1703	[Q]	1741-2	[U]	1778	[F]
1879	[I]	1913	[Q]	1704-5	[R]	1743-4	[X]	1779	[G]
1880	[J]	1914	[R]	1706-7	[S]	1745	[Y]	1780	[H]
1881	[K]	1915	[S]	1708-9	[T]	1746	[Z]	1781	[I]
1882	[L]	1916	[T]	1710-11	[U]	1747	[A]	1782	[K]
1883	[M]	1917	[U]	1712-13	[W]	1748	[B]	1783	[L]
1884	[N]	1918	[V]	1714	[X]	1749	[C]	1784	[M]
1885	[O]	1919	[W]	1715	[Y]	1750	[D]	1785	[N]
1886	[P]	1920	[X]	1716	[Z]	1751	[E][E]	1786	[O]
1887	[Q]	1921	[Y]	1717	[d]	1752	[F]	1787	[P]
1888	[R]	1922	[Z]	1718	[B]	1753	[G]	1788	[Q]
1889	[S]	1923	[a]	1719	[C]	1754	[H]	1789	[R]
1890	[T]	1924	[b]	1720	[A]	1757	[U]	1790	[S]
1891	[U]	1925	[c]	1721	[B]	1758	[K]	1791	[T]
1892	[V]	1926	[d]	1722	[C]	1759	[L]	1792	[U]
1893	[W]	1927	[e]	1723	[D]	1760	[M]	1793	[W]
1894	[X]	1928	[f]	1724	[E]	1761	[N]	1794	[X]
1895	[Y]	1929	[g]						
1896	[Z]								

Year	Mark	Year	Mark	Year	Mark	Year	Mark	Year	Mark
1795	Y	1828	H	1857	m	1891	V	1925	K
1796	Z	1829		1858	n	1892	W	1926	L
1797	A	1830	I	1859	O	1893	X	1927	m
1798	B	1831		1860	P	1894	V	1928	n
1799	C	1832	M	1861	Q	1895	Z	1929	O
1800	D	1833	N	1862	T	1896	A	1930-31	P
1801	E	1834	O	1863	S	1897	B		
1802	F	1835	P	1864	T	1898	C		
1803	G	1836	Q	1865	U	1899	D		
1804	H	1837	R	1866	V	1900	E	1932	Q
1805	I	1838	S	1867	W	1901	F	1933	R
1806	K	1839	T	1868	X	1902	G	1934	S
1807	L	1840	U	1869	Y	1903	H	1935	T
1808	M	1841	V	1870	Z	1904	I	1936	U
1809	N	1842	W	1871	A	1905	K	1937	V
1810	O	1843	X	1872	B	1906	L	1938	W
1811	P	1844	Y	1873	c	1907	M	1939	X
1812	Q	1845		1874	D	1908	A		
1813	R	1846	Z	1875	E	1909	O		
1814	S	1847	b	1876	F	1910	P		
1815	T	1848	C	1877	G	1911	Q		
1816	U	1849	d	1878	H	1912	R		
1817	W	1850	e	1879	U	1913	S		
1818	X	1851	f f	1880	K	1914	T		
1819	Y	1852	g g	1881	L	1915	U		
1820	Z	1853	h h	1882	M	1916	A		
1821	A	1854	J	1883	N	1917	b		
1822	B	1855	k	1884	O	1918	C		
1823	C	1856	l	1885	P	1919	d		
1824	D			1886	Q	1920	e		
1825	E e			1887	R	1921	F		
1826	F			1888	S	1922	S		
1827	G			1889	T	1923	h		
				1890	U	1924	I		

Up to 1931 the date letter was changed on 1st June. The Q of 1932 began on 1st January.

Gold Hall Marks

In Britain a legal standard for gold items dates, as with silver, from the early C14. Commercial gold is an alloy in which fine gold is mixed with silver and copper (and often other metals too) in order to increase its strength. The proportion of fine gold to alloy metals is measured (assayed) to establish its quality. This has to reach a certain legal standard before it can be hallmarked. Quality is measured by means of the "carat", which is a ¼th part of the weight of the object being assayed. A 22 carat piece therefore has 22 parts of fine gold to 2 parts of alloy metals.

An 18 carat piece has 18 parts of fine gold to 6 parts of alloy metals.

A 9 carat piece has 9 parts of fine gold to 15 parts of alloy metals.

The legal Gold Standards
(G.B. and N. Ireland)

Date	Standards in carats
1477–1575	18
1575–1798	22
1798–1854	22 *and* 18
1854–1932	22, 18, 15, 12 *and* 9
1932–present	22, 18, 14, *and* 9

In the Republic of Ireland the current standards are: 22, 20 (rare), 18, 14 and 9 carats.

The Marks
As with silver these are made up of:
1. Maker's mark

2. Standard mark

	To 1974		1975–present		Foreign imports	
22 carat	🔲	22	🔲	916	🔲	916
18 carat	🔲	18	🔲	750	🔲	750
14 carat	14	585	🔲	585	🔲	585
9 carat	9	375	🔲	375	🔲	375

Scottish offices used the following marks in place of the crown: Edinburgh 🔲   Glasgow 🔲 🔲

3. Assay office mark

London 🔲	Newcastle 🔲	Glasgow 🔲
Birmingham 🔲	Sheffield 🔲	Dublin 🔲
Chester 🔲	York 🔲	
Exeter 🔲	Edinburgh 🔲	

4. Date letter: Normally as silver date mark for same assay office, but with variations in border shapes.

Foreign pieces imported into Britain
From 1842 imported pieces were assayed and hallmarked; from 1876 the hallmark included a stamped "F". After 1904 each assay office was allocated a special "office" mark for foreign items. This replaced the normal office mark.

London 🔲	Birmingham 🔲	Chester 🔲
Sheffield 🔲	Edinburgh 🔲	Glasgow 🔲

International gold marks
Few countries have, over the years, evolved systems of marking gold wares as consistent, all-embracing and reliable as British Hall Marks. Some countries (e.g. France) have a complex range of marks, while others have a very limited number. The best advice is to consult a specialist book.

Leading British silversmiths and their marks
The dates given below indicate the period in which each silversmith flourished and produced his or her best work. Where insufficient information is available on this point, the date given is when the individual's name was entered (ent.) at Goldsmith's Hall in London.

Abdy, William, London, c1766–1799

Abercromby, Robt, London, c1739–1769

Adam, Charles, London, c1701–1716

Adams, George, London, ent.1840

Aldridge, Edward, London, c1739–1753

Alexander, W., Glasgow, ent.1835

Alleine, John, London, c1772–1799

Anderson, James, Edinburgh, ent.1729

Angell, George, London, c1850–1875

Angell, Jos. London, c1849–1891

Angell, Joseph & John, London, c1841–1850

Archambo, Peter, London, c1739–1769

Ash, Thomas, London, ent.1697

Barber, James, York, c1805–1857

Barnard, Edward & Sons Ltd., London, c1829–1850

Barnard, E.J. & W., London, c1829–1832

Barnard, Edward, and Emes, Rebecca, London, c1808–1828

Barnard, Messrs., London, c1894

Bateman, Peter & Anne, London, ent. 1790

Bateman, Hester, London, ent. 1774

Bateman, William, London, c1815–1840

Berthelot, John, London, c1750–1760

Bettridge, John, Birmingham, ent.1817

Boulton, Matthew, Birmingham, c1773–1809

Brind, Walter, London, c1749–1753

Brown, Robert, London, c1736–1774

Burrell, James & Co., Glasgow, c1825

Burwash, William, London, c1802–1826

Burwash, William, and Sibley, Richard, London, ent.1805

Cafe, John, London, ent.1742

Cafe, William, London, c1756–1768

Caldecott, William, London, c1755–1763

Carter, John, London, ent. pre-1773

Chawner, Henry, London, c1778–1796

Chawner, William, London, c1815–1837

Clifton, Jonah, London, c1703–1710

Cocks & Bettridge, Birmingham, ent. 1806

Coker, Ebenezer, London, c1738–1745

Comyns, William, London, ent. 1902

Cookson, Isaac, Newcastle, c1724–1757

Cooper, George, Aberdeen, c1728

Courtauld, Augustin, London, c1708–1739

Courtauld, Samuel, London, ent. 1745

Cowles, George, London, c1796–1804

Craddock, Joseph, and Reid, William, London, c1827–1833

Crespell, S. & J., London, c1764–1780

Crespin, Paul, London, c1739–1747

Creswick, T.J. & N., Sheffield, ent.1819

Crouch, John, London, c1808–1813

Davenport, Burrage, London, c1776–1789

Dexter, Francis, London, c1839–1846

Dixon, James & Sons, Sheffield, ent. 1867

East, John, London, c1668–1711

Eaton, William, London, c1837

Edwards, John, London, c1722–1752

Eley, William, and Fearn, William, London, c1797–1823

Elkington & Co., Birmingham, c1849

Elkington, Mason & Co., Birmingham, c1859

Elliott, William, London, c1810–1844

Emes, John, London, c1796–1808

Farren, Thomas, London, c1739–1769

Fawdery, William, London, c1718–1768

Feline, Edward, London, c1718–1744

Fordham & Faulkner, Sheffield, ent. 1890

Fox, Charles, London, c1819–1842

Fuller, Crispin, London, c1804–1827

Garrard, Robert, London, c1802–1822

Godfrey, Elizabeth, London, ent. 1741

Green, John & Co., Sheffield, ent. 1792

Hancock, C.F., London, c1876–1890

Hannam, Thomas, & Crouch, John, London, c1765–67

Harache, Pierre, London, ent. 1697

Harper, Robert, London, c1860–62

Harris, Charles Stuart & Sons, London, c1867–69

Harrison, Bros, & Howson, Sheffield, ent.1845

Hawksworth Eyre & Co. Ltd., Sheffield, ent.1833

Hemming, Thomas, London, c1745–1763

Hennell, David, London, c1736–1774

Hennell, Robert, London, ent. 1753

Hennell, David & Robert, London, ent. 1795

Hennell, Samuel, London, c1811–1819

Herbert, Henry, London, ent. 1747

Hicks, Joseph, Exeter, ent. 1784

Holaday, Sarah, London, c1718–1725

Holland, Henry, London, c1840–1850

Holmes, William, London, c1776–1789

Holy, Daniel & Co., Sheffield, ent. 1777

Hougham, Charles, London, c1778–1791

Hunt, John S., London, c1844–1850

Hutton, William & Sons Ltd., London, c1895–97

Hyman, Hymans, London, c1845–47

Jacobs, John, London, ent. 1739

Jones, Thomas, Dublin, c1780–82

Kandler, Charles F., London, c1726–1752

Keating, Michael, Dublin, c1774–80

Kirkby, Waterhouse & Co., Sheffield, c1792–94

Lambe, George, London, c1713–1720

Lambert, H., London, c1902–04

Lamerie, Paul, London, c1712–1749

Langlands, John, Newcastle, ent. 1732

Lawrence & Co., Birmingham, c1813

Linwood, Matthew, Birmingham, c1804–06

Lofthouse, Matthew, London, c1705–1724

Lofthouse, Seth, London, c1697–1716

Maciare & Dewar, London, c1866–68

Mann, W., London, c1857–59

Mappin & Webb, London, c1873–75

Martin Hall & Co. Ltd., Sheffield, ent. 1854

Mills, Nathaniel, Birmingham, ent. 1836

Morrison, Jas., London, c1740–1773

Murray, J., Glasgow, c1861–63

Nelme, Anthony, London, c1697–1728

Nutting, Henry, London, c1796–1804

Oliver, John, York, c1660–1693

Parr, Thomas, London, c1739–1769

Payne, John, London, c1750–1760

Pemberton, Samuel, Birmingham, c1783–85

Phipps & Robinson, London, c1790–1800

Pitts, William, London, c1778–1799

Pitts, William, and Preedy, Joseph, London, c1790–1800

Plummer, William, London, c1775–1791

Pollock, John, London, c1734–1753

Preist, John, London, c1747–1749

Pyne, Benjamin, London, c1679–1723

Reid, William K., London, c1830–1850

Richardson, Richard (III), Chester, c1734–1787

Roberts, Samuel & Co., Sheffield, ent. 1773

Roberts & Briggs, London, c1857–59

Robertson, William, London, c1752–1760

Robins, Thomas, London, c1807–1820

Rolles, Philip, London, c1675–1720

Round, J. & Son., Sheffield, ent. 1867

Rugg, Richard, London, c1752–1789

Rundell, Bridge & Rundell, London, c1803–05

Rundell, Philip, London, c1819–1824

Rutland, Robert, London, c1811–1828

Sams, Richard, Exeter, c1757–1815

Scott, Digby, and Smith, Benjamin, London, ent. 1802

Sharp, Robert, and Smith, Daniel, London, c1763–1803

Shaw, John, Birmingham, ent. 1802

Shaw, Thomas, Birmingham, ent. 1822

Sheen, William, London, c1773–1789

Sibley, Richard, London, c1837–1850

Smiley, William, London, c1844–1850

Smith, Nathaniel, Sheffield, ent. 1780

Smith, Stephen, London, c1877–79

Sobey, William R., Exeter, c1831–1851

Spilsbury, Francis I., London, c1729–1753

Sprimont, Nicholas, London, c1742–1770

Stevenson, William, London, c1801–1826

Storr, Paul, London, c1792–1834

Sumner, William, London, c1778–1810

Swift, John, London, c1728–1752

Syngin, Richard, London, c1697–1701

Tanqueray, David, London, c1713–1720

Taylor, Joseph, Birmingham, ent. 1787

Taylor & Perry, Birmingham, ent. 1829

Terrey, John Edward, London, c1818–1849

Timbrell, Robert, London, c1697–1716

Tuite, John, London, c1718–1740

Tuite, William, London, c1755–1769

Unite, George, Birmingham, ent. 1832

Videau, Ayme, London, c1739–1747

Vincent, William, London, c1773–1790

Walker & Hall, Sheffield, c1900–1921

Waterhouse, Hodson & Co., Sheffield, ent. 1822

Watson, John, Sheffield, ent. 1795

Watson, Thomas, Newcastle, c1793–1845

Wheeler, Gervase, Birmingham, ent. 1831

Whipham, Thomas, London, c1736–1772

Whipple, J. & Co., Exeter, c1854–1877

Wilkinson, Henry, Sheffield, ent. 1831

Willaume, David, London, c1697–1741

Willaume, David, London, c1718–1745

Willmore, Joseph, Birmingham, c1799–1801

Winter, John & Co., Sheffield, ent. 1773

Woodward, William, London, c1741–43

Yapp & Woodward, Birmingham, c1845

Yorke, Edward, London, c1729–1753

Continental silver marks

Holland is the only other country to have a method of silver marking in any way comparable with the British Hall Mark system. Unfortunately it was never regularly or consistently followed. Other European countries used marks from time to time, sometimes to indicate quality, sometimes the maker and sometimes payment, or otherwise, of duty. Because of their irregular and often spasmodic use, these marks are of limited use in either recognition or dating. Of more help, though not totally reliable, are the Town marks indicating place of manufacture. These were used throughout Europe and provide some guide to dating. Examples are illustrated below, but the total number and variation of such marks is so vast that identification may require specialist advice.

Two possible clues are always worth considering: an eagle mark could indicate Austrian, German or possibly Russian origin, while a fleur-de-lys is probably French. But remember: there are always exceptions to such "rules of thumb".

Quality and other marks

Austria
Standard
(950)
Mid C19

Belgium
Standard
(800)
C18

France
Standard
(950/1000)
Early C19

Italy
Standard
(950)
c1870–1930

Holland
Standard
(934/1000)
C19

Sweden
Control mark
Mid C18

Paris
Guarantee mark
Early C19

F.T.Germain
Maker's mark
Paris, *C18*

W.Jamnitzer
Maker's mark
Nuremberg,
C16

H.Swiering
Maker's mark
Amsterdam,
C18

Town marks

Amsterdam
C18

Antwerp
Early C18

Berlin
Late C18

Brussels
Early C18

Budapest
C18

Cologne
Late C17

Copenhagen
C17

Florence
C17-C18

Geneva
C18

Lisbon
C17-C18

Madrid
C18

Moscow
Early C18

Munich
Early C18

Oslo
Mid C17-mid C19

Paris
Mid C18

Rome
Late C17

Stockholm
C18-mid C19

Toulouse
C16-C17

Vienna
Mid C18

Zurich
C17-C18

Old Sheffield Plate

The process of fusing a thin sheet of silver to a thicker of copper dates from mid C18. By 1800 a wide range of articles were being produced in large quantities and a variety of styles.

Styles: Sheffield platers copied silver styles which had proved popular, and domestic ware in the styles of "Queen Anne" and "Early Georgian" were manufactured into the early C19. Such articles cannot, of course, date earlier than the 1740s. In the early C19, the fashionable Empire style was embellished with heavy ornamental designs made possible by the increasing use of plated wire.

British Plate: A process, often confused with Sheffield plate, patented in 1836. This replaced the copper element in silver plating with a silver-coloured alloy known as "German silver" though it contained no actual silver. Because it was cheaper, tougher and did not have the reddish copper to show through when worn, British plate brought about the ending of Sheffield plate production by the 1840s. It was itself superseded when even cheaper electro-plating was developed later in the century.

Aids to dating Sheffield Plate

* *Sheared edges*, c1745–1760: metal plated on one side only, revealing copper edge.
* *Single lapped edges*, c1760–1790: Silver layer was extended to lap over and conceal copper edge. Beading simple and punched in. It was usual to tin flat-ware (plates etc.) on back and hollow-ware (jugs etc.) on the inside.
* *Double lapped edges*, c1770–1810: Silvered copper ribbons soldered to edges to lap over on to copper undersides: often difficult to detect. Beading, reeding and gadrooning in common use.
* *Silver lapped edges*, c1775–1815: Both sides of copper sheet now silver-plated. U-shaped silver wire was used to conceal any copper revealed by shearing. Joins almost invisible. From 1800 shells, dolphins and oak leaves used as decoration.
* After 1815 ornamentation is much more elaborate, with vine leaves, flowers and various classical motifs.

Marks

* Useful for dating and identification. No marks were legally permitted before 1784.
* After that date makers were allowed to mark their products with individual symbols which had to be registered at the Sheffield Assay office. However, not all makers did so, continuing to sell their goods unmarked.
* Registration of marks ceased in 1835.
* From 1820 to 1835 fine quality Sheffield plate could carry a crown mark to distinguish it from lightly-silvered imported ware, especially from French manufacturers.
* For similar reasons, after 1820 makers stamped some of their products with a mark indicating the proportion of silver and copper, e.g. "BEST SHEFFIELD HEAVY SILVER PLATING 80 dwts to 8 lbs."
* Simulated silver hall marks, normally consisting of five marks, appeared on Sheffield plate from c1835.
* Marks on British plate after 1836 also imitated silver hall marks, one of the marks normally being the maker's initials.

Beware

* Electro-plated articles from mid C19 on are often referred to as "Sheffield Plate". By law, however, the term should only be applied to wares in which silver has been fused to copper, and only such wares should be so marked.
* On hollow ware a useful test is to check for a seam. Electro-plating covers a piece completely.
* The words "Sheffield Plated" indicate that the piece is electro-plated and *not* genuine Sheffield plate. Such a piece dates from mid C19.
* In North America articles produced by fusing or depositing a thin layer of silver on some other base metal are known as "Silver plate"; in Britain this term is applied to solid silver ware.

Silver shapes and dates

Teapots

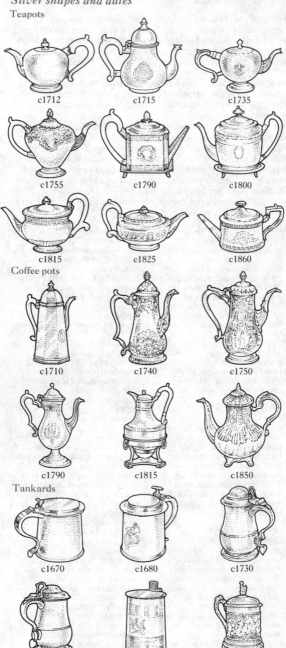

c1712

c1715

c1735

c1755

c1790

c1800

c1815

c1825

c1860

Coffee pots

c1710

c1740

c1750

c1790

c1815

c1850

Tankards

c1670

c1680

c1730

c1760

c1780

c1830

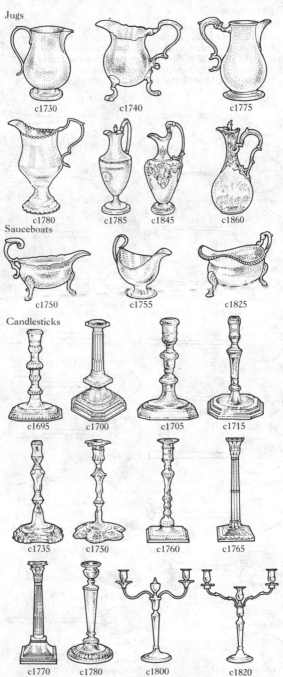

Jugs

c1730
c1740
c1775

c1780
c1785
c1845
c1860

Sauceboats

c1750
c1755
c1825

Candlesticks

c1695
c1700
c1705
c1715

c1735
c1750
c1760
c1765

c1770
c1780
c1800
c1820

Spoon shapes

The range and variety of spoons, and their evolution, has made them the most popular of all silver items for collectors. Of particular interest are the finials but beware of forgeries, especially with sets of Apostle spoons. Up to the end of the C18 spoons were generally made from two separate pieces of silver (bowl and handle); subsequently, from just one.

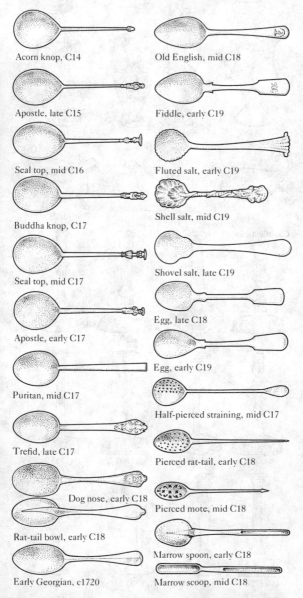

Acorn knop, C14

Apostle, late C15

Seal top, mid C16

Buddha knop, C17

Seal top, mid C17

Apostle, early C17

Puritan, mid C17

Trefid, late C17

Dog nose, early C18

Rat-tail bowl, early C18

Early Georgian, c1720

Old English, mid C18

Fiddle, early C19

Fluted salt, early C19

Shell salt, mid C19

Shovel salt, late C19

Egg, late C18

Egg, early C19

Half-pierced straining, mid C17

Pierced rat-tail, early C18

Pierced mote, mid C18

Marrow spoon, early C18

Marrow scoop, mid C18

American silver shapes and dates

Since early American silversmiths produced pieces to order, each item possessed its own characteristics, reflecting the tastes of the customer and the creative skills of the smith. Men like Paul Revere produced distinctive pieces with a vitality of line to equal, and even surpass, silverware produced in Europe.

Beaker, c1820

Spout cup, c1710

Cup, c1750

Tankard, c1740

Tankard, c1770

Mug, c1810

Coffee pot, c1715

Coffee pot, c1750

Coffee pot, c1790

Cream pitcher, c1760

Cream pitcher, c1775

Cream pitcher, c1820

Teapot, c1730

Teapot, c1815

Teapot, c1850

What you should know about:
Silver

General points

* Silver value depends on a combination of proportion, style, workmanship, balance, weight and patina. Fashions come and go, but quality pieces retain value.
* The best pieces will have no damage or alteration, will retain original decoration and carry a full set of marks correctly grouped and spaced.
* Patina, due to oxidation, age and handling, should be "glowing" and unblemished. A break in the patination is a sure sign of repair or alteration.
* Avoid pieces that have been "cleaned" with harsh chemicals and have an over-white appearance.
* Poor patina may indicate the use of substandard metal; or the piece may be an electroplate copy of a period piece; typical of recent fakes.
* Assay and other marks are a helpful guide to dating, but are by no means infallible.
* As a basic rule, the marks should follow the shape of the piece: arranged in a circle on a round-bottomed piece; in a line on a square-bottomed. Each piece of a multipart should have its own set of marks.
* All legitimate repairs must be separately marked; so new marks on a lid, spout or handle indicate a repair which reduces the value of the piece.
* Look for a patched-on hallmark; junction lines are visible on a tarnished piece when it is breathed on. Or examine under magnification.
* A patched-on hallmark may indicate an attempt to deceive. However, between 1719–59 and 1784–90 marks were sometimes taken from a spoon, watch-case or small object, and patched-on to a more substantial piece to avoid duty. Patination can be a helpful guide in distinguishing between the two forms.
* Don't be put off by the absence of assay marks on British pieces. Pieces made to commission, or in a place remote from an assay office, may only carry the maker's marks.
* Every country in which silver was used had its own assay rules, and, inevitably, exceptions to those rules. If in doubt, seek expert advice.

* Armorials should be in their original state and contemporary with the piece. They then add value and are also useful guides to dating and understanding the history of a piece.
* They should also be in original condition; check with a strong magnifying glass for any re-engraving. A second, sharp, engraving line will be seen within the lines of the original decoration.
* Armorials were often added later to increase the value of a piece. Such additions are difficult to detect but may be brilliantly sharp compared to other decoration on the piece.
* Armorials were also sometimes erased or replaced as fashions changed, and this can detract from the value. Look for signs of a patch; this may be difficult to detect if the joins form part of the decoration.

A

B

C

Decorative borders on silver:
A *Shell and scroll, C18-present*
B *Gadroon, C18-present*
C *Ovolo border, early C19*

* The areas most susceptible to damage are the joints at handles, spouts and feet, also rims. Check also for pin-prick holes where the silver has thinned through handling.

Beware

* Marriages can be done skilfully and take a variety of forms. Frequently found is a genuinely old hallmarked base or handle married to a later piece; or apostle finials to other cutlery stems.
* Because of the high price of silver in general, always exercise care when buying, and seek trustworthy advice if in the slightest doubt.

What you should know about:
Pewter and other metals

* Until c1826 the Pewterers' Company laid down stringent standards for the industry: the size and weight of different pewter objects was controlled, marks were used to designate the fineness of the alloy, and a maker was required to stamp his productions with his own individual touch-mark. After 1826, capacity marks were required by law on tavern pieces. See page 122.
* Thus it is relatively easy to distinguish between period and reproduction pieces. The latter were made in quantity from the 1920's onwards but rarely comply with the Pewterers' Company standards.
* Owners' marks, crests and coats of arms on old pewter can all enhance the value of a piece, especially if they confirm its provenance.
* C18 plates are the objects most commonly found. Most flatware made in the UK and USA was hammered to compact the metal, and this gives it desirability, unlike later reproductions which rarely have this feature.
* The best quality tankards, spoons and flatware were made of leadless hard or plate pewter, marked as described on pages 122 and 123.
* Plate pewter and Britannia metal are whiter than the inferior lay or trifle pewter, and each has a characteristic ring when struck. Britannia metal can be mistaken for silver, but never recovers its sheen if allowed to oxidize; pieces in original condition are therefore much more valuable – and difficult to find.
* Period pewter is generally better finished than reproduction. Check the seams and edges for signs of quality workmanship. Edges should be polished, where excess metal was removed, not sharp. Undersides should have concentric rings from lathe turning. Absence usually indicates a later piece made from sheet metal, not cast in the traditional manner.
* Wear should be consistent with use, and natural. Edges should be soft with wear, hinges worn, and knife cuts explicable. The characteristic patina of pewter develops after c50 years and

simulated patina on modern copies dulls the surface but doesn't have the same glow.
* In Britain and Germany particularly, Art Nouveau pewter work achieved great popularity and high standards of craftsmanship. Liberty's "Tudric" range, decorated with motifs taken from the Celtic, included tea and coffee services as well as clocks, tableware, bowls and vases. The chief German exponent was Engelbert Kayser (1840–1911), whose range was as extensive as Liberty's.

Beware
* The objects most widely faked are the higher value early-lidded tankards, and also candlesticks. Before buying check that the style and marks are correct for the period, and be suspicious if the weight, workmanship and finish is inferior. Finally, ensure that damage and oxidation is natural and reasonable.

Other metals
* Old Sheffield plate, a fusion of silver and copper, was manufactured between c1760 and 1840 when it was superseded by other processes. Fine pieces in good condition which follow the style of their silver contemporaries are in demand. True Sheffield plate turns blue when touched with nitric acid. Replated items have a greasy feel.
* The most popular forms in brass, copper, bronze and iron are candlesticks, kitchenware, trays, jardinières, boxes, ecclesiastical objects and architectural furniture.
* Most period pieces were cast and show signs of hand finishing where surplus metal was removed, or hammered from sheets of uneven thickness.
* Hollow forms, such as candlesticks, were made in two pieces until the 1830s, so a piece without seams cannot be earlier.

Beware
* Mass market products of the C19 and C20 are far more numerous than period items, but the condition and patination is usually a reliable guide to age and authenticity.

Marks on Pewter

Because of the range and quantity of pewter items produced during almost 500 years, it is impossible to give precise rules for identifying and dating by means of marks. Many of the common items for domestic use were not marked at all, particularly when produced outside London, Philadelphia and other main centres. Where marks do appear, they are not always what they seem and other factors (shape, patina etc.) should always be considered when attempting to date. Forged marks, originating in C20, are not unknown, particularly on more highly prized pieces, and again it is important to view the item as a whole.

Touchmarks

* The most consistently helpful of marks on English pewter are the makers' marks which the Pewterers' Company in London compelled its members to stamp on their wares.
* Each pewterer had his individual mark which was registered at Pewterers' Hall on special plates known as "Touch Plates" – hence the term "Touchmark" ("Touch") for such makers' stamps (which were always impressed, never engraved).
* There are 5 such Touch Plates still in existence at Pewterers' Hall, containing over 600 names with impressed accompanying touchmarks.
* Although touchmarks had been used since the late C15 the early plates were destroyed in the Great Fire of London in 1666, and the plates now in existence date from 1668 when the touchmark system was revived.
* The earliest touchmarks were small and normally consisted of the pewterer's initials. Generally, the smaller the mark, the earlier the item. Touchmarks were usually struck on handles, or the front rims of flatware.

* Subsequently, touchmarks became more elaborate, often incorporating pictorial designs or symbols. Full names appear, sometimes with addresses. These larger marks are stamped on the underside of plates, and on the lids, or inside the bases of tankards.

* When a date is included, this indicates when the touch was registered and *not* when the piece was made.

* Touchmarks ceased to be registered in 1824.

Quality marks

* Touchmarks do not indicate the quality of the alloy used, although they can give guidance as to the craftsmanship of a piece.
* Pewter is an alloy of tin and other metals, notably lead or antimony and/or copper and/or bismuth. Fine old pewter is an alloy of tin and copper, but the three types of period pewter most likely to be encountered are: 1. Lay or ley pewter (80% tin, 20% lead); 2. Trifle pewter (83% tin, 17% antimony) and 3. Hard metal or plate pewter (86% tin, 7% antimony, 3.5% copper and 3.5% bismuth). Note, however, that the proportions and constituents of hard metal vary somewhat, affecting its quality.
* Neither lay (the lowest quality) or trifle pewter carried quality marks, but hard metal pieces were marked with an X (indicating "extraordinary ware"). Some pieces also carried the legend "superfine".

* From mid C18, the best quality plate pewter was marked with an X surmounted by a crown.
* From late C17 quality pieces intended for export were supposed to be marked with a "Rose and Crown" stamp. In C18 it became not unusual to stamp this quality mark on pieces intended for sale in Britain.

Imitation hall marks

* These appear on many C18 pieces. They copied genuine silver marks (leopard's head, standard mark, date letter, maker's mark) and were placed where they would have appeared on genuine silver pieces. Though crude and not bearing close examination, they can provide useful clues to period and maker.

Excise marks

* After 1824, all measures and drinking vessels in which liquor was sold by measure, had to be tested and stamped with a mark that combined the sovereign's cypher with a local emblem and sometimes with letters and/or numbers indicating year and person carrying out the test. These marks varied from area to area. However, after 1877 the mark was standardized to a crown, monarch's initial, town number and sometimes a date letter.

Other marks

* Coats of arms, owner's initials (sometimes in groups of three letters known as "triads"), marriage marks, inn names, etc., can all be of use in confirming the period of a piece so marked. However, be sure the mark was not added later.

Britannia metal

* This is a superior form of pewter evolved in the late C18 from plate pewter. Containing approx. 90% tin, 8% antimony and 2% copper, it was widely used in C19 for factory production of a wide range of items.
* Pieces were marked with names or trade marks on the underside.
* If the mark includes a pattern number, it is Britannia metal and not one of the earlier forms of pewter.

Modern pewter

* Modern or reproduction pewter will be easily recognized from its "colour" and general condition, unless, of course, there has been a deliberate attempt at faking.

* Marks can consist of maker's name, a brand name (e.g. Liberty's "Tudric" pewter), a trade mark, or possibly a place of origin.
* Most on the market is of fairly recent date, although early C20 pewter is becoming quite collectable.

American pewter

* First pewterer's shop opened in 1635. For the next 100 years most original pewter ware came from Europe. When a piece wore out, it would be melted down and re-made by a local craftsman.

* Early pewterers either used or adapted touches they had brought with them to the New World, or simply designed their own.
* Some early American pewter bears an X quality mark, similar to that used on English hard metal pewter.
* From c1750–1850 American-made pewter became more and more available, and quality was usually good.
* Generally pieces then carry quite elaborate makers' marks. Such a mark can include full name and town, but sometimes consists simply of initials combined with some form of symbol. To complicate matters, some makers used more than one mark.

* Some fine examples of Britannia ware were produced in America, and makers' marks worth looking for are those of William Calder, Vose and the Boardmans.

Beware

* It is worth repeating that a mark in itself is no guarantee of either date or quality. Fakers often use "genuine" marks, but not always in the correct position. Be suspicious of sharp edges, where the fake die has been struck too deeply.
* Remember too that genuine old pewter quite frequently carried no marks. This makes it all the more important to gain a feel for period, style and authentic patina.

CLOCKS and BAROMETERS
Glossary

Act of Parliament clock
C18 English clock, driven by weights, mounted on a wall, with a large dial without glass and a "trunk" for the weights to hang. When timepieces were taxed in 1797, people gave up their own and relied instead on clocks of this type, installed to meet their needs by tavern-keepers. Also known as a "tavern" clock. In fact clocks of this type existed before 1797.

anchor escapement Escapement invented in England c1670. Named after the anchor shape of the linkage between the pallets controlling the escape wheel.

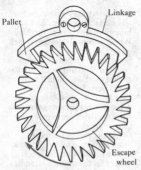

Pallet — Linkage

Escape wheel

angle barometer Barometer in which the upper part of the tube is turned nearly to the horizontal, so that the movement of the mercury can be measured across a larger scale. Such barometers often have two or three tubes set one above the other, to read at lower or higher pressures. Also known as "signpost barometers".

arbor Clockmaker's term for the axle on which a wheel is mounted.

arch Specifically, the arch above the dial, usual in longcase clocks from c1700.

automaton clock Clock with strike performed by mechanically operated figures.

backplate The rear of the two plates supporting the movement, on which details of the maker are often engraved.

balance Device counteracting the force of the mainspring on the crown or balance wheel.

balance spring Spring acting on the balance wheel to counteract the force of the mainspring, the

equivalent in watches of the pendulum, and developed shortly after c1675.

banjo barometer Type of **wheel** barometer current from 2nd half of C18 to end of C19, so called from its shape.

barrel Specifically, the barrel containing the mainspring round which the string driving the **train** is wound.

bezel The metal rim to a glass cover, e.g. over a clock face.

Bim Bam Onomatopoeic name for the strike of a type of German-produced mantel clock popular in England early C20. It sounds two strokes of different tone for the hour.

bimetallic balance Compensated balance – the equivalent of a **compensated pendulum** – made of brass and steel. These have different rates of expansion, so cancel out.

Black Forest clocks Clocks were produced in Bohemia from mid C17, but the usual Black Forest clock with automata of various kinds (the most famous of which is the cuckoo, which appeared c1730) date from C18 and C19.

bob The weight at the end of the pendulum.

bracket clock Domestic clock that originally (before C17) needed to be set high on a bracket so that its weights could hang down; later, the standard spring-driven domestic clock of C18 and C19, regardless of its stand or location.

broken arch Specifically, the arch to a longcase clock that is less than a semicircle – a sign of its early Georgian date.

calendar aperture Opening in the dial displaying the day and month.

carriage clock Type of clock developed in France in mid C19 as a portable travelling timepiece. It has an oblong dialplate, with a handle above.

cartel clock French wall clock, fashionable in England in 1740s, typically with an elaborately decorated case.

chain fusee A fusee from which a chain (rather than a gutstring) unwinds on to the barrel of the mainspring. Chain fusees became usual c1800, but earlier gut fusees were often converted.

chapter ring The part of the dial on which the numbers of the hours are inscribed. Often a separate piece, not part of the "dialplate".

chronometer Precision timepiece for navigation or science.

circular movement Movement having circular plates, a typical feature of French clocks of the early C19 and later.

cistern Chamber containing the mercury at base of the tube of a barometer.

cistern cover Piece protecting the mercury **cistern**.

clock garniture A setpiece of ornaments for the mantelpiece, incorporating a clock.

cock Bracket, attached to the plate, supporting one end of the balance spring of a watch.

compensated pendulum Pendulum compensating for the changes in its length caused by changes in temperature: mercury at the bottom of the pendulum rises or falls to keep the centre of oscillation constant; or a **gridiron** of steel and brass is used.

countwheel strike Mechanism that determines the number of strikes for each hour. Moving on with each strike, the countwheel causes a lever (the "detent") to rise and fall, until and unless it catches in one of the notches on its rim. Set at increasing intervals, these control how long the clock continues to strike. Rendered obsolete by the **rack-strike**.

crutch The arm that connects the pendulum to the pallet arbor.

date aperture See **calendar aperture**.

deadbeat escapement Improved version of the **anchor** escapement invented c1715, eliminating the slight recoil of the escape wheel as the pallets caught its teeth, so improving accuracy.

depthed Mounted with the aid of a depthing tool. On the adjustable depthing tool, a wheel and a pinion can be meshed to the optimum "depth"; then with the depthing tool the exact points for drilling holes in the plates for the arbors of the wheels can be marked.

dialplate Front **plate** of the clock, on which the **chapter ring** may be attached or painted.

Dutch strike Chiming system that strikes (on a different bell) the next hour at the half-hour. Common on Dutch and German clocks.

eight-day movement Movement requiring winding every eight days.

endstone Jewel inserted in or constituting the plate on which an arbor pivots, e.g. the balance staff or arbor of the balance wheel.

English dial English wall clock made in C19, with large painted sheet-iron dial, anchor escapement and pendulum – a type once ubiquitous in railway stations.

equation dial Dial with which to equate the time registered on a sundial and mechanical "mean" time. One hand points to the day of the month, another hand indicates how fast or slow the sundial is.

Fitzroy barometer Barometer introduced c1870 and popular into C20. Named after Admiral Fitzroy, who started the first weather forecast, in *The Times* in 1860. Typically it has a broad oblong case, with many paper charts and hints, and Fitzroy's "storm glass", intended to measure the degree of electrification in the air.

foliot Primitive form of balance, consisting of a bar suspending adjustable weights. Attached to the **verge**, it served to counterweight the thrust of the crown wheel against the **pallets**.

fusee A grooved spool, from which a line or chain unwinds as it is pulled by the mainspring of the movement. The conical shape of the fusee compensates for the diminishing strength of the spring as it unwinds.

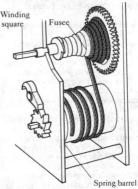

Winding square / Fusee

Spring barrel

gimbal Mounting for a ship's instrument such as a barometer, to keep it upright whatever the state of the sea.

grande sonnerie System of striking the hours and quarters, dating from late C17. As in other systems, different bells were used for the quarters and the hours; but in this system, after each quarter, the hour was struck again.

gridiron pendulum Pendulum made up of several rods, of steel or iron descending from above and of brass rising from the bottom ends of the iron rods. Brass expands in heat rather more than iron, and the length of the pendulum is thus kept constant.

half hunter A hunter with a glass giving partial sight of the dial through the cover.

hood The part of a longcase clock that contains the dial and movement.

hunter Watch with an opening front cover which protects the glass over the dial.

hygrometer Instrument for measuring degrees of wet and dry, often included in C19 barometers.

lantern clock So called from their resemblance to ships' lanterns, these clocks were made in England from c1600 into the C18. Driven by weights, not a spring, and marking only the hours, they were replaced by **longcase** and **bracket** clocks.

lever escapement A modification of the **anchor escapement** for watches (or carriage clocks). The escape wheel is restrained by one or other of the two **pallets** of an oscillating lever, made to oscillate by a pin on a roller driven by the balance wheel.

locking plate Alternative term for the **countwheel**.

longcase clock Known popularly as a "grandfather" clock, with a tall case to house the weights or pendulum and protect them from dust. First made c1660 in England.

maintaining power Subsidiary spring used to keep the movement going while the clock is being wound.

mantel clock Clock provided with feet and often appropriate decoration, to stand on a mantelpiece or shelf.

marine chronometer Precision clock for use at sea.

moonwork Mechanism to count and display the phases and age of the moon.

musical clock Clock with a train driving a cylinder with pins that strike bells to play one or a selection of tunes.

mystery clock Clock in which the motion (and source of motion) are practically imperceptible.

oignon Onion-shaped watch of French type, common in late C17 and C18.

orrery Named after the fourth Earl of Orrery, an astronomical clock that shows the positions of the sun, moon, earth and sometimes also planets.

overcoil A second spring acting on the balance spring to ensure its concentric winding and unwinding, invented late C18.

pair-case Casing that was common on continental watches and standard for English watches from mid C17 into C19: a double case, an inner one for the movement and an outer one that was usually decorated.

pallet Arm or lever that engages in an escapement wheel to halt it.

pillar One of the rods or rivets connecting the dial-plate and the backplate of a movement. The number and shape of these pillars (four, five; ringed, baluster, etc.) are a guide to classification and dating.

plate (1) The backplate of the two plates supporting the mechanism of a clock, or, in the plural, the front plate or dialplate and the backplate together. (2) The **register plate** of a barometer.

pull repeat See **repeating work**.

push repeat See **repeating work**.

quarter strike Strike (chime) that tells the quarter- and half-hours as well as the hour.

rack strike or **rack-and-snail strike** Mechanism to regulate the strike train by the movement of the hands, introduced c1676. Rack is mounted so that each blow struck gathers on one tooth, while a "snail" carried round with the hour hand controls the set of the rack, and thus the number of teeth free.

rating nut The nut and screw with which the **bob** (and so the rate of swing) of a pendulum can be adjusted.

register plate Inscribed plate of a barometer against which the level of mercury is read.

regulation dial Dial through which an adjustment can be made to length of pendulum.

regulator C18 term for precision timepiece, usually without **moonwork** or calendar, etc.

remontoire Device for rewinding the mainspring, thus ensuring its constant thrust.

repeating clock Clock with a repeating work.

repeating work Device in which the pull of a cord or push of a button will operate the strike (again). Invented 1676, so making it possible to hear the time in the dark.

rod Rod of the pendulum.

shelf clock See mantel clock.

signpost barometer = angle barometer.

single-train movement Movement utilizing the same train for "going" and for striking.

skeleton clock Clock with workings exposed by cutting away the plates.

Staartklok Dutch wall clock (meaning "tail clock"), c1800, with a pendulum and anchor escapement.

stick barometer Barometer with a straight vertical register plate from which the movement of the mercury is read off direct (as opposed to the **wheel** type).

strike/silent ring Dial or ring with a pointer to disengage or re-engage the striking mechanism.

stringing Type of veneer decoration of alternating light and dark woods, found particularly on barometers dating before 1850.

strut table clock Table clock provided with a strut to hold it steady, usual C19.

subsidiary Short for subsidiary dial.

sympiesometer Barometer patented in 1818 using gas instead of mercury to measure air pressure.

thirty-hour movement Movement requiring winding every 30 hours.

three-train movement Movement with one train for "going", a second for striking the hours, and a third for an alarm or for striking the half- or quarter-hours.

ting tang Onomatopoeic name for the quarter strike typical of Black Forest and other German clocks.

two-train movement Movement with one train for "going", another for striking.

train Set of wheels, etc, locked in drive.

turret clock Clock of type installed in medieval towers, driven by a weight suspended on a rope wound round a drum.

Even miniature clocks with this type of drive are called turret clocks.

verge escapement Early mechanism for regulating the movement. The verge is a rod with two bits or "pallets" that engage in the teeth of the escape wheel (the last wheel of the movement's train, also known as the "crown" wheel) and restrain it. The restraining force was provided either by a **foliot** or (from C17) by a pendulum connected to the verge. The verge escapement, though inferior to the **anchor** escapement, continued to be used for bracket clocks through C18.

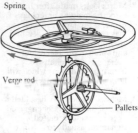

Spring

Verge rod

Pallets

Escape wheel

vernier Sliding calibrated scale read in conjunction with the fixed scale to obtain a more accurate reading on a barometer.

Vienna regulator Austrian weight-driven longcase clock (but varying considerably in size), early C19. Its glass case exposes the rapid-swing pendulum of the precision movement.

Vulliamy French-Swiss family of clockmakers, producing clocks for the English Crown in London from c1750 to 1854.

wheel barometer Barometer with a round register plate (as opposed to **stick**). The movement of the mercury is measured by a weight that floats on it, attached to a pulley or wheel that turns the pointer. Often known as a **banjo barometer**, from its shape.

Zaanklok Dutch weight-driven wall clock, C17. Its case extends both above and below the dial, because it houses a pendulum suspended well above the movement; it has glass sides so that the wheels, which may be decorated, can be seen. Usually there are sculpted figures above the dial.

What you should know about:
Clocks and barometers

Main types of clock:	
Long (Tall) case	Dial
Bracket	Skeleton
Wall	Lantern
Act of	Mantel
Parliament	Carriage

Main types of barometer:	
Stick	Aneroid
Wheel (or banjo)	

General pointers

* Best prices are paid for clocks in original condition that still work. Restoring a non-working clock to working order is expensive and even a skilful restoration will never regain the full original value.

* Most clocks made after 1698 carry the maker's or retailer's name; if the face is silver it too may carry maker's marks. Both are important clues to the origin and value of the piece, and there is a comprehensive literature on makers which will help in assessing rarity and value. See also page 134.

* Makers' names may be added to an unsigned clock, or engraved over a previously erased signature, usually to enhance the value by the addition of a more collectable name.

* Such additions can be difficult to detect; familiarity with a maker's work is necessary to judge whether the quality and style is right for the name it bears.

* On a metal face, look for hammer marks on the back, or signs of thinning where the metal was beaten forward to erase an original name.

* Faces should show the signs appropriate to age. Painted dials should show crazing, or hairline cracks. Wooden faces should have cracks where the timbers have shrunk. Metal faces should have proper oxidation; if the dial has been cleaned, check the reverse side.

* Plain metal dials were sometimes engraved at a later date to enhance the value. Be wary of a face that seems too elaborate for the case and chapter ring. As a rule of thumb, the more ornate the half hour marks, the more elaborate the face will be overall.

* Check the back of the dial for blocked holes. These usually indicate the marriage of an unrelated dial and movement; where the pillars and winding holes do not match, new ones have been drilled and the originals filled.

* They may also indicate the marriage of a chapter ring and dial plate. Check that the correcting feet are securely placed in their original holes and that decoration of the two parts is compatible.

* Sometimes holes are filled legitimately; where mistakes were made by the maker, or a worn post has been removed. Nevertheless, as a rule, beware blocked holes that cannot be explained.

* The replacement of hands does not usually diminish value, provided they are compatible in style and quality with the face.

* Examine the movement for consistent colour to all parts and signs of wear to the pinions appropriate to age.

* Check that the bell is original and not cracked; the signs are clear sound and resonance and silvery colour. Modern bells have a coarser ring.

Long (Tall) case clocks

* Check that the movement and case belong to each other by examining the block on which the movement sits for redundant holes. Their presence indicates replacement of the original movement.

* Be suspicious if this block is later than the case. The original block may simply have been replaced, having broken under the weight of the movement; but it is just as likely to indicate a marriage of movement and case.

* Double check by looking at the way the clock face is framed by the hood. It should be a good fit; i.e. disguising the edges of the dial but not masking any decoration.

* Scrape marks on the back board should match the position of the pendulum weight. A second set of marks shows that the block supporting the movement has been moved up or down, indicating a marriage.

Wall and Lantern Clocks

* Because of their relatively simple construction, wall clocks, especially the lantern type, were frequently copied in the C19 and faked in modern times. Patina and oxidation,

symmetrical engraving on the centre dial and the clear resonance of the bell help identify a genuine piece.

* The characteristic pierced fretwork crown on a lantern clock should fit well into the original feet holes. If not, it has been replaced; sometimes because of damage to the original, but occasionally with a crown bearing the signature of a maker to enhance value.

* Clocks signed "Thomas Moore, Ipswich" are particularly numerous modern pieces, treated to look old.

Act of Parliament clocks

* Modern copies are unsophisticated and easily detected because of the use of modern woods.

Dial clocks

* Avoid the numerous C19 versions with painted dials in favour of earlier wood, brass or silvered dials; but check for filled holes indicative of an earlier dial added to later movement.

Skeleton clocks

* Demand for skeleton clocks has increased the number made anew from disparate parts. All parts are on view so originals have delicate, finely pierced wheels with at least four spokes.

* The size and shape of the glass dome should be in balanced proportion to the clock; the base should be of marble or contemporary wood.

* Alteration to the clock feet, to raise or lower the height, is a sign that clock and dome were not made for each other.

Carriage clocks

* Mass produced from the mid C19 to the present, and sometimes artificially aged.

* The face should be of enamel and smooth; not thin and corrugated. Modern faces are brilliantly white with dense black numerals.

* A serial number on the back plate of more than 5 digits is modern.

* Side glasses were sometimes replaced by solid gilt panels, which will be different in colour to the case, or painted porcelain. Both detract from the value.

* It is impossible to convert from

petite to *grande sonnerie* mode, though many clocks have been modified in the attempt. Only an original *grande sonnerie* carriage is capable of striking in this mode for seven days without rewinding.

Barometers

* From the late C17, before the days of scientific weather-forecasting, barometers were important pieces of domestic equipment, and more common than is generally realized.

* Early versions by leading instrument makers such as Tompion are much sought after. Types were stick, pediment or diagonal.

* At first the wood mounts were of walnut, but later many other quality woods were used: maple, mahogany, rosewood, ebony etc.

* Early instruments should show correct patination to the wood, greeny-brown oxidation to metal (not the black of modern chemical patination) and mellow gold colour to the gilding.

* Wheel (banjo) barometers came into popular use in late C18, and were mass produced from mid C19. Even good examples of quite early date can be obtained at reasonable prices.

* Early aneroid barometers are comparatively rare and C19 examples are worth considering as potential investments. They can currently be found quite modestly priced.

* Barometers normally bear the maker's name and mark, sometimes accompanied by a date and/or registration number. Instruments by famous cabinet-makers such as Chippendale or Sheraton will command a premium.

* Marine and other special types of barometer are worth more than domestic versions, especially in good condition with a maker's mark.

Beware

* The high value of original clocks and barometers has encouraged increasingly sophisticated copies to be made. Unlike wood, metal patination is easier to induce chemically; the only sure guide is the knowledge that comes from familiarity and experience. Always seek objective advice before paying high prices.

Recognition and dating

Visual aids for dating clocks fall into two main areas: (1) the actual shape of the case itself, with all the many variations in size, style, decoration and material used. And (2) those features common to all antique clocks: the hands and dial. Fashions affecting all these factors changed continually from the mid C17, but not always at the same time. Each has therefore to be considered when attempting to reach an approximate date. The examples that follow are typical of the periods indicated but should only be used as a general guide. Remember too that new styles took time to spread and circulate. What was fashionable in London or Paris could take twenty years or more to reach North America or even provincial centres away from major cities. Craftsman also tended to follow only those fashions of which they approved.

Hour and minute hands

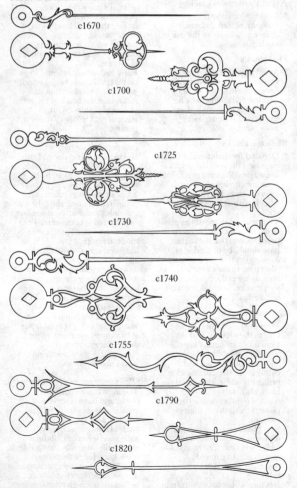

c1670

c1700

c1725

c1730

c1740

c1755

c1790

c1820

Bracket clocks

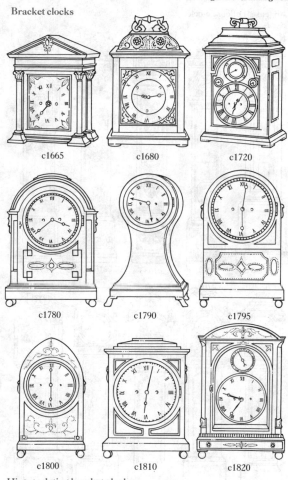

c1665

c1680

c1720

c1780

c1790

c1795

c1800

c1810

c1820

Hints to dating bracket clocks

Dials

Square dial	to c1770	pre-George III
Broken arch dial	from c1720	George I or later
Round/painted/silvered	from c1760	George III or later

Case finish

Ebony veneer	from c1660 to c1850	Carolean to mid-Victorian
Walnut	from c1670 to c1870	Carolean to Victorian
Marquetry	from c1680 to c1740	Carolean to early Georgian
Rosewood	from c1790	from mid-Georgian
Lacquered	from c1700 to c1760	Queen Anne to early Georgian
Mahogany	from c1730	from early Georgian

Longcase/Tallcase clocks

| c1660 | c1680 | c1685 | c1695 | c1730 |

| c1740 | c1765 | c1770 | c1800 | c1810 |

Hints to dating longcase/tallcase clocks

Case finish

Ebony veneer	up to c1725	Carolean to early Georgian
Walnut veneer	from c1670 to c1770	Carolean to mid-Georgian
Lacquered	from c1700 to c1790	Queen Anne to mid-Georgian
Mahogany	from 1730	from early Georgian
Softwood	from c1690	from mid-Georgian
Mahogany inlay	from c1750	from mid-Georgian
Marquetry	from c1680 to c1760	from Carolean to mid-Georgian
Oak	always	

Longcase/Tallcase dials

c1665

c1685

c1810

c1825

c1725

c1750

c1760

c1775

Hints to dating longcase/tallcase clocks

Dials

8in (20.3cm) square	to c1669	Carolean
10in (25.5cm) square	from c1665–1800	
11in (28cm) square	from 1690–1800	
12in (30cm) square	from c1700	from Queen Anne
14in (35.5cm) square	from c1740	from early Georgian
Broken-arch dial	from c1715	from early Georgian
Round dial	from c1760	from early Georgian
Silvered dial	from c1760	from early Georgian
Painted dial	from c1770	from early Georgian
Hour hand only	to 1820	
Minute hand introduced	c1663	
Second hand	from 1675	post-Restoration
Matching hands from	c1775	George III or later

Wall clocks

c1685

c1750

c1770

c1800

Hints to dating wall clocks

Dials

Square	to c1755	George II or later
Broken arch	from c1720 to c1805	early to late Georgian
Painted/round	from c1740	George II or later
Silvered	from c1760	George III or later

Case finish

Ebony veneer	from c1690	to William and Mary
Marquetry	from c1680 to c1695	from Carolean to William and Mary
Mahogany	from c1740	from early Georgian
Oak	always	

Clockmakers

Covering a period from the C17 to the late C19, the list that follows contains the names of clockmakers whose work is likely to be encountered or sought after by dealers or collectors. However, in the space available it is not possible to be in any way comprehensive, and omission carries no specific implication except to suggest further investigation. The dates given are those when the named clockmaker is known to have been active. Note that in Britain from 1698 every clock dial had to be marked with the maker's name and place of origin. In the C19 however, the name that appears is sometimes that of an English importer and not of the continental maker.

English and European

Acton, Thomas
Clerkenwell, *1675*
Addis, George
London, *1785–95*
Addis, William
London, *1745–65*
Agar, John
York, *1740*
Alcock, Thomas
London, *1635–55*
Ansell, George
London, *1800–20*
Arnold, John
London, *1760–95*
Arnold, John R.
London, *1800–30*
Atkins, George
Lon., *1785–1845*
Avenell, Edward
London, *1700–45*
Barlow, Benj.
Oldham, *1785*
Barlow, Edward
London, *1660–99*
Barr, G.
Bolton, *1790*
Barraud, Paul
Lon., *1790–1810*
Barrow, Samuel
Lon., *1690–1710*
Bartram, Simon
London, *1640–50*
Barthrop, G.
Ixworth, *1770–90*
Bateman, A.
London, *1800–20*
Bauler, James
Leeds, *1800*
Bautte, J.F.
Geneva, *1820–25*
Becker, Gustav
Germany, *c1875*
Berry, John
London, *1720–25*
Bradley, Langley
London, *1700–25*
Brayfield, Wm.
London, *1710–15*
Breguet, Abraham
Paris, *1770–1810*
Breguet, Louis
Paris, *1830–1870*
Breguet, Louis A.
Paris, *1800–1833*
Brockbank, M.

Brocot, Achille
Paris, *1850–1870*
Brown, Nathaniel
Manchester, *1780*
Brown, Thomas
Birmingham, *1765*
Brussel, Jan Van
Amsterdam, *c1750*
Bryant, John
Exning, *1790*
Bucknell, James
Crediton, *1685*
Bull, Rainulph
London, *C16*
Bull, William
Stratford, *1760*
Butcher, Benj.
London, *1810–20*
Cabrier, Charles
London, *1725–50*
Carter, John
London, *1850–60*
Carter, William
Ampthill, *1700*
Chamberlaine, Nathaniel
Lon., *1685–1715*
Charlton, John
London, *1630–40*
Chater, E.
London, *1770–80*
Child, Henry
London, *1640–60*
Christian, John
Aylsham, *1750*
Clarke, Henry
London, *1820–30*
Clement, William
London, *1685–99*
Clements, Thos.
Liverpool, *1790*
Coats, Archibald
Wigan, *1780*
Collier, Benjamin
London, *1700–20*
Coxiter, Nicholas
London, *1660–75*
Cressent, Charles
Paris, *1720–60*
Crooke, Benj.
Hackney, *1805*
Croucher, Joseph
London, *1830*
Cutbush, Edward

Maidstone, *1705*
Debaufre, Peter
London, *1690–1700*
Dent, E.J.
London, *c1840*
De St. Leu, D.
London, *1753–97*
Dicker, Thomas
Reading, *1795*
Drocourt Frs.,
Paris, *1890–1900*
Du Clair, Claude
Lyons, *c1625*
Dunster, Roger
Amsterdam, *1745*
Earnshaw, Thos.
London, *1780–99*
East, Edward
London, *1650*
Edwards, Thos.
Epping, *1680*
Ellicott, John
Lon., *1696–1735*
Emery, Josiah
London, *1780–90*
Etherington, G.
London, *1700–10*
Ettry, Joel
Horton, *c1760*
Fairman, T. H.
London, *1800–10*
Fletcher, G.
Chester, *1795*
Fowle, Thomas
E. Grinstead, *1670*
Frodsham, Chas.
London, *c1850*
Frodsham,
William James
London, *1835*
Fromanteel, A.
London, *c1632*
Fromanteel, John
London, *c1710*
Gaudron, P.
Paris, *1690–1730*
Gordon, Alex.
Dublin, *c1780*
Graham, John
Lon., *1695–1720*
Gravell, William
London, *1840*
Gregory, Jeremy
London, *1660–70*

Gribelin, Nicolas
Paris, *1637–1719*
Harris, Thomas
London, *1690*
Hedge, Nathaniel
Colchester, *1745*
Hill, Abraham
London, *1670*
Hill, Benjamin
London, *1655*
Hilton, Emanuel
Portsmouth, *1775*
Hocker, John
Reading, *1735*
Hodges,
Nathaniel
London, *1695*
Holland, Thomas
London, *1650–60*
Holmgren, Jacob
Sweden, *1811–35*
Ingold, Pierre F.
Paris, *1830*,
London, *1840*
Irving, Alexander
Westminster, *1700*
Japy, Frederic
France, *c1799*
Jacquet-Droz, P.
Neuchâtel, *C18*
Jarratt, Richard
London, *1685*
Joyce, George
London, *1690*
Jump, Richard T.
London, *c1820*
Ketterer, Anton
Germany, *1730*
Kipling, William
London, *c1705–50*
Kirk, Joseph
Nottingham, *1740*
Knibb, John
Oxford, *c1680*
Knibb, Joseph
London & Oxford,
1670–1700
Knifton, Thomas
Lothebury, *c1650*
Knottesforde, W.
London, *1680*
Lassiter, George
Wisbech, *c1830*
Lees, Thomas
Bury, *1790*

Lefroy, George Wisbech, *1785*

Legrand, E. Paris, *c1850*

Lepaute, Jean A. Paris, *1748–74*

Leroy, Chas. Paris, *1765–1808*

Le Roy, Julien Paris, *1710–1750*

Le Roy, Pierre Paris, *1740–1780*

Loomes, Thomas London, *1660*

Loor, Thomas Amsterdam, *c1740*

Lowndes, Isaac London, *1690*

Macham, Samuel London, *1710–15*

MacKinlay, Peter Edinburgh, *1836*

Martin, Edmund London, *1790–95*

Massy, Jacob London, *1715–20*

Masterson, R. London, *1640*

McReadle, Thos. Stranraer, *c1825*

Million, William London, *1670*

Mynuel Paris, *1700*

Neve, Henry London, *1700–05*

Nicasius, John London, *1650*

Norris, Edward London, *1680–85*

Norton, Eardley London, *1780*

Oakley, William London, *1810*

Overzee, Gerard London, *1685*

Paine, William Trowbridge, *1785*

Peckover, Richard London, *1737–56*

Perigal, Francis London, *1755*

Poole, Robert London, *1775–80*

Quare, Daniel London, *1675–99*

Ramsey, David London, *1610–50*

Rayment, Richard Bury St. Ed., *c1700*

Regnault Paris, *c1750*

Robertson, David Perth, *c1835*

Sanderson, John Wigton, *1725*

Simmons, Ebenezer London, *1816–76*

Simmons, George London, *1840–42*

Simmons, John London, *1753–56*

Smith, James London, *1775–85*

Smith, Robert Dunstable, *1690*

Stephens, Joseph London, *1760–70*

Stogdon, Matthew London, *1720–70*

Street, Richard Lon., *1680–99*

Style, Nathaniel London, *1750–70*

Taylor, Thomas London, *1650–80*

Thomson, Wm. Perth, *c1770*

Thwaites, John London, *1800*

Tomlinson, Wm. London, *1700–30*

Tompion, Thomas Lon., *1671–1710*

Troughton, Ed. London, *1780–1830*

Upjohn, Thomas Exeter, *1745*

Valentine, C.F.D. London, *1810–20*

Viner, Charles E. Lon., *1780–1820*

Vokes, E.J. Bath, *c1860*

Vulliamy, Benj. Lon., *1775–1820*

Vulliamy, Benj. Lewis London, *1815–50*

Vulliamy, Justin London, *1730–75*

Webster, Robert London, *1680–99*

Webster, William London, *1730–50*

Wheeler, Thomas London, *1665–99*

Wigson, William London, *1800–05*

Wilson, Joshua London, *1705–10*

Windmills, Joseph London, *1690–99*

Windmills, Thos. London, *1700*

Wise, John London, *1670–99*

Wynn, Henry London, *1685*

Yardley, James Stratford, *1765*

American

Adams, Nathan Boston, *1796–1825*

Allen, Jas. Boston, *c1684*

Allenbach, Jacob Phil., *1825–40*

Archer, Walter New York, *c1715*

Austin, Isaac Phil., *1785–1805*

Bachelder, Ezra Denver, *1793–1840*

Badley, Thos. Boston, *c1712*

Bagnall, Benj. Boston, *1740–60*

Bailey, Calvin Hanover, *1800–10*

Bailey, John Hanover, *1790–1815*

Balch, Benjamin Salem, *c1837*

Balch, Daniel Newburyport, *1760–90*

Baldwin, A. Lancaster, *1810–30*

Barker, B. New York, *c1786*

Barnes, Thos. Lichfield, *c1790*

Basset, George F. Phil., *c1797*

Bentley, Eli Tawney Town, *c1790*

Burnap, David E. Windsor, *c1780*

Chandlee, Benj. Nottingham, *c1714*

Cheney, Benj. Hartford, *1745–50*

Cheney, Timothy Hartford, *1745–50*

Crow, Thomas Wilmington, *c1770*

Currier, Edmund Salem, *1820–30*

Curtis, Lemuel Concord, *1815–20*

Doolittle, Isaac New Haven, *1742–1790*

Downes, Ephraim Bristol, *1826–1828*

Faris, William Phil., *c1755–90*

Harland, T. Norwich, *c1775*

Hollingshead, Joseph & John Burlington, *c1780*

Ives, Joseph Brooklyn, *1820–30*

Jerome & Darrow Bristol, *1827–40*

Lane, Aaron Elizabethtown, *c1790*

Lyman & Howe, Pittsfield, *1785–1800*

Pope, Joseph Boston, *1790–1810*

Rittenhouse, David Phil., *1750–90*

Sawin, John Boston, *c1822*

Schoonmaker, Isaac Patterson, *c1825*

Selig, Conrad Reading, *1800–25*

Shourds, Samuel Bordentown, *1770*

Stretch, Peter Phil., *1715–25*

Taber, Stephen New Bedford, and Providence, *c1790*

Tanner, John Newport, *1740–60*

Terry, Eli Plymouth, *1792–1852*

Thomas, Seth Plymouth, *1810–30*

Wellington, C.L. Hingham, *c1850*

Wheaton, Caleb Providence, *1785–1822*

Wilder, Ezra Hingham, *c1800*

Wilder, Joshua Hingham, *1810–20*

Willard, Aaron Boston, *c1815*

Willard, Alex J. Mass., *c1825*

Willard, Benjamin Boston, *c1770*

Willard, Simon Boston & Roxbury, *c1825*

Winters, Christian Easton, *c1800*

Wood, David Newburyport, *c1765–90*

Wood, John Phil., *1770–93*

GLASS
Glossary

air-beaded Glass holding bubbles of air resembling beads.

air-twist Twisting, spiral pattern formed in the glass by an enclosed bubble. Technique evolved in England from c1740 to c1770. In that period the spirals become increasingly complex.

ale glass Drinking glass with long stem and tall, thin bowl. C18. Not to be confused with the modern beer-glass.

annulated Ringed.

Baccarat Factory in northern France famous for tableware and coloured paperweights.

baluster glass Glass with stem in shape of a baluster (either "true" if the thicker swelling is beneath or "inverted" if it is above). Dating from late C17.

balustroid Resembling a baluster type stem, but lighter and slimmer. 2nd quarter C18.

Beilby glass The Beilby family in Newcastle were the leading English painters and enamellers of glass in C18 (until c1778).

bottle glass Coloured glass used for utensils such as bottles, as distinct from quality or clear glass.

bowl Hollow vessel; or that part of a glass above the stem which holds the liquid.

Bristol glass Coloured glass (e.g. blue) like that made in quantity in Bristol in C18. Cf. **Nailsea.**

cased glass Glass wrapped with a second glass layer. Cf **flash.**

cast glass Glass shaped by a mould.

champagne glass Today, a small glass with a semi-spherical bowl, little resembling an C18 champagne glass, which has a **double-ogee** shape.

Clichy weight Factory set up mid C19, in French town of Clichy. Famous for paperweights with decorative patterns.

coin glass Glass or goblet with a coin inserted in the knop of the stem. Originating in England, early C18.

cordial glass Glass evolved in C17, with a small bowl for a strong drink.

crystal glass See lead crystal.

cullet Scraps of glass, used to help fuse new glass.

diamond-cut Cut in diamond or lozenge shapes.

double-ogee bowl Bowl of drinking glass with a complex curved profile, resembling a

larger bowl with an S-profile above a smaller one.

dram glass Small short-stemmed glass, usually, with a rounded bowl, the lower portion of which is normally solid.

enamel Coloured, painted decoration, fired on the glass – an ancient technique revived by the Venetians in C15.

facet-cut Glass cut criss-cross into straight-edged planes or facets. Popular between c1760 and c1810.

filigrana (filigree) Glass with thread-like pattern running through it. Developed C16 in Venice, since used widely.

firing glass Thick, sturdy C17 glass with short stem and solid foot, made to resist the hard wear of drinking toasts – when clinked together or rapped on the table they sounded like a volley of muskets.

flash Second layer of glass, typically incised or cut, laid over the inner glass.

flute glass Glass with tall, slender bowl, sometimes of great size. Evolved in the Netherlands C17.

fluting Grooving, or vertical cuts between ridges, in the shape of the lip of a flute.

frit The mixture or flux from which glass is made.

frosted glass Variant of ice-glass.

Hyalith glass Coloured glass, either sealing-wax red or jet black, made in Bohemia from 1803 and 1817 respectively.

ice glass Glass with an uneven, rippling surface, like disturbed water. Technique developed in Venice and Liège C16.

inclusion Flaw, fault or mark in precious stones or glass.

jelly glass Glass, C18, with conical bowl and short stem, sometimes with handles.

knop The same word as "knob": a rounded projection or bulge, e.g. in the stem of a glass.

lead-crystal Glass with lead in it, from which it gains a specially clear brilliance. Technique developed for cut glass made in England and Ireland C18.

Lithyalin glass Type of glass invented by Egermann in Bohemia, 1828: meant to imitate precious stones, it is opaque, coloured, and usually marbled.

lustre Alternative term for a chandelier, current from C18; or a thin film of metal laid over the glass, like porcelain lustre.

mercury twist An **air-twist** of silvery colour.

milk glass Glass made with tin oxide, which turns it an opaque white. Developed in Venice, C15, where it was known as "lattimo". Technique soon reached Bohemia and remained popular in Germany till C19.

millefiori Multi-coloured or mosaic glass. In a process known since classical times different-coloured threads of glass were laid together to make a rod that was then sectioned. Today seen most commonly in glass marbles and paperweights.

mixed-twist With **opaque twists** of more than one colour.

Nailsea glass Nailsea, near Bristol, produced opaque glass with bold decorative streaks from late C18. Now any such glass is commonly called "Nailsea".

Newcastle baluster Type of **balustroid** glass, associated with Tyneside, mid C18. Features are more than one knop and a conical bowl.

ogee bowl Bowl of drinking glass with a profile of S-shape.

opaque twist Twist or spiral created in the stem of a glass by laying in a strand of milk or coloured glass; found in especially English glasses of 3rd quarter of C18.

pedestal-stem Glass with thick stem narrowing towards the bottom, usually fluted. Early and mid C18.

pontil Rod with which the glass is removed from the blowpipe.

pontil mark Mark made by the pontil, e.g. on the bottom of a glass. Can be a means of dating.

potichomania Imitation of oriental porcelain by paper designs stuck inside glass, popular mid C19.

pressed glass Technique developed in early C19. Glass is pressed, not blown, in the mould.

prunt Blob of glass applied for decoration to the glass body.

ratafia glass C18 glass used for drinking the liqueur ratafia. Resembles an ale-glass, but is even more slender, the stem merging into the profile of the bowl.

roemer (rummer) Type of goblet, usually with prunts on the thick stem. Often in green ("Waldglas"); made in Bohemia from c1500.

ruby glass Glass containing gold or copper, which makes it red. Technique, perfected in late C17 in Germany, is particularly associated with Bohemia in Czechoslovakia.

St Louis glass Glass made at St Louis in Lorraine, France, from late C18; famous for coloured glass and paperweights.

step-cut Cut in a series of layers or steps, e.g. the foot of a bowl or drinking glass.

tazza Italian for cup or basin: specifically, a type of glass with a wide bowl, tall stem and spreading foot, made in Venice from late C15.

tear Air-bubble in the glass (usually in the stem of a drinking glass) in the shape of a tear-drop. Technique developed in England in early C18; from it the **air-twist** evolved.

terraced Descending in layers, e.g. an outspreading foot on a drinking glass.

three-piece, two-piece Glass made up of two, or three, blown pieces.

turnover With a rim that turns over, as a cuff does.

twist See **air-**, **opaque**, etc.

What you should know about: Glass

General pointers

* Fashion dictates prices as much as age and intrinsic quality. Good art glass (Tiffany, Lalique, etc) fetches the best prices, and etched/engraved C18 English glass is perennially popular. High prices are paid for early paperweights, American pressed glass and "Mary Gregory" originals. By comparison, much C18 Continental glass is underrated and good value.

* All types of glass have been copied and reproduced in the C19 and C20, in the USA sometimes using original moulds. This makes collecting a challenge. To recognize true originals, handle glass frequently to become familiar with period shapes, decoration and techniques.

* Strong lead glass, which lends itself to cutting, etching and engraving, was the predominant material in use in England from the early C18, but several decades later on the Continent and in America.

* The earliest lead glass has a greenish tinge; it becomes progressively more transparent and colourless through the next 150 years.

* Lead glass has a pleasing ring when tapped with the fingernail, though thicker pieces may not have this characteristic.

* Lead glass has a bluish tinge under ultra-violet light; however, not all lead glass is necessarily old. Glass which looks yellow to brown under ultra-violet light, or stays the same colour, is unlikely to be old. Oxidated pieces will not respond to this test.

* Coloured glass is unlikely to be old. Until c1860 its use was mainly restricted to bottles, decanters and tumblers; after that date its use spread to many other items.

* The presence of a bubble is no indication of age; most glass with bubbles is C20 and cruder than period glass.

* Most genuine C18 tablewear has a pontil mark on the base. If it has been ground off there may be a polished circle where it was removed. The presence of a pontil mark is no guarantee of age, however, so look for other corroborative signs.

* Old glass should show other signs of the manufacturing process; look for vertical creases in the bowl, and a nick or lump in the rim where surplus glass was sheared off. Lack of these marks is cause for suspicion.

* The foot of genuine early glass should be wider than the rim. Any repairs that destroy this proportion, such as grinding to remove a chip, considerably reduces the value.

* To detect recent engraving place a white handkerchief inside the glass. Old engraving looks grey, and is darker than the surrounding glass. New engraving looks too white and powdery.

* Genuine Jacobite and Williamite glass is generally restrained and subtle in its display of engraved political symbols. A proliferation of motifs suggests the engraving was added at a later date.

* Documents, makers' marks, date marks, details of provenance and ownership all add considerable value to a piece of glass, since in their absence there is no certain means of dating.

Types of glass

* *Cased glass* Glass of one colour covered with one or more layers of different colour.
* *Cut-glass* Decorated with facets based on geometric patterns.
* *Engraved glass* Decoration using diamond point. See page 139.
* *Etched glass* Decoration using an acid as etching agent.
* *Frosted glass* With a matt or otherwise opaque outer surface.
* *Lacy glass* Pressed glass with stippled background. Originated in Boston, U.S.A.
* *Lime glass* A substitute for lead glass discovered by William Leighton, mid C19.
* *Lutz glass* Thin glass striped with coloured strips.
* *Vaseline glass* Decorative glass, also known as "yellow opaline".

Beware

* There are no foolproof methods of authenticating glass, and many experts have been fooled in the past. Always buy from reputable sources, willing to provide a descriptive receipt and re-purchase the piece if its provenance proves to be mistaken.

Glass engraving

Engraving on glass is an ancient craft dating back to the Ancient Egyptians. Over the centuries it has been carried out in a number of ways. Those which are of particular interest to the collector are given below. A knowledge of these is important, since many old glasses and other pieces have been engraved and cut at a later date to enhance their value.

Methods of Engraving

* *Diamond Point* Where the required design was produced by a diamond or graver.
* *Wheel Engraving* Where the design was effected with copper wheels, varying in size from a pinhead upwards, the wheels being fed with a mixture of either oil or water and sand. This engraving could be highlighted by polishing part of the engraving. Also, the depth of engraving could be varied to produce high and low relief effects, combined with polishing.
* *Stipple Engraving* Here the required design was effected by the use of a diamond needle and hammer to produce a series of dots or short scratched lines. The closeness of the dots and their intensity produced a shading effect.
* *Acid Etching* This required the surface of the glass or vessel to be covered with a varnish or resin, and the design then scratched through with a needle or other sharp tool. The surface was then exposed to hydrofluoric acid fumes to etch through the scratched design.
* These methods continue in use today.

English Engraved Glass

* Decoration on glass in C18 and early C19 fell into two categories: either to make the glass or vessel more attractive, or to indicate a use; to record a sentiment, event, toast, or to support a current cause.
* During the C18 there was little attempt to emulate the Dutch and German engravers whose work was invariably of high artistic merit and quality, and whose chosen subjects were diverse. On English glass, it was expressed quite crudely in flowers and foliage, birds and insects. In the earlier wheel engraving there was a predominance of floral designs, hence in the early 1740's and onwards, these glasses were referred to as "flower glasses". Crude attempts at portraiture were also made.

* It was not until the third quarter of C18 onwards, with some notable exceptions, that the skill of the engravers had progressed to a state where attempts at high and low relief carving and polishing were attempted.

Jacobite glasses

* Jacobite glasses, which began to be engraved c1730, have commanded much attention and popularity among collectors. The dating and the significance of the various motifs on these glasses is still the subject of debate and disagreement, but considered opinion is that few of them can be dated to before Culloden in 1746. Jacobite engraved glasses continued to be produced through the various stem formations (plain, air-twist, opaque and faceted) until the death of Prince Charles Edward Stuart in 1788. Countless numbers of old glasses have been later engraved. There were also the counter Jacobite glasses supporting the Loyalists but these are considerably fewer in number.

Decanters

* Decanters were also engraved from about 1750. A few shaft and globe were Jacobite decorated, but examples are rare. Later in the century (about 1760), shouldered and tapered decanters were engraved, with bands of floral decoration, husks and swags. The egg and tulip design was often used. A certain number of these decanters were engraved with the name of a wine, this usually being in a floral cartouche.
* In the early C19 Irish decanters were engraved with decoration of social, political and especially patriotic significance, but these are rare. Also, patterns such as bands of laurel leaves, chains, stars and the vesica pattern were often combined with cutting; the star, slice and facet being a favourite combination.

Drinking Glasses: Dates and Shapes

The generally accepted grouping for pre-C19 drinking glasses is that devised by E. Barrington Haynes in his seminal work *Glass Through the Ages*, first published by Penguin Books in 1948. His system divides drinking glasses into 13 groups, each with its own sub-groups. Most glasses can be placed in one of these. The 13 groups are as follows:

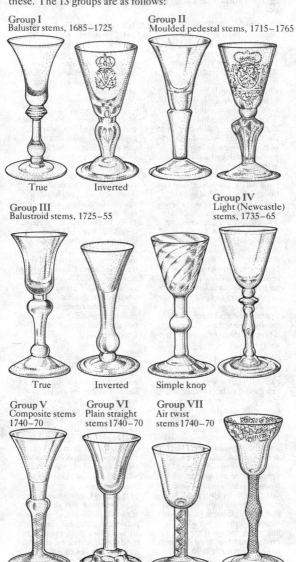

Group I
Baluster stems, 1685–1725

True   Inverted

Group II
Moulded pedestal stems, 1715–1765

Group III
Balustroid stems, 1725–55

Group IV
Light (Newcastle) stems, 1735–65

True   Inverted   Simple knop

Group V
Composite stems 1740–70

Group VI
Plain straight stems 1740–70

Group VII
Air twist stems 1740–70

Unknopped   Swelling knop

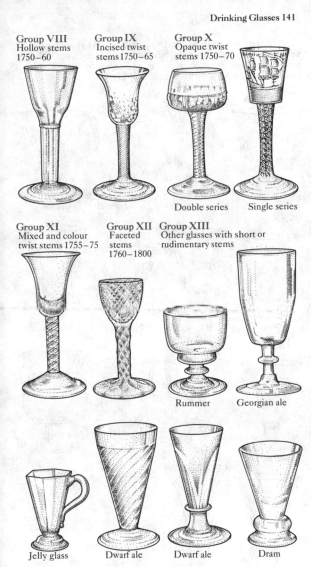

Group VIII
Hollow stems
1750–60

Group IX
Incised twist
stems 1750–65

Group X
Opaque twist
stems 1750–70

Double series   Single series

Group XI
Mixed and colour
twist stems 1755–75

Group XII
Faceted
stems
1760–1800

Group XIII
Other glasses with short or
rudimentary stems

Rummer   Georgian ale

Jelly glass   Dwarf ale   Dwarf ale   Dram

Types of Air twist

Multiple spiral   Lace   Lace outlined   Spiral gauzes

Spiral gauze
and corkscrew   Multi-ply
corkscrew   Spiral gauze
with core   Spiral cable

Each of the Groups illustrated on pages 140–41 shows wide variations in stem formation, bowl shape and foot form. The following illustrate those shapes most frequently met, with the names by which they are generally known.

Bowl shapes

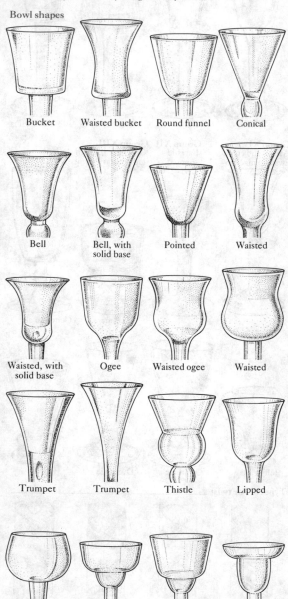

Bucket

Waisted bucket

Round funnel

Conical

Bell

Bell, with solid base

Pointed

Waisted

Waisted, with solid base

Ogee

Waisted ogee

Waisted

Trumpet

Trumpet

Thistle

Lipped

Cup

Pan-topped

Bucket-topped

Saucer-topped

Stem formations

True
baluster

Ridged true
baluster

Inverted
baluster

Collar

Simple
knop

Acorn
knop

Annular
knop

Annulated
knop

Angular
knop

Ball
knop

Cone
knop

Cushioned
knop

Cylinder
knop

Drop
knop

Flattened
knop

Mushroom
knop

Shoulder
knop

Swelling
knop

Wide angular
knop

Dumb-bell
knop

Bobbin
knop

Ovoid
knop

Quatre-foil
knop

Silesian
stem

Feet shapes

Solid
conical

Plain
conical

Conical with rim
folded under

Folded

Firing

Flanged

Pedestal

Stepped
square foot

Domed
square foot

Terrace-domed
solid
square foot

Domed
and folded

"Beehive"
foot

ART NOUVEAU and ART DECO
Glossary of names and terms

Aalto, Alvar 1898–1976 Finnish architect and designer of furniture, notably bentwood chairs, made from early 1930s.

Andersen, David Oslo firm making furniture and metalwork, founded 1876.

Argy-Rousseau, Gabriel 1885– French glassmaker, specializing in **pâte-de-verre.**

Art Deco In design, the style that succeeded **Art Nouveau** and dominated the 1920s. From Art Nouveau it inherited high standards of craftsmanship and interest in new materials. Though influenced by modern art movements, esp. Futurism, Art Deco enjoys ornament, by contrast to "modernism" of the type of De Stijl and Bauhaus.

Art Nouveau C19's "own" style, although it did not fully develop until the 1880s. Is usually divided into two "schools": the floral or at least organic style of England and most of the Continent, and the more straight-edged, geometric look of the **Glasgow School** and Vienna. The major influence on both "schools" was the Gothic revival, no longer imitated but transmuted. Gothic ornament lies behind both the pronounced verticals of the Glasgow School and the extreme curvaciousness of the mainstream. Similarly, Art Nouveau developed out of the medievalist Arts and Crafts Movement but shifted ground to embrace modern materials and techniques.

Barnsley, Sidney 1865–1926 "Cotswold School" designer (with Ernest Gimson) of Arts and Crafts furniture.

Bindesbøll, Thorvald 1846–1908 Danish painter, designer and potter, known for his simple, bold Art Nouveau forms.

Boucheron Jewellers established in Paris in 1858. At first conservative, but not unaffected by Art Nouveau, they later became leading Art Deco jewellers.

Brandt, Edgar 1880–1960 French designer of Art Deco metalwork. His factory, established in 1919, produced mainly ironwork furnishings, but also bronzework.

Bugatti, Carlo 1855–1940 Italian Art Nouveau furniture and interior designer, accused even in his own day of excessive weirdness. His son Ettore designed and manufactured the famous Bugatti racing car.

cameo glass Glass "cased" or composed of two or more layers, which are carved, or commonly etched away, to achieve a relief design. Carved cameo was an old technique; etched cameo, developed notably by Gallé after 1889, was a new Art Nouveau and Art Deco development.

Cardew, Michael 1901–1983 English artist potter, pupil of **Bernard Leach,** working at Winchcombe Pottery 1926–1939. His inspiration was oriental porcelain.

Carlton ware Brand-name of Wiltshaw & Robinson Ltd, a Stoke-on-Trent pottery founded in 1897.

Chaplet, Ernest 1836–1909 French potter, associate of the painter Gauguin. Working for **Haviland,** he produced oriental-inspired glazed ware, notably his "barbotine" or coloured-slip ware and **flambé.**

Chermayeff, Serge 1900– Russian-born modernist architect and designer, working in Britain in 1930s.

Chiparus, Demêtre Rumanian sculptor, working in Paris in the 1920s, specializing in painted bronze and ivory figures – typically costumed dancers in exotic poses.

chryselephantine Made of gold and ivory – or, more loosely, of ivory and another metal, e.g. bronze. Applied to Art Deco statuettes of this genre.

Clarke, Arundell Retailer of modernist and Art Deco furniture in London.

Cliff, Clarice 1899–1972 Artistic director of the Newport, Staffordshire, pottery A.J. Wilkinson Ltd, employing many of the leading British painters of the 1930s. She produced her own "Bizarre" and "Fantasque" range, typically Art Deco in their colourful super-bright patterns.

Coates, Wells 1895–1958 Modernist architect and designer from Canada, working in Britain in 1930s.

Clutha glass Brand-name of range of art glass produced from about 1885 by Couper Ltd of Glasgow to designs by **Christopher Dresser**. Opaque, greenish and textured by bubbles and streaks, it was inspired by excavated ancient glass.

Crown Devon Brand-name of the Staffordshire pottery Fielding & Co. Introduced in 1913.

Cymric See **Liberty**.

Dali, Salvador 1904– Spanish Surrealist painter who also designed some famous Surrealist furniture, e.g. a lobster telephone and a Mae West's lips sofa.

Daum Frères French glassmakers, active from the early 1890s in Nancy, where they were associates, but independent of, of Emile Gallé. Specialists in several new Art Nouveau and Art Deco techniques, including **cameo** glass, their own "martelé" or faceted glass (an effect like hammered metal), **pâte de verre** and **etched** glass.

Decoeur, Emile 1876–1953 French artist potter, specializing during 1920s in relatively simple, plain stoneware.

Décorchement, François Emile 1880–1971 French glassmaker, specializing in **pâte de verre** Art Deco vases and *objets d'art*.

Doulton London pottery firm established in 1815, but important for its art pottery only from 1860s, when it revived brown stoneware and salt-glaze ware. Its leading potter was Tinworth and it had links with the **Martin** brothers. In 1870s the Barlow sisters decorated ware with animals and scenes. In 1880s and 1890s many different artists made or decorated fancy ware – "siliconware", or enamelled china. In 1902 Doulton received the royal warrant. "Royal Doulton" figures were introduced in 1913, since when more than 2000 designs have been produced. Many are highly collectable.

Dresser, Christopher 1834–1904 English designer chiefly of pottery and glass. Pottery firms he worked for include Ault, Linthorpe and Pilkington. He had great interest in Japanese work, and had American connections, notably with **Tiffany**.

Elton, Sir Edmund 1846–1920 English potter, active from 1880, noted for multi-colours and novel shapes. Signature "Elton".

etched glass Glass modelled or surface-treated with acid, sometimes in quite high relief ("deep-etched"). Developed and much favoured in Art Nouveau and Art Deco (see also **cameo**).

Favrile Brand-name of **Tiffany's** iridescent glass.

Fielding & Co See **Crown Devon**.

flambé Alternative name for the Chinese porcelain bright red glaze "sang-de-boeuf" (see page 91), now usually applied to imitations and variations on it produced in France in late C19 and early C20.

Foley Staffordshire pottery, established by H. Wileman in 1860. In 1880 it was bought by E. Brain. In 1925 it became "Shelley Potteries Ltd". Foley is known for its "Intarsio" polychrome ware; Shelley particularly for its Art Deco services.

Gallé, Émile 1846–1904 French glassmaker from Nancy, Lorraine, the leading spirit of Art Nouveau glass. He is perhaps more important for technique than design. In 1884 he advertised his "new colorations" or kinds of translucent glass; in 1889 he developed **cameo** glass; in 1897 he introduced "marquetry in glass", applied glass in fantastic colours.

Gimson, Ernest 1864–1920 English designer of Arts and Crafts furniture: with a workshop in Gloucestershire, he was the leading member of the "Cotswold School", known for its plain wood finishes.

Glasgow School Style or group of designers led by Mackintosh, offering from the 1890s a drastically streamlined Gothic, which greatly influenced Continental Art Nouveau.

Goldscheider Viennese porcelain factory, founded 1886. Known for its Art Nouveau vases and Art Deco figures.

Gray, Eileen 1879–1976 Irish furniture designer working in Paris. She made her name for lacquerwork furniture influenced both by modernist movements such as De Stijl, and by ethnic art.

Haviland (1) Porcelain factory founded by the American David Haviland in France in 1842. It was bought out in 1885 by its director, Ernest **Chaplet**. (2) In 1892 David's son Theodore Haviland started his own factory in France, now known for its Art Deco tableware.

Heal, Ambrose 1872 – 1959 English cabinetmaker and retailer, a leading figure of the Design and Industries Association, founded 1915. The DIA was a successor of the Arts and Crafts Movement, advocating decent machine-made furniture.

Hoffmann, Josef 1870–1956 Austrian architect and designer, a founder of the **Wiener Werkstätte**. He had contacts with the **Glasgow School** and made comparable furniture. He also designed porcelain and glass.

Jensen, Georg 1886–1935 Danish designer of jewellery and silver. He set up a workshop in Copenhagen in 1904, and quickly became famous for his prizewinning teapot with a cover shaped like a rose. He collaborated with other Danish artists, notably Johan Rohde, to produce elaborate but robust work for international sale throughout 1920s.

Joel, Betty London makers of Art Deco furniture, typically of laminated wood.

Knox, Archibald 1864–1931 English designer of Celtic-inspired Art Nouveau silver and pewter for **Liberty's.**

Lacloche Frères Paris firm of jewellers, leading the market in Art Deco styles.

Lalique, René 1860–1945 French designer of Art Nouveau jewellery, into which he introduced undisguised glass. From 1909, he made his own

crystal and opalescent glass, and after 1920 emerged as the leading designer of Art Deco glass, in an enormous range.

Leach, Bernard 1887–1979 English artist potter, inspired by oriental ware (he spent much time in Japan, Korea and China) and successful in producing ware that could be ranked as "art".

Le Verrier, Max French metalwork caster and designer, known for his Art Deco bronze and **spelter** figures.

Liberty, Sir Arthur Lasenby 1843–1917 Liberty founded his Regent St, London, store in 1875, at first selling Japanese textiles, then furniture, silver, pewter, jewellery, glass and ceramics, much of which was produced for him in original Art Nouveau styles, e.g. his "Cymric" silver and jewellery and "Tudric" pewter.

Loetz German glassmaking firm established at Klöstermühle, Bohemia, known for its iridescent glass, first produced in 1873.

Mackintosh, Charles Rennie 1868–1928 Scottish architect and designer of furniture. See **Glasgow School.**

Marinot, Maurice 1882–1960 French painter, who turned glass designer between 1922 and 1937. Building up in layers, he handled semi-molten glass as if it were sculpture, achieving remarkable effects by catching air-bubbles between the various skins.

Martin brothers, Martinware Pottery firm, active in London

1873–1914, known for its grey stoneware, often in grotesque shapes or with incised decoration.

Minton Old-established Staffordshire pottery firm, producing a variety of signed art pottery in C19 and into C20. Minton's Art Pottery Studio, a training academy, was set up in London, in 1870.

Moorcroft, William 1872–1946 Staffordshire artist-potter. Known especially for his "Florian" and "Aurelian" ware from 1898, he worked for MacIntyre's from 1898, independently from 1913. Continuing successfully between the Wars, he is known for his vases with floral designs in coloured slip.

Morgan, William Frend de 1839–1917 English designer of pottery, particularly tiles, an associate of William Morris, also a novelist. He drew inspiration for his ceramics from Renaissance maiolica and Islamic, particularly Iznik, lustreware.

Moser, Kolomann 1868–1918 Austrian graphic artist and designer, a founder of the Wiener Werkstätte. He designed Art Nouveau furniture and *objets d'art* in many materials.

Moser, Ludwig 1833–1916 German-Bohemian glassmaker, with a factory at Karlsbad from 1857. He made engraved glass and later iridescent glass of the type of Tiffany's "Favrile".

Mucha, Alphonse 1861–1931 Best known for his Art Nouveau posters, Mucha also designed jewellery and other pieces c1901. Czech born, he worked in Paris and USA. His graphic art is predominantly floral, and richly intricate.

pâte de verre Powdered glass in a paste, refired to obtain a translucent effect dear to Art Nouveau.

Preiss, Ferdinand German sculptor, working in Berlin, of Art Deco figures, typically dancers in bronze and ivory.

Rhead, Frederick 1856–1929 From a well-known pottery family, Rhead worked for Wedgwood and then for a variety of potteries.

Rosenthal Bavarian porcelain factory, founded in 1879, employing a variety of artists to design both Art Nouveau and Art Deco ware.

Rousseau, Clément 1872–? French Art Deco furniture designer, combining simple forms in rich materials (ivory, sharkskin, ebony and other exotic woods).

Royal Dux Brand-name of the German porcelain factory founded 1860 in Dux, now Duchov, Czechoslovakia. Notable for busts, figures and vases.

spelter Zinc, treated to resemble bronze, for which it was a cheaper substitute. Widely used in the 2nd half C19.

Stickley, Gustav 1857–1942 American furniture-maker, who from 1898 developed a "Craftsman" style indebted to William Morris.

Tiffany, Louis Comfort 1848–1933 Designer son of established American goldsmith Charles Louis Tiffany, and known above all for his art glass. He founded his glass company in 1892 and in 1896 developed his iridescent "Favrile" glass, from which he also made lamps. His jewellery (for his father's company) dates from 1902, his ceramics from 1905.

Tudric See **Liberty**.

Voysey, Charles Francis Annesley 1857–1941 English architect and designer of furniture and textiles. He exhibited with the Arts & Crafts Society from 1893.

Waals, Peter Dutch cabinetmaker, who from 1901 worked for **Gimson** and **Barnsley**. After their deaths Waals continued the workshop until 1937.

Wiener Werkstätte The "Vienna Workshops" were founded in 1901, under the direction of **Hoffmann** and **Moser**. Best known for their Art Nouveau designs, they produced furniture, textiles, metalwork, glass and ceramics until 1932.

What you should know about:
Art Nouveau and Art Deco

* Art Nouveau (1890 to 1914) and Art Deco (1920 to 1940) are terms which cover numerous and disparate decorative styles which continue to influence designers working today. At its most characteristic, Nouveau designs are curvilinear and based on natural forms, whereas Deco has been described as "domesticated cubism".
* Best prices are reserved for handmade pieces from the top name designers, especially pieces which significantly influenced the development of a style. Competition from museums and wealthy collectors is fierce.
* Next in value are objects of high quality, finish and artistic merit which particularly epitomize the style of the period. Collectors concentrate on well-provenanced pieces in perfect condition from the leading factories.
* Finally there is a wealth of mass-produced material which reflects the fashionable motifs of the time and which can cost little more than a comparable object made today.
* Condition is paramount in assessing prices. Except for unique or important works, even slight damage will reduce the value. Many pieces were produced in quantity and survive in perfect condition.

Furniture
* Many Art Nouveau designers eschewed machines and revived the highest standards of craftsmanship. Particularly sought after are the flamboyant continental inlaid pieces of Gallé, de Feure, Colonna, Gaillard, Lardry, Guimard, and Carabin.
* British and American work is simpler and more rectilinear. The best pieces came from the workshops of Voysey, Grison and the Barnsley brothers in England and Stickley and the Greene brothers in the USA.
* Charles Rennie Mackintosh originals are rare and very valuable; even Mackintosh-style commercially-made furniture has a high market value, though more commonly found.
* Art Deco designers embraced the values of the machine age and favoured modern materials.

Prototypes from the leading Bauhaus designers, Breuer and van der Rohe, and Jazz age designers in America, Wright, Deskey and Frankl, are eminently collectable, as are any pieces that exemplify the spirit of the age.

Sculpture
* Bronze and ivory pieces were produced in quantity in the 1920's and 30's particularly in Vienna and Paris. Ivory was handcarved and bronze often handpainted, so no two pieces are identical.
* Fakes, which are numerous and often cast in original moulds, are rarely as well finished. Look for crudely carved ivory hands and feet, and a poor join between the ivory and bronze.
* Cracked and discoloured ivory substantially reduces value.
* Mass produced copies in plaster or spelter have little investment value.
* Nudes and erotic figures are much in demand and the works of Preiss, Chiparus, Colinet and Zach in particular command high prices.

Glass
* Gallé was the outstanding craftsman in glass of the Art Nouveau period, producing textured, multicoloured and technically complete pieces. His work influenced the Daum Brothers who are also increasingly collectable.
* Although he was producing glass in the Art Nouveau period, Lalique is the giant of the Art Deco period; his glass works produced over 10 million pieces, mostly marked, to a high standard and extremely collectable. Other noted manufacturers are Degues, Genet et Michon, Hunebelle and Verlux.
* Best prices are paid for one-off pieces known to have been made by the masters. Prices for mass-produced replicas correlate to the degree of technical skill involved in their manufacture. Thus cameo glass and mould-blown pieces are especially popular with collectors.
* Signatures have been forged and it is sensible to ask for documentary support for the provenance of a piece.

Lamps

* Tiffany iridescent and mosaic-glass lamps influenced the designs produced at the factories of Steuben, Quezal and Brooklyn J Hardel. All are collectable. There are many modern copies which lack the quality and finish of originals.

Typical Tiffany lamp

Jewellery

* Art Nouveau jewellery falls broadly into two categories; pieces designed individually for wealthy clients which are now very highly priced, and more modest, sometimes mass-produced items.
* The favoured materials were silver, enamel, horn and semi-precious stone. Motifs are largely based on flower, bird and insect designs. Haircombs, brooches and belt buckles are still relatively numerous.
* The work of Lalique, before he turned to glass, is very valuable along with the work of those jewellers he influenced: the Vever brothers, Gaillard and Wolfers. Liberty's produced an attractive range which is popular with collectors.
* From the Art Deco period look for powder compacts, cigarette cases and brooches, especially those signed by Jean Després.

Ceramics

* Studio or art pottery was made in the late C19 and early C20 by artists working well away from the fashionable centres of Art Nouveau; their work owes more to Japanese models than contemporary decorative styles.
* It was an age of lively experimentation, and the best pieces are not only beautiful, but early examples of new or revived techniques. Salt-glazed stoneware, matt glazed and painted pieces by the leading masters are all collectable.
* Particular favourites with collectors are the grotesque stoneware birds of the Martin Brothers, early Rookwood wares, noted for their rich green and brown glazes, and the wafer thin Rozenberg wares.
* The work of Art Deco studio potters has always commanded high prices but the colourful mass-produced designs of Clarice Cliff, and Carlton ware are increasingly popular. Look for pre-1935 pieces and rare shapes and patterns.

Metalwork

* British designers excelled in silver craftsmanship and revived the art of pewterware. Knox designed the mass-produced Cymric silver range and Tudric pewter range for Liberty's.
* Ashbee's Guild of Handicraft produced individual pieces using silver decorated with stones and enamel which have great beauty and rarity value. More numerous are the Continental pieces of Hoffmann, Moser and Peche which reflect the Guild's influence.
* Other collectable names are Rex Silver and George Jensen in silver, Dresser's Japanese-inspired electroplate pieces, Kayser-Zinn pewterwork, and early American Arts and Crafts community work sold through the shops of Roycroft and van Erp.

Beware

* The popularity of Art Nouveau and Deco ensures a ready availability of modern copies and reproductions. Ignorant or dishonest dealers will not scruple to pass off new as original. The golden rule is "Let the buyer beware!" Only buy from dealers of repute and pass over pieces which are not adequately provenanced – unless, of course, you are prepared to pay the asking price for a decorative piece or are willing to buy simply because you like it. Really satisfying purchases can often be made "on a hunch" based on liking a piece which no-one else rates very highly.

RUGS and CARPETS
Glossary

abadeh Strong, highly coloured Persian rug, with design usually including tree-of-life and diamond-shaped medallion.

abrash Oriental carpets made by nomads are especially subject to variation within a colour; this is termed "abrash".

abrisham Persian silk.

allover Rug with an allover, repeating pattern.

aniline dye Industrial dye. Aniline dyes, introduced into Oriental carpet manufacture c1870, are considered much inferior to the traditional vegetable dyes.

baff A knot.

border Stripe or series of stripes surrounding the **field** of a Persian carpet; generally the edge decoration.

boteh Type of **motif**, essentially a leaf form, but curled at the tip, resembling European Paisley pattern.

candy Side cord of rug.

chain Term sometimes used for the threads of the warp or weft.

chrome dye Modern industrial dye now used widely in the East, more fast than **anilines.**

corridor carpet Long thin carpet, also known as a "runner".

dhurri Indian equivalent of *kelim* (*q.v.*).

doruye Rug with different design on each side; reversible.

dragon-lung Male dragon symbol found on Chinese rugs.

feng-huang Chinese female dragon-phoenix symbol, opposite of **dragon-lung.**

field Area of a carpet within its borders.

flat or **flat-woven carpet** Carpet without a pile; see also **kilim.**

Ghiordes knot Type of pile, also called "Turkish". The "knot" is formed by passing a thread round two "chains" of the warp and through the space between.

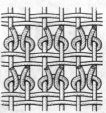

guard stripe Stripe immediately surrounding the **field** of the Persian carpet, even inside the **inner stripe.**

gul Persian word for "flower"; describes the stylized geometric pattern, concentric like a flower, that recurs in many variations, particularly on Turkoman carpets. It is often possible to identify the maker's tribe by the gul, which served as a kind of emblem. However, guls were sometimes taken over by a conquering tribe.

hatchli Carpet with design based on a cross.

herati pattern Design common on Persian rugs. It has a repeating unit consisting of several elements, usually floral ones, arranged in two-way or four-way symmetry round a centre, typically a rosette.

inner stripe Stripe between the **field** and the **border** (or central stripe) of a Persian carpet.

ipek Turkish silk.

kaba Prefix meaning "coarse".

kar-haneh Workshop.

Kashmir Area in northern India producing silk and wool rugs.

kenare Long, narrow carpet, the Persian term for a "runner" or side carpet, flanking the main, central carpet.

kermes Persian term meaning "red" or "crimson".

kilim (ghilim, khilim) Rugs without a "knot" or "pile"; also known as "flat" carpets.

kufic Type of Arabic calligraphy, often used in stylized form on many Islamic artefacts, including carpets.

kurk Softest wool, from the sheep's chest.

mamluk Egyptian rugs dating from C15 or C16.

medallion The centrepiece of a Persian carpet, essentially of disc or diamond shape.

mihrab Hollow or niche in the wall of a mosque that faces towards Mecca; often adopted as a structural element of the design particularly in Turkish rugs.

mir Persian rug with palm-leaf motifs.

mira Palm-leaf motif.

moquette Heavy imitation velvet, used for upholstery; also used as an alternative to knotting to produce an apparent pile, e.g. on Axminster carpets.

motif Item or element of a design, whether geometric, stylized or naturalistic.

mud Finely-woven rugs made in area around Khorassan in Iran, with geometric designs.

mudjur Turkish prayer mat, usually of wool.

namas Rug on which to pray, typically not more than 3ft (91cm) long, and a little less wide.

needlepoint or needlework Woven carpets decorated with needle and thread, sometimes to imitate knotted carpets.

nil Indigo.

nomad rugs Rugs woven by wandering central Asian tribes, never entirely symmetrical and usually with a fringe at each end.

outer stripe Stripe surrounding the **border** of a Persian carpet.

pambe Cotton (Iran).

pamuk Cotton (Turkey).

pendant Smaller design element attached usually on each side of a **medallion**.

pile Short pieces of thread or yarn "knotted" to the warp and weft of a carpet, constituting its upper surface.

pillar rug Chinese rug so made that it can be arranged round a pillar.

pole Motif resembling a pole linking medallions along an axis.

prayer rug Rug on which a Muslim normally kneels when he prays. It is personal and precious, so often finely worked, but invariably small. Frequently it incorporates a **mihrab** design.

runner Long, narrow rug. See also **kenare**.

rutakali Horse blanket.

saph Design used on Turkish prayer rugs.

savonnerie French rug in the Oriental style, with cut pile. From C17.

Sehna (Senneh, Sinneh) Type of pile, also called "Persian". The "knot" of the pile is formed by passing a thread round two "chains" of the warp and out beside the second.

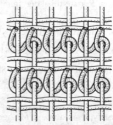

Sereband Area in C. Iran, giving name to rugs with an allover **boteh** design.

Shah abbas Floral design named after famous Persian ruler.

sileh S-shaped motif, common on Sumak and other Caucasian rugs.

Sinkiang Modern Chinese rugs from province of Sinkiang. They have geometric designs and bright colours. Also known as "Samarkands".

spandrel Element of a design, closing off a corner: two spandrels make an arch shape.

specular Symmetrical, or "mirror-like". Specifically, on carpets, a design that is symmetrical both lengthwise and crosswise but not lengthwise and crosswise together.

stylized Said of a form or object that has been reduced to a pattern.

suf Embossed.

tabachi Wool of very inferior quality.

tikh Hooked knife used in carpet making.

vase pattern Technique of weaving producing a vase pattern, associated with southern Iran (and the **Sehna** knot). The vase is not the only or the dominant **motif** of a vase-pattern rug.

veramin Persian rug made from top-quality wool, richly coloured and decorated, usually with flower and leaf designs.

warp The lengthwise threads of carpet, as opposed to the crosswise threads of the "weft".

weft The crosswise threads of a carpet, as opposed to the lengthwise threads of the "warp".

zar measurement of approx. 36in (91cm).

Regions, Makers and Styles
Middle Eastern

Agra A main centre of rug production in India, from Mogul times (late C16). Designs and colours derive from Persia, but with native motifs.

Afshar Persian tribal rugs from south of Kirman.

Ainabad Kurdish rugs also known as Bibikabads, from village in NW Iran.

Bakhtiara Semi-nomadic tribal rugs woven near Isfahan.

Baluchistan Region covering SW Pakistan and SE Iran where rugs resembling Turkoman types are produced.

Birjand Trade name for rugs of coarse type sold through Meshed.

Caucasian Like Turkish carpets, Caucasian carpets usually have Ghiordes knots and geometric designs. In Caucasian examples, however, the geometric grid of the design is dominant, and usually includes stylized motifs. Tribal types or centres of rug production in the region include: Baku, Daghestan, Gendje, Kazakistan, Kuba, Leshgi, Shirvan, Sumak, Talish, Tchi-Tchi.

Dorukhsh (Dorosh) Fine quality C19 carpets from Kainat area in E Iran.

Gorovan Rugs woven in village near Herez in Iran. Usually of inferior quality.

Herez Major weaving centre in NW Iran.

Isfahan Modern rugs woven in Isfahan; or quality rugs sold in Meshed.

Kashan Town in central Iran, famous from C16 for its silk carpets. In the best, silk was used in warp, weft and pile, and of all Persian carpets, Kashan are regarded as supreme.

Kashgai Tribal and village rugs from Fars, S Iran, esp. Fars lion rugs.

Kazak From Kazakistan in the Caucasus, a region known for its bright (fine reds and yellows) geometric designs.

Khorassan Generic name for carpets woven in eastern province of Iran, often misused.

Kirman Region in southern Iran, known especially for its "vase-pattern" carpets.

Kuba Region in Armenia. Its carpets are of Caucasian type, but known particularly for a stylized dragon motif and for bright, stylized floral designs.

Kum City in central Iran with important modern weaving industry, known for its calligraphic (Kufic) designs.

Kurdish Generic name given to tribal weaving from NW Iran.

Malayer Fine Kurdish type weaving from village near Arak.

Mehreban Area near Herez; sometimes a particular quality of rug.

Persian Persian rugs have great variety of design and colour, attributable to the influence from other arts and from China that revolutionized rug-making in C16 Iran. They may feature an arabesque pattern, a geometric pattern, a floral pattern, or incorporate naturalistic motifs, e.g. horsemen. Specifically "Persian" is a design based on a central medallion surrounded by dense stylized floral motifs. Persian centres of rug production or tribal types include: Bakhtiara, Bidjar, Fereghan, Hamadan, Herat, Herez, Isfahan, Kashan, Kashgai, Kirman, Kum, Meshed, Nain, Saruk, Sehna, Shiraz, Tabriz.

Polonaise Silk carpet of a type evolved in Isfahan in Iran in C16, but also made in Kashan, with a symmetrical floral design in soft, almost pastel colours, enhanced by gold and silver brocade. Carpets of this type found in the collection of a Polish prince gave rise to term "polonaise" in C19.

Qum see **Kum**.

Saraband Term applied to rugs

woven in Arak.

Serab (Sarab) Rugs from village of same name near Herez in Iran.

Shirvan Rugs from Shirvan in the Caucasus; also known as "Baku" or "Kabistan". Appreciated for the quality of their fine, but short pile, they have a wide range of decoration, extending to motifs generally associated with Persian rugs.

Sumak (Soumak) Region of the Caucasus, known for its flat-woven carpets or "kelim", often decorated with a running pattern in the weft. Unlike other kelim, Sumak carpets are usable one side up only.

Tabriz Town in NW Iran, the original capital of the Persian Safavid dynasty. Typically its carpets are designed round one, or several, medallions, while the ground is filled with a dense multitude of floral "shoots".

Turkish Also known as "Anatolian". Like Caucasian carpets, Turkish rugs usually have a geometric design, for example a repeating arabesque, producing an overall pattern; if the design is more structured, its elements are simple (e.g. a "mihrab") and recognisable motifs are few. Turkish types or centres of rug production include: Bergama, Ghiordes, Karabagh, Kirsehir, Ladik, Milas, Ushak, Yuruk.

Turkoman Carpets from western Turkestan. Made by nomads or semi-nomads, usually with a Sehna knot, these carpets show a limited repertoire of geometric patterns, dominated by a repeating "gul" or stylized flower. They are famed for their soothing, subtle colours. Turkoman tribes include: Salor, Tekke, Yomud.

Other

Aubusson Town in France, where tapestries, coverings and carpets have been produced since C17. The carpets have a tapestry-weave (that is, do not have a knotted pile) and are known for their large floral designs.

Axminster Town in Devon, England, where moquette or pileless carpets were made from mid C18 till 1835, when the factory was moved to Wilton. At Wilton, "Axminster" mechanically woven carpets have continued to be made.

Gobelins Name of the French royal factory mainly producing tapestries for the king from C18.

Sprague, W.P. Philadelphia carpet factory making finger-tufted rugs at end of C18.

Wilton Town in Devon, where there has been a carpet factory from about 1740. At first using a moquette weave, Wilton switched to knotted carpets in C19, and also mechanized the process.

Pronunciation Guide

Mis-pronouncing a name or word can be embarrassing when making an enquiry about, or buying, a carpet, so here is a list of those terms most likely to be needed, with their phonetic pronunciations. Stress syllables printed in capitals.

Word	Pronunciation
Abadeh	AB-ah-day
Afshar	AF-shar
Aubusson	OH-byu-sohn
Bergama	ber-GAH-mah
Bidjar	BEE-jar
Bokhara	bo-KHAR-ah
Boteh	BO-tay
Dhurri	DAR-ree
Dorukhsh	do-ROSH
Doruye	DOR-ru
Ghiordes	YOR-dez
Gul	goohl
Hamadan	HAM-ah-dan
Hatchli, hatchly,	HATCH-lee
Herat	heh-RAT
Herati	heh-RAH-tee
Hereke	heh-ree-KAY
Herez, Heriz	heh-REEZ
Isfahan	Iss-fah-hahn
Isparta	ee-spah-tah
Karabagh	Kar-ah-BAGH
Kazak-istan	kah-ZACK-ee-stahn
Kashan	kah-SHAHN
Kashgai, Gashqai, Qashqa'i	kash-GAI
Kirsehir, Kayseri	KAI-za, KAI-za-ree
Kelim	kil-LEEM
kenare	ken-ah-RAY
Khorassan	KHOR-ah-san
kirman	KER-man
Kum, Qum	ghoom
Kurk	koork
Meshed	meh-SHED
Mihrab	MEHR-ab
Milas	MEE-las
Mir	meer
Mira	MIR-ah
Mud	mood
Mudjur	MOOD-jah
Muh	moo
Nain	nai-EEN
Pambe	PAM-beh
Pamuk	PAM-ook
Qashqa'i	*see* Kashgai
Qum	*see* Kum
Salor	say-LOR
Sehna, Senneh	sen-NAY
Seraband	SAR-ah-band
Shirvan	SHUR-van
Sumak	soo-mack
Tabachi	tah-BAH-chee
Tabriz	ta-BRIHZ
Tekke	TEK-key
Ushak	OOH-shak
Veremin	VER-ah-min
Yomud	yoh-MOOD

What you should know about:
Rugs

* In general, the older the rug the greater its investment potential. "Antique" rugs, over 100 years old, command the highest prices; though "old" rugs, over 50 years old, are also sought after.
* Next in importance is richness and harmony of colour, fineness and the interest of the design, and the patina which naturally dyed fibres acquire with age.
* The best rugs are those made by the tribal peoples of Asia Minor. More recent Chinese, Indian and Pakistani rugs, characteristically of soft wool and floppy, have little investment value.
* A hand-made rug has the pattern visible on the back as well as the surface. Part the pile and look for rows of knots at the base of the tuft. Absence of either indicates a machine-made rug of little interest to collectors.
* Rugs of synthetically-dyed fibres, introduced in the 1920s, are often garish and lack strength. Chemical dye will come off on a white handkerchief wetted with saliva, and has an unpleasant smell. Some vegetable dyes will also leave a stain, but slight by comparison.
* The back of an old rug will have a polished appearance and the knots will be flattened.
* The foundation threads at the base of the pile should be yellowish-grey with age, even if the rug has been cleaned.
* Check tufts with a magnifying glass. In old rugs the colour should shade gradually from deep at the base to pale at the tip. Three distinct bands of colour indicates a newer rug artificially aged.
* Never buy a rug that has been attacked by mildew. Signs are light coloured patches on the back and rotten fibres which snap when the rug is folded or twisted.
* Checks rugs for holes and wear by holding up to a strong light. Weak areas can be strengthened and repaired if not too extensive, but the cost of repair should be reflected in the price.
* Repairs can be detected with the palm of the hand as raised or uneven areas of pile. Provided repairs are done skilfully with correctly matched colours using vegetable dye, they do not substantially affect the value.
* Top prices should only be paid for complete rugs. Many have had worn areas removed. Check that the pattern is contained within the frame and does not run beyond the carpet edge. Check that the end borders match the side ones and have not been replaced.
* Fringes are especially vulnerable to wear and removal. It is better to buy a rug with a replaced fringe than one in which the fringe has been removed and a new one made by fraying the edges of the rug. Always check that the threads are firm and have not begun to unravel.
* Dates (in arabic characters) woven into the rug are helpful, but can be misleading. Sometimes weavers copied earlier rugs, including the date. Dates can be altered to increase the apparent age; check carefully for signs of new weaving, especially around the second numeral.
* The most important factor in valuing a rug is its country of origin, and where it was made there. Other points to consider are age, condition, rarity, demand and the quality of manufacture and design.
* Top of the scale are fine silk rugs from Persia and Turkey. Quality wool rugs from Persia and the Caucasus command high prices. Modern rugs and those from other areas are relatively less expensive but no rug, of reasonable quality, condition and pedigree, will be cheap. A "bargain" may indeed be just that, but do take the trouble to check out the claims made for it.

Beware

* Modern rugs are frequently distressed and antiqued in order to realise higher prices. Remember that not all rugs that look old really are; *vice versa* a well-cared-for antique may look almost pristine. It is well worth paying for a second opinion before spending a lot of money.
* Many so called "Isfahan" rugs were in fact made in or around Meshed. They are much inferior to the genuine Isfahan, and should be marked and priced accordingly.

ballock dagger Dagger (or knife) with **quillon** terminating in small spheres.

basket hilt Guard covering whole hand, usually perforated or made up of several metal bands.

bluing Colouring (by heat) of metal, to protect it from rust and for decoration.

blunderbuss Handgun with a barrel that widens or flares at the end, to scatter the shot.

bore Inside of the barrel; or the measurement of its diameter.

bowie knife Sheath knife introduced in America in early C19, named after James Bowie of Texas. It has a cutting blade curving to a point for thrusting.

boxlock Type of **flintlock**, where the entire firing mechanism is enclosed within the breech.

breech Rear end of the barrel (opposite end to the muzzle).

breech-loading Gun loaded, not down the barrel, but through an opening in the breech.

broadsword Large sword with broad blade, *cf* **smallsword** or **rapier**.

butt Rear end of **stock** of a gun; the end placed against the shoulder or held in the hand.

carbine Short, light **long arm** suitable for use by a horseman.

cartridge Pre-packed charge of primer or gunpowder; in modern systems is combined with the bullet.

chamber Space where ignition takes place – in the breech of the barrel.

chape Fitment to a scabbard. Either the buckle by which the scabbard was attached to a belt, or the tip or cap protecting its end.

claymore Scottish Highland longsword.

close helmet Helmet covering the whole head and neck.

cock The spring-tensioned arm holding the igniting agent. "Cocking a gun" means setting the spring in tension. It is held in tension by a **sear**. A gun at "half-cock" is cocked and ready to fire, but is held by a second sear to prevent it going off accidentally.

couse Medieval broad-bladed spear.

cuirass Breastplate, or half armour. Normally worn by a horseman ("cuirassier").

daisho Pair of Samurai swords, worn together. One, the "katana", was "dai" or long; the other, the "wakisashi", was "sho" or short.

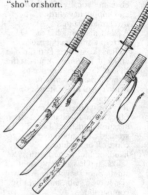

derringer Type of pistol, named after those made by Henry Deringer (with one "r"!) in mid C19. Small, with a single barrel, fired by percussion lock.

dirk Dagger with pointed blade, carried by naval officers; or a Highland dagger.

diplomatic sword See **dress sword**.

dog lock Type of **flintlock** with a safety-catch or "half-cock". So called because the shape of the **serpent** commonly resembles a dog's head.

double-action A gun that may be cocked or may be "self-cocking", as required. See **single-action**.

dress sword Sword worn as a badge or distinction, not for use.

express rifle High-bore rifle with a light, high-velocity bullet, introduced in mid C19 for game shooting.

firangi Indian sword with an imported European blade (the word means "foreigner").

flintlock Type of firing mechanism. The flint held in

the **serpent** or **jaw** strikes the **steel** or **frizzen** and creates a spark to fire the priming in the **pan**.

fore end The part of the **stock** under the barrel, *cf* **butt**.

forte Thickest and strongest part of blade, near hilt.

French lock Most common type of **flintlock**, developed in France early C17. Like other flintlocks, the "French" lock has both full **cock** and half-cock, and the **steel** and **pan-cover** made in one piece. Unlike others the **sear** catch is not on flanges but in the notches of a tumbler, attached to the cock by a "cock-screw".

frizzen or **frizzle** In a **flintlock**, the metal on which the flint strikes to create the spark to ignite the priming. Also known as the "steel".

frontal Piece of armour used either for covering the face or protecting a horse's forehead.

fuller Groove running down the centre of a blade.

full-stocked With the stock extending the full length of the barrel.

fusil Small flintlock musket.

gorget Piece of armour to protect the throat.

greaves Pieces of armour protecting the legs below the knees.

gusset Chain mail covering joint between parts of suit of armour.

hair trigger Trigger requiring minimal pressure to fire it. Sometimes both a hair trigger and an ordinary trigger are provided.

Halberd Similar to a double-headed axe, but with projecting spike and mounted on a pole. C16.

half-stocked With the stock extending only part way down the barrel.

hanger Short sword, originally hung from the belt.

hammer Usual term for the **cock** in a **percussion lock**.

hilt Hand-grip of a sword.

jambiyah Arabian name for type of dagger in use throughout the Muslim world; has a sharply curved blade, bending away almost at a right angle.

jaw A small vice (worked by a screw) to hold the pyrites or flint of a **flintlock**.

kabuto Japanese Samurai helmet.

kard Turkish or Persian straight-bladed dagger.

katana See **daisho**.

katar Indian dagger, with a

pointed blade and a pommel like a bar.

kettle hat Iron helmet, C14/C15.

khandar Indian sword with two-edged blade and a long pommel for a two-handed grip.

khanfar Persian dagger, typically with a curved pommel.

khanjar Indian dagger with curved blade, often with hilt of another material, e.g. jade.

kindjal (kindjhal) Caucasian short sword or dagger with a double-edged broad blade, without quillons.

knuckle bow Extension of the quillon curving back to protect the knuckles.

kris Traditional Malaysian and Indonesian dagger, often with a wavy or crinkly blade, and a hilt set at an angle. There are several different regional designs.

kukri Heavy, curved Nepalese sword, as used by Ghurkas. Often has one or two small knives attached.

lame Metal plate, particularly one of the overlapping metal plates attached beneath a helmet or breastplate in a suit of armour.

left-hand dagger Dagger held in the left hand (in the right was the rapier), mainly to parry the opponent's sword.

lock Firing mechanism of a gun.

lockplate Support or base holding the firing mechanism on a gun barrel.

long arm Firearm with a long barrel, for sighting and aiming.

matchlock Type of firing mechanism. Ignition was achieved by lowering a "slowmatch" held in a lever or **serpent** into the priming **pan**.

miquelet Type of **flintlock**. Its cocking mechanism differs from other types: the **sear** operates not on a tumbler but against lugs.

morion Helmet common in C16 and C17, round, with a rim, usually with an upturned front peak.

mortuary sword Straight-bladed soldier's sword of C17, with a **shell** and a basket hilt.

musket Heavy **long arm**, the standard weapon of the foot-soldier from late C16 to late C18, when supplanted by the **rifle**. To be fired, it had to be supported on a crutch or rest.

needle gun Type of gun fired by a pin ("needle") that detonated the primer (in the cartridge).

nimcha North African Muslim sword, with a knuckle bow.

nipple In a percussion lock, a hollow pointed cone on which a cap containing fulminate was placed.

over-and-under Gun with two barrels, one set over the other.

pan The shallow depression in which the priming was placed.

pan cover Cover to the **pan**, protecting the priming till it was fired. In the developed **flintlock**, was automatically moved aside by the firing mechanism as the **serpent** descended.

patchbox Compartment in the butt of a gun for storing accessories.

pepperbox Revolver with several revolving barrels (and often a central one).

percussion lock Type of firing mechanism introduced in C19. Gunpowder priming, ignited by a spark, was replaced with

chemical fulminate, ignited by the stroke of a hammer.

pike Spear-like thrusting weapon mounted on a long shaft. Used by infantry, C16-C17.

plug bayonet Bayonet designed to fix into the barrel of a musket or rifle.

pogmoggan Bone or stone fastened to end of slender rod. Used by North American Indians.

pommel Knob or end of a handle, e.g. of a dagger.

poniard Small slender dagger.

pricker Metal pin with which to clean the touch-hole of a piece, once standard equipment.

proof mark Official mark certifying the efficiency of the barrel. Metallurgical testing or proving of barrels was instituted as early as C17.

quarrel Crossbow arrow with square pointed head.

quillon Cross-piece of a sword, dividing hilt and blade, to protect the hand or provide a grip for fingers.

ramrod Rod for ramming ball, bullet or shot down the barrel.

rapier Sword with a pointed blade designed to pierce (unlike a **sabre**).

revolver Any gun with several chambers or barrels, which may be revolved. However, a gun with revolving barrels is now called a "pepperbox revolver"; otherwise "revolver" means a single-barrelled gun with a revolving cylinder containing several bullet-holding **chambers**.

ricasso Part of sword blade next to the hilt, roughened, not sharp, on which the fingers may grip.

rifle, rifling Gun with a barrel that has internal spiral grooves, to spin the bullet; spiral grooving. Spinning equals out the imbalances of the bullet, which might otherwise make it veer in flight.

sabre Sword curved to slash or cut, unlike a **rapier**.

sashqua, sashka Cossack (also Caucasian) sword; gently curved, without quillons.

scabbard Sheath for daggers, swords, bayonets, etc.

scale armour Small steel plates fastened or riveted together, so resembling fish scales.

scimitar Eastern curved sword, only suitable for striking, not thrusting.

sear The catch which holds the gun cocked or half-cocked, and is released by pulling the trigger.

self-cocking See **single-action**.

serpent The arm or lever holding the match, pyrites or flint by which the priming was ignited. So named because of its usual S shape. Also **serpentine**.

shako Conical or cylindrical peaked helmet, C19.

shamsir (shamshir) Persian or Indian sword with a curved blade, short quillons and pommel set at a right angle.

shell or **shellguard** Disc resembling a shell set beneath the quillon as a further protection to the hand; a "double shellguard" has two such discs.

sidelock With the lock fitted not above the breech, as usual, but beside it.

single-action Gun that can be fired by pulling the trigger, without cocking. Also called "self-cocking".

smallsword Light fencing or duelling sword.

skean-dhu Small dirk worn by Scottish Highlanders, normally in their stockings.

snapha(u)nce Early type of **flintlock**, lacking the safety feature of "half-cock".

snaplock Term covering both **flintlock** and **snaphance** arms.

steel Another name for the **frizzen**.

stiletto Thin steel dagger, for stabbing, C16 and C17.

stock The wooden (or sometimes metal) support for the barrel of a gun; the means by which it is held.

swept hilt Hilt bent into a flourish or loop serving as a guard to the hand.

taaweesh War club used by North American Indians.

tachi Japanese Samurai sword, of long, gently curved shape, with a single cutting edge.

talwar, tulwar Any Indian sword ("talwar" is Hindi for sword),

but usually with straight quillons (sometimes rounded at the end) and a disc-like pommel.

tang The end of the blade of a sword that the hilt covers.

tasset One of a series of overlapping plates in a suit of armour, extending down from the waist, to protect the groin and thighs.

tanto Japanese Samurai dagger, used together with the **tachi**.

tiller Central arm of a crossbow or the stock of an early firearm.

touch hole Hole giving access (from the pan) to the gunpowder (in the breech).

tsuba The guard of a Japanese sword.

two-stage barrel Barrel made in two parts.

tube lock Variety of **percussion lock**. The fulminate is contained not in a cap over the **nipple**, but in a tube.

turn-off barrel Barrel that can be unscrewed, or must be unscrewed for loading.

vent Alternative name for **touch-hole**.

wakisashi See **daisho**.

watered steel Steel with a decorative pattern typical of Islamic blades, from the Middle Ages to C19. The pattern is produced naturally in steel of a high carbon content, but is enhanced by etching.

wheel lock Type of firing mechanism using a spring-driven wheel. The wheel was wound or turned against the spring, then released by the trigger, which at the same time brought a piece of pyrites held in the **jaw** or **serpent** into sharp contact with it, producing sparks to fire the priming in the **pan**.

yataghan Turkish sword with a short hilt and no guard. Both curved and straight blades are found.

What you should know about:
Armour

Armour, in one form or another, has been in use since c1500BC and maybe earlier. Even today steel helmets and bullet-proof jackets are a standard part of the soldier's equipment. For the collector, however, armour normally means medieval plate armour and the variations and adaptations which evolved from it. Body armour was still worn, particularly in the cavalry, until the early C19, but the increasing efficiency of firearms rapidly reduced its use to ceremonial occasions only. Oriental armour developed very different styles from those of the West, and is often collected as a separate subject.

General pointers

* Collecting armour is a very expensive hobby. Genuine full suits of armour rarely become available, and then fetch thousands of pounds/dollars. Such a suit must have full and verifiable authentication.
* Most of the suits of armour, and indeed many individual items, on the market are fairly modern reproductions and should be described as such.
* Even reproduction armour is comparatively expensive and good quality C19 complete suits, often made in Germany, France or Spain, are particularly sought after.
* Buying armour is therefore not for the novice. Learn to distinguish periods and styles, and be on guard against "marriages" of items which do not belong together.
* Condition, general wear and patina are all important factors in assessing a piece of armour. If you feel something is "wrong" but are not certain what, seek expert advice. Never buy armour in a hurry.

English Civil War armour

* Mid C17 armour, and particularly that of the English Civil War (1642–49) is a popular subject for collectors.
* Especially sought after are the lobster-tailed "pots" of Cromwell's cavalry. These had a three-bar face protector attached to a pivoted peak which could be raised if required. Make sure that visor and the lobster-tail neck protector belong to the helmet. Marriages are quite comon, so check joints and hinges to ensure they are original.
* Genuine C17 armour sometimes carries an armourer's mark, plus small dents from a pistol ball fired at close range to test or "prove" the strength of

the breast plate. Do not rely totally on such marks, however; they are sometimes faked.

Repairs and reproductions

* In addition to "marriages", genuine repair work may have been carried out by a blacksmith many years ago. This is acceptable as long as it is reflected in the price.
* Modern reproductions have probably been gas welded. This process can produce burn marks on the surface, which will be absent on a genuinely old piece of armour.
* Approach cleaning with care. Do not attempt to refurbish armour with a power drill or wire brushes; leave such work to an expert. Instead use wire wool and oil, or even just fine grade wet-and-dry emery paper.
* Be careful not to damage or remove any marks which may be concealed beneath rust.
* Treat leatherwork with saddle soap.

Oriental armour

* Emphasis was on chain mail combined with plate, leather or fabric, rather that on full plate armour. Consequently less has survived in original condition.
* The Japanese, however, favoured lamellar armour which consisted of lacquered metal plates laced together. Their helmets are very distinctive, with wide neck-pieces and a metal mesh protecting the face.
* Japanese armour is of excellent quality and highly sought after. Again the advice is: know what to look for before you buy.
* Chinese armour was usually of inferior quality. Beware of attempts to pass it off as something more valuable.
* Genuine Indian and Middle Eastern armour is colourful and varied. However, beware crude bazaar copies.

Chain mail of inter-locking metal rings

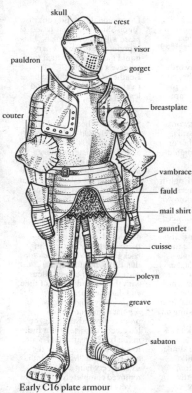

skull

crest

visor

pauldron

gorget

couter

breastplate

vambrace

fauld

mail shirt

gauntlet

cuisse

poleyn

greave

sabaton

Early C16 plate armour

Half-armour late C16

Breast and back plates with leather coat, C17

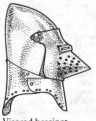

Visored bascinet, late C14

Kettle hat, late C15

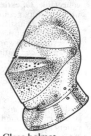

Close helmet, mid C16

Combed morion end C16

Lobster-tail "pot", mid C17

Hourglass gauntlet

What you should know about: Edged weapons

Types

Swords	Pole weapons
Daggers and dirks	Bayonets

Swords

* Long-bladed medieval swords often had a pommel of shaped metal at the top of the hilt, to balance the blade. The shape of the pommel may give a clue to dating.
* Very few genuinely old swords have their original scabbards. Made of thin wood, leather or velvet, scabbards deteriorated relatively quickly.
* C17 swords are sought after, particularly those of the English Civil War period. Marriages and reproductions are not unknown, so look for pitting and other signs of genuine wear, correct hilt to match the blade, and any other evidence of authenticity.
* The C18 and C19 provide the most fruitful and rewarding period for the sword or dagger collector. There are a number of clearly defined areas in which to specialize, with genuine pieces nearly always available at reasonable prices depending on condition.
* American swords go back to before the War of Independence. Hilts are similar to European designs, while pommels and quillons often carry an eagle's head motif.
* Japanese swords are very collectable. Of extremely fine workmanship, genuinely old, signed pieces justifiably command high prices. However, such swords were mass-produced during the Second World War, and since then reproductions have become widely available. Make certain which you are buying, and that the price is right.
* Middle Eastern and Indian swords can be found in a great variety of types and designs. Many are of quite recent date, being produced well into C20.

Care and maintenance

* Always wipe a blade with an oily cloth after it has been handled. This prevents rust marks caused by sweaty fingers.
* When cleaning, do not use a metal brush. A brush with a soft bristle gives the best results.
* Hot water with a small amount of detergent should remove deeply ingrained dirt or grease.

Dry thoroughly to prevent rust.
* A non-abrasive silicon-based paste will remove tarnish. This is preferable to the ordinary liquid metal polish which tends to leave a deposit.
* Leather scabbards should be treated regularly with a good leather polish.

Beware

* Swords have been faked fairly extensively. On early swords, spurious makers' marks are added, while later military swords have faked presentation inscriptions etched or engraved to give a totally false connection with some famous person or memorable event like The Charge of The Light Brigade.
* Faked etching will have a different depth from the original blade etching, and there will be a difference in background colour. Check too that the signs of aging are correct, with fine lines filled with the dirt and grease of time, and that there are no suspiciously bright edges.
* A great number of mass-produced swords and daggers have been exported from India in the last 20 years. Blades are roughly forged and carry the etched legend "Made in India" usually very faint and often removed completely. They are of very inferior quality and have absolutely no claim to be called antiques.

Bayonets

* The first bayonet, mid C17, was simply a dagger plugged into the barrel of a musket after it had been discharged ("plug bayonet").
* The French are credited with the invention of the socket bayonet (end C17), which allowed the weapon to be fired while the bayonet was fixed to the musket.
* The socket bayonet was in world-wide service until the end of C19 when it was gradually replaced by the spring-loaded knife bayonet.
* The spring-loaded knife bayonet, produced from the beginning of the C20, offers the widest range and choice for the collector.
* Even bayonets have been faked, so buy rare antique specimens with due care.

Types of edged weapons

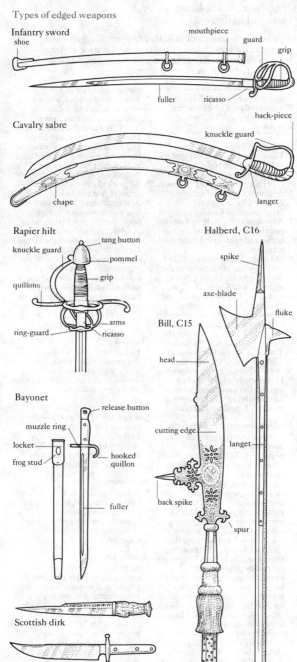

Infantry sword
shoe
mouthpiece
guard
grip
fuller
ricasso
back-piece

Cavalry sabre
knuckle guard
chape
langet

Rapier hilt
knuckle guard
tang button
pommel
grip
quillons
arms
ring-guard
ricasso

Halberd, C16
spike
axe-blade
fluke

Bill, C15
head
cutting edge
langet
back spike
spur

Bayonet
release button
muzzle ring
locket
frog stud
hooked quillon
fuller

Scottish dirk

American Bowie knife

What you should know about:
General Militaria

The accountrements of military life – actual equipment, ceremonial items, honours and commemorative material – have an undoubted fascination, prices are reasonable and all are collected with great enthusiasm.

Types

Powder flasks	Medals
Badges, insignia and buttons	Ephemera
Regalia	Uniforms

Powder flasks

* Flasks can be found dating back to C16, but the most popular field for the collector is the early C19 pieces in copper and brass.
* Sought after manufacturers include Dixon, Sykes, Hawksley and Bosch.
* American colonial horn flasks carrying vignettes or scrimshaw command high prices in original condition.
* Other desirable American flasks are those made for use with the New England flintlock pistol and the early Colts. Designs included "Clasped Hands" and "Stand of Arms". Excellent reproductions of these are sold, some aged and faked to appear original. To check, remove the cap and look inside the flask. Traces of new solder, combined with the bright metal of the "new" thread, are a giveaway.
* Flasks made of soft leather attached to a tin frame were, in fact, intended for shot and not powder. Equally collectable.

Badges, insignia and buttons

* These reasonably priced items have become enormously popular in the years since World War II. They cover items produced by all the countries taking part in both World Wars, as well as pieces from C19 and even earlier.
* Badges and insignia, whether metal or fabric, are beginning to command quite respectable prices, when not long ago they could be found in bargain lots.
* Brass cap and helmet badges are especially popular and examples can be found dating back to the mid C19. Before that date in England there were no standard cap badges as such, although a King's Crown badge appeared on swords, belts, buckles and shoulder plates.
* British Regimental badges almost always include a crown as part of the design. The pattern of this crown will give a useful clue to dating.
* Some badges struck abroad (e.g. in India) were crudely made and even cast in lead. They are nevertheless genuine.
* However, all too many fakes and re-strikes are in circulation to catch the unwary. They tend to be lighter than genuine badges and have a waxy feel.
* Be particularly wary of rare items in fine condition.
* American metal badges are far less numerous than British ones, but there is a wide range of fabric unit and other insignia. Beware of mass-produced copies.
* Dating British buttons is straightforward. After 1767 the regimental number was embossed on all buttons (which were generally of pewter). Pewter buttons were not finally replaced by brass ones until mid C19. For details consult any of the excellent books available.

Regalia

* Usually refers to Nazi regalia of the period 1924–1945. Not really to be classified as antiques, though highly popular with many collectors.

Medals

* A vast subject of world-wide interest and range, the best advice is to consider what country and aspect are of special interest, study the available literature, and then specialize.

Ephemera

* Posters, postcards and cigarette cards are very popular, but any printed items, particularly connected with famous battles or events, are extremely collectable.

Uniforms

* Although a considerable amount of space is required for display and storage, uniforms are collected and fetch quite good prices for genuine articles in good condition.
* Headgear (helmets, kepis, busbys, shapkas etc.) are especially popular because they require less space, and because they have been less subject to the effects of time and wear.

Types of powder flask

Musketeer's,
mid C17

Embossed leather,
C18

American cow-
horn, mid C18

C19 flask with
graduated neck

Flask to go with
early Colt

Leather-covered
shot flask, C19

Badges

British military badges, showing different styles of crown: *l. to r.*
Victoria "high-ears" pattern; George V; naval crown; Elizabeth II.

Types of helmet

Lancer's shapka,
mid C19

Officer's home
service helmet, C19

Hussar's busby,
late C19

German pickel-
haube, 1914

German, 1915
(modified 1939)

French infantry,
1914–18

British, 1915–45
U.S. 1917–41

American,
1941–present

Japanese,
1941–45

What you should know about:
Firearms

For the collector, anything earlier than C18 will be rare and expensive, provided it is genuine and authenticated. Demand for C18 and early C19 flintlocks is keen, but good examples can usually be found. Percussion and breech-loading firearms form a very popular section on their own, and prices reflect this – as do the number of reproductions and "repaired" items to be found.

Types

Matchlock	Percussion lock
Wheel-lock	Breech-loaders
Snaphaunce	Revolvers
Flintlock	Repeating rifles
Pennsylvania	Automatic
(Kentucky) rifle	weapons

* Flintlocks vary enormously in quality and price. An authenticated pistol by a well-known maker will command a high price; because of this, faking is not unknown. Always check for fresh looking file or cut marks.
* If necessary, ask for the lock-plate to be removed. Behind it may lie evidence of tampering.
* Look for newly drilled holes or the wrong kind of screws, both of which could indicate that the lock has been altered or replaced. In a genuine piece the screws will all be hand-cut.
* Legitimate repairs to sear or main spring are acceptable if declared and reflected in price.
* Many English pieces have a proofmark stamped on the barrel. By its size, shape and design, a proof mark will reveal the year it was stamped. Such proof marks indicated that the barrel had been "proofed" and found up to the official standard.
* Such "marked" barrels were, however, sometimes married to foreign stocks and furniture, either at the time or much later. So use any mark as just one clue, and not a guarantee that the piece is totally original and authentic. America had no comparable system.
* Another clue can be the maker's name, usually to be found engraved on the lock plate.
* Others marks (owners' names, coats-of-arms etc.) engraved on the metalwork, should be regarded with an open mind unless authenticated.
* If an unmarked flintlock is being offered very cheaply then it may well originate from the Middle or Far East. Such "trade" guns were being made well into C20. If the price is *not*

cheap, it could still be such a piece, so be wary.
* The parts of a Colt revolver were individually numbered, and those with matching numbers are highly desirable. If the numbers do not match, it may be because a part had to be replaced quite legitimately during the weapon's working life. However, check to see if any attempt has been made to change numbers.
* Always take care when purchasing a Colt revolver. A great many late C19 models of less than top quality, made for the Middle Eastern market, have come back into circulation. These have been sold as "genuine" standard "Army", "Navy" or "Pocket" Colts. They have also been doctored to conceal their origin and fake highly priced models. As a safeguard, check all serial numbers, also ramrods, cylinders, and barrel lengths, as these may have been altered.

Note
Each country has its own laws affecting the collecting and owning of guns. It is the responsibility of a collector to make absolutely certain that he or she is conforming to these laws.

Beware
* The "feel" of a weapon is important. If it feels top-heavy and uncomfortable in the firing position, take a closer look, particularly if it is a highly priced piece.
* If the metalwork does not fit exactly into the stock or butt, ask why. Examine closely for any indication of cutting away, building up, or apparent repair, especially round the lock on a flint or percussion piece.
* If there is rusting on a piece, is it consistent on barrel, furniture and lock? It should be.
* Cased sets of pistols should be carefully checked to confirm that all the items included belong together, and that some are not later additions.

Types of firearms

Flintlock pistol, late C18

jaw-screw
cock
frizzen
lock-plate
butt cap

Flintlock musket, end C18

pan
cock
frizzen

ramrod

match
pan and cover
sear spring
serpentine
sear
trigger

shank for winding key
pan cover
jaws
wheel case
main spring
cocking spring

Matchlock mechanism,
early C16

Wheel-lock mechanism,
late C16

Flintlock mechanism, C18

pan
frizzen spring
main spring
tumbler
sear spring

Left: exterior of lock plate; *right:* inside lock plate

Forsyth "scent bottle"
percussion lock, early C19

American Maynard lock,
mid C19

hammer
hand and spring
firing pin
ejector rod
chamber
bolt
main spring

Colt solid-frame revolver, late C19

Gunmaking

In the early days of gunmaking, manufacturing tended to be concentrated in capital or other important cities: London, Paris, Nuremberg etc. As demand increased other centres became increasingly famous (Birmingham, Charleville, etc.). In C18 America arsenals were set up at Harpers Ferry and Springfield, Mass.

Early production was by craftsmen, all guns being handmade. Pieces bearing the names of these master gunsmiths (particularly those based in London) are eagerly sought and highly priced. Because of this, their inscriptions are sometimes faked, so never rely solely on a maker's mark when buying.

Leading gunsmiths & gunmakers

Adams, Robt. & Jas., London, mid C19

Allen, Ethan, Mass., early/mid C19

Borchardt, Hugo, Berlin, late C19

Brander & Potts, London, early C19

Brander, W., London, early/mid C18

Brander, W.B., London, C18/C19

Byrne, Michael, England, mid C18

Collier, Elisha, U.S.A., early C19

Colt, Samuel, Hartford, Conn., mid C19

Cooper, J., England, mid C19

Cooper, J.M., Philadelphia, mid C19

Davidson, Joseph, England, early C19

Deringer, Henry, Philadelphia, early/mid C19

Dickert, Jacob, Lancaster, Pa., late C18

Dreyse, J.N. von, Germany, mid C19

Egg, Durs, London, early C19

Enty, John, London, early/mid C19

Freeman, John, London, mid C18

Ferguson, Patrick, Scotland, C18 (d. 1780)

Forsyth, Alex. J., Scotland, early C19

Freund, Johan, Suhl, early C19

Gandon, London, mid C19

Grant, Stephen, London, C19

Griswold, A.B., & Co, New Orleans, C19

Hall, John, London, mid C18

Hall, John Hancock, U.S.A., early C19

Harman Barne, London, mid C17

Heylin, London, late C18

Innis, F., Edinburgh, late C18

Johnson, R., Middletown, Conn., mid C18

Jover, England, late C18

Lacey & Co., London end C18/early C19

Lacey & Reynolds, London, mid C19

Le Bourgeoys, Marin, France, early C17

Lefaucheux, Eugène Gabriel, France, C19

Lepage, Paris, mid C19

London Armoury, mid C19

Luger, George, Germany, C19/C20

Manton, John, London, early C19

Moore, C., England, early/mid C19

Mortimer, H.W., England., late C18

Newton, Grantham, late C18

Nock, Henry, London & Birmingham, late C18/early C19

North, Simeon, Middletown, Conn., C19

Pape, W.R., Newcastle-upon-Tyne, mid/late C19

Parker, W., London, early C19

Pauly, Johannes, Switzerland, early C19

Pickfatt, Charles, London, C17/C18

Potts, T.H., London, mid C19

Purdey, James, London, mid C19

Reid, James, New York, mid C19

Remington, U.S.A., mid C19

Richards, J. & W., England, early C19

Richards, T., England, late C18

Rigby, John, London & Dublin, late C19

Scalafiotti, Bart., Turin, late C18

Sharps, Christian, U.S.A., mid C19

Shaw, Joshua, U.S.A., early C19

Silk, R., London, end C17

Smith, Saml. & Chas, London, mid C19

Smith, Horace & **Wesson**, Daniel, U.S.A., mid C19

Staudenmayer, S., London, early C19

Storey, Joseph, England, early C19

Tranter, Wm., London & Birmingham, mid C19

Turner, S., London, late C18

Twigg, T., London, late C18/early C19

Twigg & Bass, London, late C18

Unwin & Rodgers, Sheffield, mid C19

Waters & Co., England, late C18

Waters, John, Birmingham, C18

Webley, Philip & John, Birmingham, C19

Webster, Wm., England, early/mid C19

Westley Richards, Wm. England, C19

Winchester, Oliver F., U.S.A., mid C19

Witton, John, London, mid C19

Wogdon, London & Dublin, mid/late C18

Wogdon & Barton, London & Dublin, early C19

The Chronology of Arms

C14 Armour in general use: of the type called "Gothic" armour. Specialist centres had emerged for the production of fine swords, e.g. at Toledo, Milan, Passau. Also from this period first records of "handcannon"; otherwise longbow and crossbow were used.

C15 Armour became increasingly complex: chainmail gave way to armour made entirely of metal plate. In Italy, a new kind of sword, the rapier, was developed for thrusting rather than slashing and cutting. In Italy, Germany and Turkey, cannon began to revolutionize siege warfare. The matchlock firearm (arquebuse) was introduced, though without any significant effect on the battles of the period.

The C17 musketeer transformed the art of warfare in Europe

C16 The age of the *Landsknecht*, the professional soldier, of whom the most feared were the Swiss. Besides his halberd the *Landsknecht* also carried a musket, whose technical development was progressing rapidly. However, although barrels now began to be rifled, the musket was still much less accurate than the bow. The major improvements were in the firing mechanism. The wheel-lock was invented c1525, followed, c1550, by the invention of the flintlock. Swords, the weapon of the nobility, became finely worked and precious objects. Guards for the hand became usual, decorative as well as practical.

C17 Because it could not stop a musket-ball, armour was reduced mainly to cuirass and helmet. The smallsword, lighter but also sturdier for use in defence, replaced the rapier. Guns began to be worn rather than carried, and the pistol was developed. Longarms acquired the type of stock they still have today. The snaplock mechanism replaced all other types in Europe. As the century progressed special types of guns began to proliferate: the blunderbuss; the fowling piece or sports gun; the carbine.

C18 In this century both armour and swords became largely obsolete for practical purposes, and were worn purely for effect or ceremonial. Even duels were fought with pistols. The pike was replaced by a bayonet fixable to the musket. Only the helmet remained useful. In the domain of firearms, there were no major developments; rather this was a period of increasing refinement – safer cocking, better performance in the wet, greater accuracy. In the last quarter of the century, new emphasis was placed on the rifle in Britain, France and America.

C19 From the early C19 experiments with fulminates led to the development of the percussion lock. Then c1820 the percussion cap was invented. From the 1830s experiments were made with self-expanding bullets. New impetus was given to what were actually old ideas, such as breech-loading, repeating guns, and cartridges. By 1850 the musket and the flintlock had been entirely abandoned by the military in Europe and America, and the era of the breech-loading, cartridge-firing, repeating rifle had arrived.

Technological advance was constant, patent following patent. From about 1850, many fine gunmakers whose names are still famous emerge – Colt, Webley, Remington, Smith & Wesson and Luger.

Pepperbox revolvers, so popular in the first half of the century, gave way to the cylinder revolver. In 1891 cordite was introduced, and the automatic pistol was developed immediately afterwards. Technological advances in artillery were about to make as great an impact on the art of war as the introduction of cannon in C15.

DOLLS
Glossary

autoperipatetikos Greek for "walking about by itself", the common term for C19 clockwork dolls.

baby house A dolls' house. These survive from C17.

ball-jointed With limbs that move by swivelling on a ball, as opposed to "stiff-jointed".

bébé French doll, modelled as a child about 8–12 years old. Made by Bru and others in 2nd half C19.

bent-limb Doll made only to sit, with limbs fixed in bent position.

bisque Made of biscuit pottery. E.g. doll with bisque head, all-bisque doll.

blonde bisque Term for early bisque dolls tinted slightly pink.

character doll Similar to a **portrait doll**, but not representing anyone specifically; has a naturalistic physiognomy.

composition doll Doll made of cheap materials such as wood pulp, paper pulp and size.

estate-made Made on the estate of a great house by a staff craftsman, as was common C17–C19.

Frozen Charlotte Doll made of china that could be used in the bath, Germany, C19.

googlie eyes Eyes that can be moved, e.g. by means of a string in the back of the head. From first years of C20.

gutta-percha Not to be confused with rubber, but similar to it, a synthetic substance used for making dolls in 2nd half C19.

intaglio eyes Eyes modelled by incising into the bisque.

marotte Type of **poupard** that plays a tune when spun round.

open-closed mouth Doll's mouth modelled in such a way as to appear open.

paperweight eyes Glass eyes coloured through using the same technique as for marbles or paperweights.

parian Stoneware developed in C19 and good for modelling e.g. dolls' heads; loosely, any bisque doll that is not painted.

Parisienne French doll, made from 1860s to 1880s by makers such as Jumeau or Rohmer, having a bisque head and usually a kid-leather body.

pate Crown of a doll's head, beneath the wig if it has one. Can be made in a variety of materials and means, depending on the maker. In better dolls, usually of cork.

portrait doll Doll modelled to represent somebody well known.

poupard Doll without a lower body but set instead on a stick, which is usually covered by the doll's clothes.

poured wax Dolls moulded in wax.

Pouty Character doll with a pouting expression, of which Kammer and Reinhardt's model 117 is a famous example.

printed doll Rag doll with fabric covering on which facial and body features were printed.

Queen Anne doll Carved and jointed wooden doll of fixed facial type made in C18.

rooted hair Hair not moulded, but in tufts, in the wax scalp.

shoulder head Doll's head made in one piece with neck and collar, and inserted into body.

stump doll Doll made of a single piece of wood, without joints.

three-faced Like a **two-faced** doll, but with three. A speciality of Carl Bergner.

turnabout Rag doll with two different faces, one of which would, at any one time, be covered by a bonnet.

turnover doll Rag doll made with two different heads, one of which would be covered by the reversible skirt.

two-faced Doll with a revolving head, able to show a choice of two faces.

voice box Device by which the doll can talk, cry, etc.

waxed Composition doll dipped in wax to give a surface finish.

Doll Makers

By the beginning of this century there were in excess of 1,500 active doll manufacturers in Europe alone. However, only a relatively small number of these are important from the collector's viewpoint. The following list includes the majority of those whose products are particularly sought after and which normally realize good prices.

Adam Sisters American makers, based in New York, of the "Columbian" and other rag dolls.

Baehr & Proeschild German makers of bisque dolls active from late C19 to 1930.

Alt, Beck & Gottschalk German maker, active from 1854. Known for bisque dolls' heads. Monogram mark.

Bergner, Carl German maker, active at Sonneberg 1890–1909, known for two- and three-faced dolls.

Bing Artists' Dolls Based in Nuremberg, Germany, they specialized in "art" and character dolls after First World War.

Bru & Cie French maker, active 1866–99, the leading manufacturer of the time. Factory produced a great variety of dolls in various materials, taking great pride in their fashionable costumes; also a range of special dolls, e.g. "Le Dormeur". Maker's mark is "Bru" or a circle round a dot, incised.

BRU J^{NE}R

Chad Valley Co. English manufacturer of rag dolls, active from 1897.

Dean's Rag Book Co. English maker of printed rag dolls.

Dorst, Julius German maker (Sonneburg) of wooden dolls, active from 1865 to early C20.

Dressel, Cuno & Otto Long established German firm. Their dolls sometimes have distinctive red waxed booties. Produced waxed as well as composition, bisque and celluloid dolls.

Jutta
1914.

Ellis, Joel American maker from Springfield, Vermont, who patented a jointed wooden doll in 1873.

Fleischmann, Adolf German maker specializing in papier mâché dolls from mid C19 to 1930.

Gaultier Parisian porcelain factory producing bisque dolls C19/early C20.

Greiner American maker of very collectable bisque dolls active in Philadelphia mid C19. Maker's mark: "Greiner".

Handwerck, Heinrich German maker of bisque dolls, active late C19/early C20.

Heubach German manufacturer, active 1820–63 (Gebrüder Heubach) and again from 1887 until after 1920 (Ernst Heubach). Noted for finely modelled bisque heads, and specialized in character dolls. The bodies are fabric or composition and the clothes usually attached.

Johnson, Mason & Taylor American rag doll makers, C19.

Jumeau, Pierre François Prolific French maker, active 1842–99. Known for "Parisiennes" and a distinctive Jumeau expression. Maker's mark varies: "Breveté SGDG Jumeau"; "Tête Jumeau"; "Medaille d'Or" (referring to gold medal won at 1878 Exhibition); "Bébé Jumeau"; "DEP" (indicates later date); "1907" (ditto).

BÉBÉ JUMEAU

Kammer & Reinhardt German maker, active from 1886 into C20. Known particularly for character dolls, introduced in 1909. Maker's mark: "K & R".

Kestner, J.D. German maker, active from early C19 to early C20. Dolls of high quality but limited range, bisque-headed. Some stamped "Gibson Girl" on chest. Maker's mark is "JDK" with a number, or simply a number.

J.D.K

Kley & Hahn German maker known for bisque dolls, early C20.

Kling, C.F. Long-established German company producing glazed porcelain dolls from mid C19.

Kruse, Käthe German maker, active from 1912 at Bad Kosen, near Nuremberg. Her aim was to create imitation babies, that were "art" dolls not character dolls. Some were even filled with sand to simulate a baby's actual weight. Maker's mark: "Kruse" and a number on the sole of the left foot.

Lenci Italian maker, active in Turin after World War II, making pressed felt dolls. Characteristically the eyes are giving a sideways glance. Maker's mark on sole of left foot.

Lowenthal & Co. German makers of papier mâché and other dolls, C19.

Marseille, Armand German maker, active from 1865 till after 1920. Known mainly for bisque heads, but also made composition heads. Prolific.

A.M.

Montanari, Augusta & Richard London makers of poured wax dolls, mid C19.

Müller & Strassberger, German makers, particularly of papier mâché dolls, C19.

Peck, Mrs Lucy English maker of poured wax dolls, active 1891–1921.

Petzold, Dr. Dora Berlin maker specializing in character dolls 1919–1930.

Pierotti Family London based family business producing wax dolls through C19 and into C20.

Putnam, Grace Storey American maker famous for her "Bye-Lo Baby" doll early in C20.

Robery & Delphieu French makers of "bébé" dolls, later C19/early C20.

Rohmer French maker, active 1857–80, known for "Parisiennes". Maker's mark:

"Mme Rohmer. Breveté SGDG Paris".

Samhammer, Philip, German maker of wax dolls, late C19/early C20. No known mark.

Schilling, Barbara & Ferdinand Max Produced papier mâché and wax dolls in Germany, late C19/early C20.

Schmidt, Bruno German maker, active at Walterhausen 1900–1925, known for character dolls in a variety of materials. Maker's mark: "BSW" and a number.

Schoenau & Hoffmeister German maker, active from 1901. Quality variable. Maker's mark: "SPBH", the PB being set in a star.

Schoenhut Co. Philadelphia company who produced a popular series of wooden dolls with spring-jointed limbs, early C20.

SFBJ Stands for "Société de Fabrication de Bébés et Jouets". Founded in 1899, merging Jumeau, Bru and others. Thus a wide variety of wares. This led to a decline in quality. Marked "SFBJ", often also "Paris", and a number ("60" is common).

Simon & Halbig German maker, active at Grofenhain and Ohrdruf from 1870 into C20. A general porcelain manufacturer, supplying dolls' heads to the industry. Usually very good quality bisque and fine, soft modelling. Maker's mark: "Simon & Halbig" or "S & H", with a number.

Steiff, Margarete German maker, active 1877 to the present. Known for soft toys and fabric dolls, and particularly for dolls in uniform and teddy bears. Maker's mark: Steiff button in left ear.

Steiner, Hermann German maker, active in Sonneberg 1921–25. Known for character dolls.

Steiner, Jules Nicholas French maker, active 1855–91. Steiner experimented with moving parts – clockwork walking dolls, dolls that raised their arms while crying, etc.

Walker, Izannah Generally accepted as the lady who produced the first rag dolls in America. Based in Rhode Island, she patented her method in 1873.

What you should know about:
Dolls and Toys

Dolls

* Most collectors are interested in dolls made before World War I. Original condition is important. Clothes should be retained even if shabby, and dolls should never be repainted.

* Early papier mâché dolls attached to a fabric body were made 1800–50, sometimes dipped in wax before painting. Most were made in Germany but American dolls are keenly collected, especially those which reflect contemporary dress taste.

* The realism of wax dolls with human hair, made in England from 1850 to 1900, is prized, particularly the work of Charles Marsh and the Montanari and Pierotti families.

* Bisque head dolls with swivelling heads and glass eyes, made from 1855, are collectable and often marked with the factory name. Look for the products of Bru, Steiner, Jumeau, Greiner, Simon & Halbig, Armaud Marseille and Gebruder Heubach.

* The same factories produced glazed porcelain head dolls from 1850. The emphasis changed from adult dolls to baby dolls after 1875. Automata are particularly valuable. Some have porcelain marks which aid dating.

* Character dolls, copied from live models, were produced in large quantity but only limited numbers from each mould. Many have makers' marks and mould numbers. Particularly valuable are early Kämmer and Reinhardt models, especially model 117, and any doll with pouting features.

* Teddy bears have become collectable recently, particularly early German Steiff versions with working growl.

Beware

* Reproductions abound, particularly of dolls. Hair and clothing styles are important clues to period and no doll with machine stitched clothes can be earlier than the sewing machine (invented 1850). Another "giveaway" is nylon hair which indicates a modern copy.

* Trademarks are no guarantee of authenticity. The best test is side-by-side comparison with a known original.

Toys

* Collectors look for pieces in good condition, not excessively battered or worn.

* Repainting destroys the investment value.

* Items of social or historical interest attract the keenest prices, especially in their original packaging; examples include toy theatres, farms, dollshouses, shop sets, factories and fire stations, trams, ships, cars and soldiers.

* Toys with a history linking them to an owner, particularly the aristocratic or famous, are much sought after.

* Toys with working and moving parts, including clockwork, are popular; particularly those made between 1870 and 1914 in the factories of Bing, Märklin, Lehmann and Carette in Germany, Martin and Rossignol in France, Bassett-Lowke in the UK and Ives in the USA.

* Trains were at first crude, powered by clockwork or steam, but by 1920 were accurate scale models of the real thing. Collectors look for early Märklin, Bing and Hornby models.

* The taste for cast iron money boxes with mechanical parts worked by a coin has spread beyond the USA. Crudely painted, poorly finished fakes are now found, indicating that rare examples are in demand.

* Early diecast lead soldiers were flat or semi-flat until the Britain's hollow-cast technique led to a wider range of more realistic figures from 1900. Examples with oval bases and paper labels in their original box fetch the best prices and soldiers are still the most desirable items for collectors, though farm animals are gaining in popularity.

* Interest is gaining progressively in wooden toys, especially Victorian games, early jigsaws, maps of the children of the world, C19 Noah's arks and novelty balls made of interlocking parts.

* Rocking horses are very popular. Early home-made C19 American horses fetch best prices but even commercially-made Victorian models are a good buy. It is worth comparing prices of modern craftsman-made pieces.

OTHER COLLECTABLES

It is probably true to say that there is nothing that has been produced by man in his long history that is not collected by someone, somewhere. From buttons to buses, each theme has its devoted enthusiasts. Even the original London Bridge was bought and re-erected block by block in the United States. Some themes (like bridges!) are minority interests, while others are collected by many thousands of people world-wide. We have already covered the great antiques collecting subjects in these pages, and it therefore seems appropriate to conclude with concise pointers on the other most popular areas for seekers after bygones and other collectables. These are useful and practical hints to have ready at hand, but remember that almost without exception, each theme has a range of specialist books available for further reading.

Antiquities

* Objects made before AD600 in Europe, and pre-Columbian in America, are generally classed as antiquities.
* Most countries have strict laws governing the excavation and export of antiquities. Objects legitimately on the market come from collections formed in the C18 and C19. Nevertheless there is much robbed material on the market, particularly Chinese bronzes, Etruscan and Roman ceramics and pre-Columbian artefacts.
* Only buy well documented pieces from reputable dealers, with an export licence and museum certificate of authenticity. If in doubt seek museum assistance.
* Collectors tend to specialize by period or type and are usually very knowledgeable about their subject. They will pay good prices for rare pieces, or works of artistic merit, even if in fragmentary condition. *Vice versa*, the commoner an object is, the more condition is important. Antiquities are fragile and susceptible to corrosion; in particular, bronze infected by verdigris (bright green encrustation) should be avoided; conservation is expensive, and the corrosion may have destroyed valuable detail. Cleaning of any antiquity should be undertaken by experts.
* Watch out for forgeries. Particulary common are imitations of ancient glass, made in Israel, Turkey and Egypt, Roman coins from North Africa, erotic Samian ware bowls and lamps made in Southern Italy. They are difficult to detect so take expert advice.
* Marriages are also quite common; genuine ancient glass or ceramic fragments are made up into vessels, but rarely to a known and recorded shape.
* Reproductions also confuse the collector. Unscrupulous dealers will pass off pieces made for museum shops as genuine. Look for makers' marks. The Köln Ehrenfield glass works produced reproductions of ancient types from 1879. Usually flawless, they are collectable in their own right.
* Provided these caveats are borne in mind, antiquities represent an under-valued sector of the market; fine objects can be bought inexpensively and are likely to appreciate.

Jewellery

* Pre World War II jewellery is now so popular that many inexpensive modern copies are manufactured. To avoid mistakes it is vital to learn how to recognize the stones, stringing and setting methods appropriate to the period.
* Value depends on age and condition, the intrinsic value of the materials, and current fashions. Unique or handmade pieces generally fetch more than mass-produced, and a famous previous owner can affect the value considerably.
* Gold, silver and platinum are usually marked, which aids authentication. The scrap value of the metal content is a guide to the premium being asked for the artistic worth.
* Diamond jewellery has an intrinsic as well as antique

value. Do not rely solely on the glass-scratch test for diamonds, since there are other less valuable stones which will produce a similar effect. Good-sized diamonds fetch more than small ones or off-cuts, and the "brilliant cut" is preferred to "rose cut" which has fewer facets.

* The value of cameos depends on the material and the skill of the carving. Cameos of semi-precious stone are worth considerably more than shell cameos which were produced by the million.

* Necklaces of strung coral are still fairly common; prices depend on colour which in turn depends on fast-changing fashions, but generally reds and pinks are preferred to white, black or orange. Coral cameos are particularly desirable.

* Jet was used for jewellery from 1880, but demand exploded when Queen Victoria made mourning jewellery fashionable. Glass, enamel and onyx were also used. Morbid associations limit the appeal, but early hand-carved pieces and brooches with a glass-covered locket in the reverse are collectable.

Netsuke

* Netsuke are Japanese carved toggles, originally made to secure a portable medicine box (*inro*) or similar item, which hung from the waist on a cord. Usually made of wood or ivory, they date from about C16.

Ivory netsuke, c1880

* There is keen competition for signed netsuke by acknowledged masters of the art, as well as for those depicting rare or novel subjects. Otherwise, charming netsuke can be collected fairly

inexpensively, but avoid incompetent workmanship, dull subjects, damaged pieces or early C20 copies. The best pieces are hand-carved.

* Ivory is not necessarily more valuable than wood, especially since ivory netsuke were mass-produced for export in the late C19. However, inlaid netsuke often command a premium.

* Copies and fakes are numerous. Some are genuine period ornaments (*okimono*), converted to netsuke by boring a cord hole. In genuine netsuke, the hole is designed to be almost invisible; in fakes the holes are often clumsily obtrusive.

* Recent copies lack patina. The grain in genuine ivory is only visible at certain angles, whereas simulated ivory grain is always visible and very regular. Signatures on fakes are often moulded, not carved.

Bottles

* Until c1870 heavy taxation on glass made bottles expensive, and many owners had them personalized by the application of an embossed seal.

C17 wine bottle with seal

* The very earliest bottles (pre-1650) are very rare and expensive, and in general the older a bottle, the higher the value. Those with seals fetch at least twice as much as those without, and the more detailed the seal, especially if it includes a date, the greater the value.

* In commercial bottles collectors are concerned with rarity of shape and colour, and the interest of the name, label or trademark.

* Bottles for gaseous liquids, complete with their marble, cork, plunger or stopper, fetch

the best prices, followed by those with humorous pictorial embossing.

* Only collect bottles in perfect condition – even a slight chip reduces the value. The grey or white film, or iridescence characteristic of a bottle that has been buried for a long time cannot be removed and, except in the case of very rare early pieces, destroys the value.

Scent bottles

* Scent bottles display every technique of the glass maker's art and are collected for their novel shapes, colours and decoration. Even some commercial bottles have a value.

* The best buys are C18 bottles of coloured glass, decorated with gilt and enamel with silver or gold caps; later C18 James Giles bottles, faceted and gilded on opaque white glass; and Art Deco bottles designed by Daum, Gallé and Lalique.

* Porcelain bottles made at Chelsea, Bow and Worcester in the late C18 are also popular and are often modelled in the shape of human or animal figures; particularly collectable are the bottles from the "Girl in a Swing" factory. Large numbers of C19 forgeries exist which are hard to distinguish from the originals. Seek a guarantee of authenticity.

* Bottles must be in perfect condition, with caps or stoppers complete, to command good prices (except for very rare items).

Potlids

* The perfecting of colour printing on ceramics, c1840, led to the fashion for making pictorial lids. These were originally found on small pots made to contain ointments, cosmetics or meat pastes.

* More than 300 designs were produced between 1840 and 1900. All are well documented.

* The best lids are the early flat tops (1845–60) and convex tops (1860–75). Later lids have weaker colours and heavy texture. Post 1900 reissues can usually be detected by the lack of crazing.

* Lids made by the firm of Felix Pratt, especially those signed by engraver Jesse Austin, are particularly collectable.

* Avoid lids with poor colour and bad registration, where successive layers of colour do not precisely overlie each other. Damage and restoration devalues even rare pieces.

Boxes

* Small enamelled boxes were made in England from 1750 to 1840. Battersea boxes are considered best for their rich colour and fine line. Late C18 are much more valuable than C19 boxes which were mass produced as cheap trinkets.

* Boxes with all-over decoration, erotic scenes on the inside lid, snuff boxes with spoons set in the lid, and Bilston boxes in the shape of animals, birds and heads all command a premium.

* Samson forgeries made in Paris from 1860 have a value if marked with an S monogram. Modern copies are detectable by the screening dots visible under a glass.

* Silver snuff boxes command higher prices than those of wood, porcelain or horn. Otherwise higher prices are paid for larger boxes, 5–6 in (12.5–15 cm) long, interesting decoration, well known makers (e.g. Nathaniel Mills, William Eley, Edward Edwards) and pristine condition.

* Snuff boxes with erased or re-engraved inscriptions are considered damaged and less valuable. Vice versa, the inscription of a well-known person or one which connects the piece to an historic incident adds a premium.

* Vesta boxes took over from the tinder box with the invention of the wax match, c1830. Most collectable are silver boxes with gilded interior and intact interior springs. Boxes with assay marks of Chester, London and offices other than Birmingham are more desirable.

* Pre-1850 card cases of silver are much more valuable than later cases of other materials. Except for early filigree, cases are marked, and Birmingham silversmiths are most collectable. Many have repoussé pictures of famous landmarks, particularly castles and value depends on the rarity of the scene. The slightest damage halves the value.

* C18 silver tea caddies are the most sought after. Single caddies are valuable, but pairs

or sets of three command a high premium, higher still if complete with original tea-chest to house the caddies.

* Good decoration, armorials and the mark of a leading silversmith all contribute to value.
* Of the later caddies, look for C18 Sheffield plate, sets of opaque-white glass with enamelled decoration which includes the name of the tea, and metal lined wood caddies decorated with marquetry, boulle or needlework.
* Caddies in the shape of apples and pears are also popular, but copies exist. Original C18 caddies are of beech, fruitwood, box or walnut with brass or silver locks and hinges and foil lining.
Copies are of white wood with steel or tableware hinges.

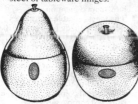

Pear- and apple-shaped fruitwood tea caddies, both early C19

Papier Mâché

* A light, cheap substitute for wood, usually used for small tables, writing cases, desks, trays and boxes. Usually has very elaborate decoration of flowers, birds and rural scenes, embellished with mother of pearl, polished after painting or japanning. Wine coasters and trays are particularly desirable.
* More restrained, pre-1840 pieces, especially furniture, are worth more than later pieces.
* Some pieces are marked with manufacturer's name, and others have the distinctive style of collectable artists. Names to look for are Henry Clay, Jennens & Bettridge, Spiers of Oxford and B. Walton & Co, and the work of artists Edwin Haseler (flowers) and Frederick Newman (peacocks).
* Chinoiserie subjects are common, often crude, and not popular. Equally, mother of pearl inlay is only valued if restrained and illustrates an identifiable topographical scene.

* Avoid damaged pieces which are plentiful.

Sewing Antiques

* Lace bobbins have colourful names, many distinctive types and a wide range of decoration, which makes collecting them all the more fascinating.
* The commonest type of bobbin has a spangle at the base, usually of nine glass beads threaded on brass wire. Price depends on the quality of the beads, particularly the larger central one. The value is enhanced if the spangle includes coins, medals, unusual buttons or carved shell.
* Inscriptions on the shaft add human interest and value: look especially for dates, name of the owner and village, records of a betrothal, marriage, birth or death, cryptograms and political slogans. Best of all are bobbins inscribed with the name and execution date of a murderer by a relative of the victim.
* Hollow bobbins which contain miniature bobbins, balls, or "church window" apertures are more valuable than plain. A complete set of bobbins with one to six pewter rings named after Henry VIII's wives are keenly sought.
* Damage decreases value, although C19 hybrid bobbins spliced or dowelled from different parts, are collectable.
* As a general rule, the price of thimbles reflects the intrinsic value of the material and the fineness of the decoration. Gold thimbles are rare and even plain examples are costly. Silver thimbles are next in value, followed by the base metals. Hand-painted enamel and porcelain have a high value for their rarity, whereas prices for other materials, such as ivory, tortoiseshell, mother of pearl and glass depend upon the fineness and quality.
* Flowers and scenery were the commonest form of decoration on silver; lesser value thimbles have the name of a town inscribed round the base, or a crude picture; intricate, skilfully modelled scenes attract higher prices. Thimbles celebrating important royal or national events are highly prized.
* Trade marks and advertising slogans can increase the value of base metal thimbles, but most

sought-after are patented types:
the Dorcas ventilated thimble,
the non-slip, and those with a
needle-threader or cutter
attached.
* Thimble cases collected in their
own right are worth more with
the original thimble inside.
Look especially for pre-1850
silver, gold, enamel, hardwood
and leather examples and for
cases with needle
compartments and novel shapes.
* Beware of modern silver
thimbles which lack patina but
resemble C18 and C19
originals.

Scientific instruments
* The very finest and earliest
instruments are now so rare that
anything offered as pre-C18
should be treated with caution
especially if cheap.
* Copies of notable instruments
have been made for a variety of
reasons, legitimate and
otherwise, from the C19, and
some are valuable in their own
right. Beware, though, the
modern fake which is described
as a C19 copy.
* Genuine period instruments
exist in sufficient quantity to
enable a collection to be made.
Pieces by renowned makers are
very expensive, but competent
instruments made by
anonymous craftsmen still have
investment potential.
* As a rule value depends on age,
materials used, decorative
features, quality of
workmanship and condition.
Restoration should ideally be
done so that the repair can be
seen; though complete and
perfect working instruments
fetch more, there is a ready
market for skilled restorations.
Patina should never be
removed.
* Armillary spheres demonstrate
the movement of the planets in
the solar system. Pre-
Copernican examples, with the
earth in the centre, are virtually
all recent copies. C18 examples
are most in demand, whilst
clockwork versions (orreries) are
worth many times more than
hand-turned.
* Michael Butterfield, the
original maker of Butterfield
pocket sundials, died in 1724,
but the name lives on, engraved
on innumerable C18 and C19
versions. Originals are very rare.
The most desirable copies have
a silver octagonal base plate and

Armillary sphere

bird-shaped gnomon.
* The most valuable compasses
were those made between 1670
and 1800, of gold, silver, gilt
and ivory. The best examples
are finely engraved with the
latitudes of important cities on
the lid. Less decorative
compasses of the period 1800–
1900, liquid compasses, and the
later card compass can be
bought inexpensively and are
likely to appreciate.
* Pre-1745 microscopes are rare
and require expert appraisal
before buying. After that date
microscopes began to be made
in quantity, brass mounted on a
box base with accessory drawer.
Makers of note are Cuff,
Adams, Martin, Dollond and
Cary. The Culpeper-type with
characteristic S-shaped legs is
also valuable. C19 compound
and binocular microscopes were
a great technical improvement
on their predecessors. The
finest examples were made by
Abrahams, Aransberg, Beck,
Lealand, Powell, Ross, Leitz
and Zeiss. Cased models with
complete accessories fetch the
most.
* Apothecaries' scales can
generally be dated by
inspector's marks and royal
cipher on the weights.
Manufacturer's marks are also
commonly found on the
weights. The earlier the date,
the better the value, but only
pre-1720 complete sets with
drawers for the weights fetch
the high prices.
* The octant (one-eighth of a

circle), invented by Hadley in 1731, was followed by the sextant (one-sixth of a circle), invented by Campbell in 1757. Both measure angular distance and continued to be made until 1920. Early examples in wood are now very rare. Brass was commoner after 1780, and the most valuable examples have engraving of a maritime theme. Ivory, ebony, silver and platinum parts also add value. Good names are Cary, Troughton, Berge and Bardin.

* Precision theodolites for measuring height and orientation were made from 1730. Pre-1840 versions by leading instrument makers, such as the Troughton brothers and William Simms, command a premium over more utilitarian, but more accurate, later models.

* The early telescopes developed between 1605 and 1760 are too rare to be found outside museums. From 1758 on, John Dollond's achromatic lenses cured many earlier problems and led to many more telescopes being made; hand-made C18 examples of mahogany and brass have greatest appeal to collectors. Large floor models on cabriole legs are priced higher than hand-held or table top versions. Decoration and famous names (Dollond, Bradley, Molyneaux, Scarlet, Hearn) add value. Machine produced C19 and C20 telescopes are inexpensive, unless they have regimental insignia or an owner's name. Avoid any telescope with damaged lenses or dented cases.

* Waywisers for measuring distance were used from the late C17, and many were made for the Post Office pre-1840 when charges related to distance rather than weight. The names of makers Heath and Wing, or Fraser and Cole, engraved on the dial, or GPO insignia, add to the value.

Medical instruments

* The value of sterilization, discovered by Lister in 1872, spelt an end to instruments which could not be boiled, so most collectors are interested in the ivory or wood-handled instruments of the C18 and early C19.

* Complete sets of bleeding knives and surgical instruments in their original cases fetch the best prices.

* Other collectable instruments include scarifiers, stethoscopes, trephines, instructional aids, douches, artificial limbs and even false teeth, provided they are unusual, an early example, or made of fine materials such as silver or ivory.

* Medicine chests with complete and labelled contents, spoons and balances are worthwhile collecting, and a special compartment for poisons adds value.

* Apothecary jars with blue decoration on white background can be dated by the design around the cartouche. Angel designs were common from 1650 to 1700, birds from 1700 to 1780, and cherubs thereafter. All early examples are collectable.

Cameras and photographs

* The earliest cameras available to collectors, and the most valuable, are the wet plate cameras of 1840–80; these have a silver wire inside the plate carrier which dry plate cameras do not. Manufacturers' names and patent numbers are a clue to date. These cameras are admired for their craftsmanship, so all-wood cameras of two

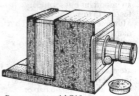

Box camera, mid C19

concentric sliding boxes are more desirable than the rarer bellows versions.

* George Eastman's invention of the dry plate in 1879 led to the popularity and mass production of cameras, though again collectors are more attracted to quality of workmanship and materials than technical features: handmade mahogany and brass pieces are the most desirable.

* The more functional roll cameras of 1888 to 1920 lack the aesthetic appeal of contemporary plate cameras, but fetch reasonable prices in good condition.

* 1920–40 was the period of greatest technical innovation, when technical features were quickly superseded. Collectors go for cameras which represent milestones along the way, regardless of aesthetic considerations. There is much interest in early Leica, Zeiss, Contax and Rollei models.
* By extension, the first examples of post-war innovations in camera technology should be of interest to collectors in the future.
* Old negatives and photographs are increasingly collectable. Prior to 1870 the main interest is in their technical, rather than artistic, merit. Thereafter, the subject, photographer and aesthetic merits are paramount. Caution is required, however, when faced with an attribution to a famous photographer which cannot be proved. Many fakes are now known. Pictures of famous subjects are collectable, but the price should reflect the quantity of prints in circulation and the age of the print; new prints from old negatives command less interest.

Musical boxes, phonographs and gramophones

* Musical boxes must be in working order to achieve good prices. Decorative features are an important but secondary feature to this basic rule. Movements can be repaired but damage to the comb or cylinders cannot, and seriously affects value.
* After 1875 most musical boxes are mass-produced and of inferior quality. Earlier pieces with a wooden inlaid flap or glass top are most in demand, but later handmade boxes, particularly those with a set of four or six interchangeable cylinders compare in value.
* Rare types with special effects or features which improve the quality of the sound, are highly prized, particularly Overture, Forte piano, Mandoline and Orchestra boxes.
* Disc boxes were popular, especially in America from 1885 until superseded by the phonograph. The Symphonion and Polyphon were marketed in Europe, the Regina in America. Collectors go for rarity, technical innovation and the availability of discs for playing on that model. Examples of

innovations that attract high prices are coin-operated boxes, multiple disc players, automatic disc changers and orchestrations with percussion and bells.
* Edison patented the phonograph in 1877 in America, while in a separate development, Emile Berliner patented the gramophone in Europe in 1887. The chief difference is that phonographs play cylinders and gramophones play discs.

Edison phonograph

* Both developed rapidly over the next three decades and successive innovations can be dated accurately by the patent number.
* All early models are of interest to collectors, particularly those with finely decorated cabinets and shapely horns. For this reason prices fall substantially for the post 1920 models.

Typewriters

* Patents were taken out on typewriters as early as 1828 in America, but Remington made the first commercially successful machine in 1873. As soon as the office potential was realized, demand soared and hundreds of manufacturers filed patents after 1890.
* Collectors look for pioneering machines which represent a stage in the development of typewriters, and rare pre-1900 models. Post 1914 machines hold little interest for collectors.
* Patent numbers are a useful guide to date; most machines were produced within three years of the patent being filed.
* Early manufacturers of note include Fitch, Yost, New Century, Williams, Empire Fay-Sho, Oliver, Crandall and Blick.

Late C19 typewriter

* Condition is paramount in assessing value, and a perfect machine, with contemporary ribbon, undamaged transfer motifs, gilding, enamelling and paintwork sells for much more than a damaged or restored item. Accessories such as instruction manual and carrying case, add further value. Avoid machines with defective nickelling to the metal parts which is expensive to repair or restore.

Pop ephemera

* There are few hard and fast rules to guide collectors of pop ephemera and it is a market in which prices fluctuate wildly.
* Best prices are reserved for ephemera connected with the giants of the pop world whose work is acknowledged to have been lasting and influential: Bill Haley, Elvis Presley, Jimmy Hendrix and the Beatles are obvious examples.
* Some knowledge of the rarity of a piece of ephemera is essential to avoid expensive mistakes. Unique items, such as the original artwork for a famous album cover, demonstration records and tapes, and musical instruments fetch more than relatively common autographs, posters and magazines.
* Other items of value include objects which predate the pop musician's achievement of fame, personal possessions, and objects connected with significant events in the artist's career.
* Significantly higher prices are achieved for the ephemera of artists who are no longer alive, partly because of the "legendary" characteristics they acquire and partly because this limits the amount of ephemera which is in circulation.
* Perhaps the best rule in such an uncertain market is to collect for personal pleasure rather than potential investment.

Posters

* Virtually any poster that dates from before World War II has a value, but the precise value depends on many factors including artistic value, a famous designer, humour, social historical value, or the fact that a poster has had a significant impact on advertising styles.
* Very high prices are achieved by the posters of Alphonse Mucha whose work epitomized the Art Nouveau style, but works by lesser known and anonymous artists working in the same idiom are eminently collectable.
* Transport posters are a rich field for the collector, since shipping and railway companies, motor manufacturers and petrol companies all commissioned work of high artistic merit to promote their names. The value of a poster is increased if it has subsequently become famous through reproductions.
* Posters advertising products which have become household names and whose slogans have become part of the language are highly valued.
* War recruitment posters include the most famous of them all, James Montgomery Flagg's finger-pointing Uncle Sam which Orwell used to sinister effect in his book *1984*. Some collectors specialize in derivatives of this theme.

* The effect of damage on poster prices depends on the rarity value; a common poster needs to be in pristine condition to achieve the best price and even creasing has an adverse effect.

Cigarette Cards

* For collectors, the golden age of cigarette cards begins with colour printing in 1885 and ends around 1918. After that date, cards were printed in such quantity as to have little value.
* Between 1885 and 1902 numerous small tobacco companies issued cards which are keenly collected for their rarity: MacDonald, Alberge and Bromet, Taddy and Ainsworth are among the most valuable.
* Certain pre-1902 subjects are particularly popular: monarchs, sporting figures, military heroes (particularly Boer War), ships and contemporary celebrities. Sets command a small premium, but since collectors enjoy building up their own sets, a rare individual card in good condition can have significant value.
* Cards became an important component in the battle for markets between 1902 to 1918 and technically accomplished cards, with good colour and gilding, were produced as customer loyalty incentives. The first cards were produced by Ogden's, Wills, Carreras, Gallahers, Churchman and Players.
* Some cards of the period 1918 to 1940 are sought after because they refer to contemporary events or fashions. Of these, Edward VIII coronation cards and portraits of 1920's/30's beauties and actresses are most collectable.
* Albums were introduced c1930 and album sets fetch a small premium if in mint condition.
* After 1945 trade cards were occasionally revived, notably by tea companies, but collectors have so far shown little interest in this period.

Postcards

* The buoyancy of postcard prices is stimulated by the very diverse interests of collectors. Some collect cards which illustrate developments in postal history, others specialize by subject. However, in collecting for investment it is better to study the demand for a particular category rather than trying to cover the whole range.
* C19 cards are more valuable than C20 as a rule, and used cards are preferred because the postmark is a guarantee of date and authenticity.
* Continental souvenir cards of the 1880's and 90's and "patriotics" of the Franco-Prussian war are keenly sought by collectors of early cards. They also value cards which illustrate changes in postal regulations, such as imprinted stamps and those which restrict messages to the front.
* Cards published for national events (exhibitions, jubilees, coronations) with a commemorative postmark, sell for a premium.
* Postcards of the period 1900 to 1940 are extremely numerous and value depends on subject, artist and condition, though gimmick cards, cards of unusual materials and album sets consistently perform best.
* Patriotic, propagandist and satirical cards are an important category. First World War cards are more valuable if posted from the front and bear censor's or Field Post marks. Irish Home Rule and Easter Rising cards, and Nazi, Communist and Fascist cards of the 1930's find a ready market.
* Cards signed by artists achieve high prices. Key names are: Mucha, Kirchner, Wain, Thackeray, Browne, May, Hassall, Hardy, Payne and McGill.
* In general, social historical subjects, transport, and ethnographical subjects, and cards illustrating coins, flags and heraldry are more keenly collected than architecture, scenery and portraits.
* An interesting collecting area is post cards depicting your own town or area. These can often be purchased cheaply.
* Unusual postmarks can enhance the value of a card, particularly commemorative marks, early machine franking, and postmarks from remote places.

Costume

* Costume prices are generally a reflection of rarity. Pre-1830 costume is scarce, 1830 to 1900 garments are more numerous, whilst early C20 clothing is still relatively common. Within these period divisions, value is related to condition, quality, decoration and colour, though a famous former owner, or a desirable couturier's label can lift the value considerably.
* Condition is critical since stitching, fastening and

laundering details are an important part of the appeal to collectors. Beware of areas that have obviously been treated, cleaned or repaired, in case important evidence has been lost. Ancient repairs and alterations, however, can add interest to a piece.

* Elaborately trimmed, decorated or embroidered pieces have a particular appeal to collectors. For this reason, floral embroidered waistcoats, evening gowns, christening robes and country smocks are all popular.

* Black is an unpopular colour, and the large quantity of C19 mourning garments rarely fetch as much as equivalent items in other colours. Colour should be bright, consistent and not faded by sunlight.

* Couturiers began labelling their work around 1861; but labels were frequently removed. Collectors are always on the look out for unlabelled garments whose worth may have gone unrecognized.

* Many dresses were designed as an ensemble with matching accessories. Shoes, veils, hats, handbags, gloves, stockings, prayer books to accompany dress, all add value.

* Prices can be good for apparently insignificant garments if there is a keen specialist market; examples include garters, corsets, underwear, nightdresses and servants' clothing, as well as theatrical costume and fancy dress.

Goss and crested ware

* In 1887 Adolphus Goss obtained permission to reproduce city and borough coats of arms on porcelain miniatures, sold as souvenirs. They proved so popular that china producers all over the world followed his example. Strictly, "Goss" refers to objects produced at the Falcon pottery and bearing the Goss mark; all other pieces are known as crested ware.

* Genuine Goss is of higher quality than rival products, noted for the accuracy of hand-painted armorials, brilliance of colour, and quality of the parian body, developed by the pottery's founder, William Goss.

* Products made 1888–1914,

marked W.H.Goss with the falcon emblem, are considered the best. Miniature buildings, Roman urns and royal event souvenirs are especially popular.

* During 1914–1920 military shapes were produced in quantity. Ships and despatch riders are scarce, and objects inscribed with a battle date are worth most.

* Later pieces marked "W.H.Goss England" were produced after Cauldon Potteries took over the Goss firm, and are of much lower value.

* Other crested wares sell for half the price of comparable Goss wares. Rare shapes and commemorative pieces are most in demand, but theme collecting is popular.

* Only perfect pieces command top prices. Firing flaws are common and can be ignored but cracks, chips, faded colours and worn gilt reduce the value by half or more.

Fairings

* Fairings were sold at resorts and fairgrounds between 1860 and 1914. Those with solid bases, from the Conta and Boehme factory in Saxony, are collectable; later hollow-based imitations are not.

* The unmarked, earliest fairings are the most valuable, because the detailing is crisper. Later fairings have softened-out lines due to mould wear, and can be dated by the incised serial number (1865–80), impressed arm, dagger and shield mark plus serial number (1880–91) and "Made in Germany" mark (1891–1900).

* Fairings on the theme of marriage are commonest and least valuable. Bicycling and political subjects are rarer and more valuable. Mistakes in assembling the parts of a fairing can enhance the value, particularly when a part has been transposed from a different subject.

Wemyss ware

* The distinctive style of Wemyss ware – reminiscent of majolica and enamel work – derives from the influence of continental artists working in the Fife pottery in the 1880s. Karel Nekola became the leading artist until his death in 1915.

The moulds were sold to the Bovey Tracy pottery in 1930 and Karel's son, Joseph, perpetuated the style until his death in 1952.

* The fragility of Wemyss ware, and its popularity for nursery use, accounts for the relative rarity of pieces in good condition and the high prices paid for pristine examples. Even chipped pieces sell well, but cracks affect price.

* Otherwise, the artistic quality is the paramount influence on price. Large pieces by Karel Nekola, early pieces with a red border, rare shapes such as cats and carps and unusual subjects – nasturtiums, gorse, flamingoes – all attract collectors' interest.

* Late pieces are less desirable, but the quality of Joseph Nekola's work ensures keen interest in pieces from the Bovey Tracy period.

Beware _____
* Unmarked pieces, which are usually copies from another factory or reject pieces.

Tins
* Huntley and Palmer pioneered the use of tins as packaging; the earliest, dating from the 1840s, were handmade with intricately decorated paper labels glued to the surface. Such tins are now rare and valuable, and rust free examples even more desirable.

* Next in terms of value and rarity are the machine-made, transfer printed tins of 1860–80. Again, the few that survive in good condition are valuable.

* With the invention of cheaper offset lithography for colour printing on tins, production expanded in the 1880's and 90's. Only the more ornamental and attractive designs of this period are worth much.

* The first shaped tins were made around 1888, and are valuable if they can be securely dated to this first stage of shape experimentation. Most are embossed to simulate picture frames, or gently curved.

* Between 1900 and 1920 imaginative shapes of every description were produced in quality. Tins which resemble wood, wicker or leather, and unlikely shapes such as "book" tins, now sell well in good condition. Christmas and commemorative tins are popular but too numerous to be very valuable, but food tins sent to troops printed with messages of encouragement, are highly collectable.

* The latest tins of interest to collectors are those with moving parts made between 1920 and 1939. Windmills, aeroplanes, vehicles, prams, coconut shies and shooting galleries must be in perfect condition to be valuable.

* This is still a good area for the novice collector.

Tools
* Tool collecting is still in its infancy and interest focuses on the famous makers, since their work is easiest to date. Given that many craftsmen made their own tools, as part of their apprenticeship, there are many tools by anonymous or unknown makers which have potential value.

* Price differentials will undoubtedly emerge between the good and the mediocre, the rare and the common, with premiums for complete sets of tools in boxes fitted with individual compartments.

* Prices for pre-1830 tools are generally much higher than those for later examples, though rarity and quality are also important. Thus C18 planes are preferred to C19, except for metal planes by Spiers, Norris and Preston which are admired for their sophisticated construction. Smoothing planes are less valuable than tools made for a specific task, such as mitre, dovetail and moulding planes.

* Wooden braces, particularly of rosewood or box, are generally preferred to metal ones. An exception is the Marples brass-framed "Ebony Ultimatum" which is most valuable in mint condition.

* Lathes attract the highest prices of all tools, especially if they are well equipped. Those made by Holtzapffel or Evans, with special ivory and ebony turning tools, are highly prized.

Fishing tackle
* Finely engineered reels made from the early C19 onwards are enjoying considerable popularity. Collectors concentrate on rare early examples or on building up a complete set of a

manufacturer's output.

* Reels made by Hardy Bros of Alnwick are keenly collected. Other notable makers are Charles Farlow, S. Allcock, Alfred Illingworth, P.D. Malloch and Ogden Smith.
* Reels with makers' marks are more valuable.
* Though mint condition reels are rare, avoid those with worn, cracked, bent or replaced parts, and highly polished reels which have had their original finish removed.
* Engraved or scratched owner's initials reduce value, unless the owner is famous.
* Fish trophies in bow-fronted cases with a descriptive label mounted by expert taxidermists (e.g. J. Cooper & Sons) fetch good prices, but avoid trophies in poor condition.

Railway Antiques

* Railway relics fall into one of three periods: pre-1921 when over a hundred companies operated services at same time; 1921–1947 when companies were amalgamated into four regional groups; and post 1947 when railways were nationalised to form British Railways.
* The value of relics from the earliest period depends on the size and longevity of the company. Relics of small, short-lived companies are obviously rarer, and more valuable, than those of the larger companies, into which most were absorbed. Tickets, timetables and route maps or posters of defunct companies are prized.
* Relics of the second and third periods are still plentiful. Interest focuses on the lines which remained outside the major groups' control, especially narrow gauge lines, or relics of lines which closed post-Beeching. Anything of interest to a preservation society has a value; otherwise, items bearing insignia – lamps, crockery, clocks, office equipment, carriage equipment and posters – are the most valuable. Particularly in demand is any kind of memento or relic connected with the Great Western Railway.
* Railway locomotive nameplates fetch the best prices of all railway relics, headed by those from famous engines, followed by those with florid lettering or unusual insignia.

Treen

* The term "Treen" is used to describe any small wooden object normally associated with everyday domestic, trade, professional or rural life.
* Most articles of treen have been turned on a lathe and are not normally the work of a cabinet-maker or joiner. The term is not applied to articles larger than a spinning wheel.
* Carving, poker-work, inlay and painting are all common forms of decoration.
* Some C19 items can still be purchased reasonably inexpensively, and there are a large number of possible subject areas in which to specialize.
* Earliest examples generally available date from late C17, though these are often difficult to distinguish from later reproductions.
* C18 treen drinking vessels and other utensils are often most attractive pieces, finely turned and in a variety of quality woods: maple, walnut, mahogany and lignum vitae.
* Such C18 pieces are sought after, but the collector has to be on guard against late Victorian reproductions. These tend to be of poorer quality mahogany and are generally cruder and less elegant in execution.
* Patination should be present, but faking is not unknown.
* Fine carving, especially if combined with skilful turning and attractive graining, adds greatly to value. Mottoes and quotations, carved or in poker-work, are also desirable, but beware later additions to genuine but plain items.
* General antique shops are always worth searching for treen, while junk shops can sometimes provide the odd worthwhile piece. Prices should reflect condition, type of wood and any special features.

Mauchline ware

* A distinctive range of treen souvenir ware, usually of varnished sycamore and transfer printed with colourful designs.
* Ware was produced by A and A Smith in Mauchline, Ayrshire (and later in Birmingham), from c1820 until the 1930s.
* Items produced included various types of boxes, needle-cases, napkin rings, spill holders and wooden eggs.

INDEX

A
Aalto, Alvar 144
Abrahams 178
Adam, James 50
Adam, Robert 23, 30, 50
Adam Sisters 171
Adams 178
albarello 67
Alberge & Bromet 182
Allcock, S. 185
Allen, Robert 86
Allen, T. 87
Alt, Beck & Gottschalk 171
Andersen, David 144
andiron 96
antiquities 174
Aransberg 178
Argy-Rousseau, G. 144
argyle 96
armoire 10, 28
armour 160
    scale 158
arms and armour 156–69
    chronology of 169
    glossary 156–9
Art Nouveau & Art Deco 144–9
Arts and Crafts Movement 51, 144
Ashbee 149
auctions 7, 8
Augustus Rex ware 86
Ault 145
Austin, Jesse 176
autoperipatetikos 170

B
baby house 170
Baccarat factory 136
Ball, William 85
Bancroft, Joseph 87
banjo barometer 127, 129
Baohr and Proeschild 171
Barlow sisters 145
Barnsley, Sidney 144, 147, 148
Barnsley brothers 148
barometers 124–7, 129
    aneroid 129
    Fitzroy 125
    signpost 127
    stick 127, 129
    wheel 127, 129
Bassett-Lowke 173
Baxter, T. 89
bayonets 162
    plug 158, 162
Beatles, The 181
Beck 178
beds 20
bellarmine 56
Berge 179
Bergner, Carl 171
Berliner, Émile 180
biggin 96
Billingsley, William 84, 87, 89

Bim Bam 124
Bindesboll, Thorvald 144
Bing Artists' Dolls 171, 173
"blanc de Chine" 83, 90
Blick 180
blunderbuss 156
bobbins 177
bonheur du jour 10
bookcases 21
Boreman, Zachariah 84
Böttger, Johann 52, 86
bottles 175–6
    scent 176
Boucheron 144
Bouelle, A-C. 50
Boullemier, A. 87
Bovey Tracy pottery 184
Bow 82, 84, 86, 88
    polychrome wares 82
    blue and white wares 82
bowie knife 156, 163
bowls 90, 97, 136
boxes 176–7
    Battersea 176
    Bilston 176
    counter 96
    freedom 96
    pounce 96
    snuff 176
    vesta 97, 176
boxlock 156
Bradley 179
Brain, E. 145
Brameld family 88
Brandt, Edgar 144
brandy saucepan 96
Breuer 148
Briand, Thomas 83, 84
Bristol 52, 82, 84, 87, 89
Britannia metal 96, 123
British Antique Dealers Assn (BADA) 7
British plate 96
broadsword 156
Browne 182
Bru & Cie 171, 173
Bugatti, Carlo 144
Bugatti, Ettore 144
bureaux 22
    bureau bookcase 21, 22
Butterfield, Michael 178
buying antiques 7, 8

C
cabinets 23
caddy 96, 176–7
Calder, William 123
Cambrian Pottery 84
Camelford, Lord 87
cameras 179–80
Campbell 179
candlesticks 117
canteen 96
canterburies 24
Carabin 148
carbine 156

card case 96, 176
Cardew, Michael 144
Carette 173
Carlton ware 144, 149
Castleford ware 56
carpets see rugs
cartouche 96
Cary 178, 179
caster (castor) 44, 96
"Castle painter" 86
caudle cup 96
Caughley porcelain 82, 83, 87, 89
celadon 90
cellaret see wine coolers
centrepiece 96
ceramics, Art Nouveau and Art Deco 149
Chad Valley Co. 171
Chaffers, Richard & Partners 85
chafing dish 96
chair backs 36–41
    American 40–1
    Continental 39
    English 36–8
chairs 25–6
    see also chair backs
chaise longue see sofas
Chamberlains 84
Champion, R. 82, 84
Chantilly 83, 88
Chauffeuse 7
Chelsea 82, 83, 84, 86
chenet 96
Chermayeff, Serge 144
chest of drawers 27
chests 27
chiffonier 10, 23
china 56
Chinese Imari 90
Chinese porcelain 94
    export porcelain 83, 90
Chinese pronunciation 94
Chiparus, D. 144, 148
Chippendale, Thomas 50, 129
    Gentleman and Cabinet Maker's Directory 50
Christian, Philip 85
chronometer 125, 126
chryselephantine 144
cigarette cards 182
Cirou, Ciquaire 83
claret jug 96
Clarke, Arundell 145
Clarke, William 83
Clay, Henry 177
claymore 156
Clichy weight 136
Cliff, Clarice 145, 149
clockmakers 134–5
clocks 124–35
    glossary 124–7
    hands 130
    recognition and dating 130–3

clothes press 28
Clutha glass 145
Coalport 83, 84, 87, 88, 89
coaster 96
Coates, Wells 145
Cobb, John 50, 51
coffee pots 116, 119
coffers 27
Coke, John 87
Colinet 148
Collections 53
Colonna 148
commodes 24
Contax cameras 180
Cookworthy, William 52, 82, 86, 87, 88
Cooper, J. & Sons 185
Copeland 57
costume 182–3
counter box 96
Couper Ltd. 145
cow creamer 56, 96
cradle 20
Crandall 180
creamware 56
credenza 23
Crown Devon 145
cruet 96
Cuff 178
cuirass 156
cupboards 28
cups
  caudle 96
  dram (porringers) 96
  stirrup 97
Cymric see Liberty
cyphers 55

D
daggers 156, 157, 162
  ballock 156
  left-hand 157
daisho 156
Dali, Salvador 145
Daum Frères 145, 148, 176
Davenport 10, 84
Davenport, Captain 29
Davenport, John 84
de Feure 145
dealers, antique 7, 8
Dean's Rag Book Co. 171
decanters 139
Decoeur, Emile 145
Décorchement, F. E. 145
Degues 148
delft (delftware) 56
derringer 156
Design Registration Mark 54, 55
Deskey 148
Després, Jean 149
Derby porcelain 82, 84, 86, 87, 88
  cypher 55
Design & Industries Assn. (DIA) 146
desks 29–30

see also bureaux
deudarn 10
dinanderie 96
Dingyao 95
dirks 156, 162, 163
dog lock 156
Dollond, John 178, 179
dollmakers 171–2
dolls & toys 170–3
Dorst, Julius 171
Doulton 145
douter 96
dram cup 96
Dressel, C. & O. 171
dresser 28
Dresser, Christopher 145
dry edge 84
du Paquier, C. I. 89
Duesbury, William 82, 84, 86
dumb waiters 30
Duvivier 87

E
earthenware 56
Eastlake, Charles L. 50
  Hints on Household Taste 50
Eastman, George 179
écuelle 56
Edison, Thomas 180
Edwards, Edward 176
Eley, William 176
Elfe, Thomas 50
Ellis, Joel 171
Elton, Sir Edmund 145
Empire Fay-Sho 180
Enghalskrüge 56
épergne 96
escritoire 10
etuis 96
Evans 184
excise marks 123

F
faience 56
fairings 183
Farlow, Charles 185
fauteuil 10
Favrile 145
Fielding & Co. see Crown Devon
firangi 156
firearms 156–9, 166–7
fishing tackle 184–5
Fitch 180
Fitzroy, Admiral 125
Fitzwilliam, Earl 88
Flagg, J. M. 181
flatware 56
Fleischmann, Adolf 171
Flight, Barr and Barr 89
flintlock 156, 166, 167
Foley 145
Frankl 148
Fraser & Cole 179
freedom box 96
French lock 157
French polish 19
Frye, Thomas 82

Fukugawa 90
furniture 8, 10–51
  alterations and restorations 18
  Art Nouveau & Art Deco 148
  copies 19
  drawers 16
  early oak 31
  fakes 19
  glossary 10, 11
  handles 46–7
  legs and feet 42–4
  marquetry 11, 17
  marriages 18
  mouldings 49
  patination 13
  pediments 48
  periods and styles 14–15
  recognition and dating 36–49
  repairs 18
  veneers 11, 17
  walnut 35
  woods used in 12, 13
furniture makers and designers 50–1
fusil 157
Futurism 144

G
Gaillard 148, 149
Gallé, Emile 144, 145, 148, 176
garniture 56
Gaultier 171
Gebrüder Heubach 173
Genet & Michon 148
Gibbons, Grinling 50
Gilbody, Samuel 85
Giles, James 176
Gillow's of Lancaster 50
gimbal 125
Gimson, Ernest 50, 144, 145, 147
girandole 11
Glamorgan Pottery 88
Glasgow School 144, 146
glass 136–43
  Art Nouveau and Art Deco 148
  cameo 144
  camera 144
  Clutha 145
  drinking 140–3
  engraved 138, 139, 145
  etched 138, 145
  glossary 136–7
  Jacobite 139
goldmarks 111
Goldscheider 146
Goldsmiths' Company 98
gorgelet 90
gorget 157
Goss China 183
Goss, Adolphus 183
Goss, William H. 183
gramophones 180
Gray, Eileen 146

greaves 157
Greene brothers 148
Greiner 171, 173
Grison 148
Gropius 51
Guanyao 90
Guanyin 90
Guild of Handicraft 149
Guimard 148
gunmakers & gunsmiths 168
guns *see* firearms

H

Hadley 178
Halberd 157
Haley, Bill 181
hallmarks 98, 111
  imitation 115, 122
  International 111
  see also goldmarks; silvermarks
Hancock, George 87
Hancock, Robert 82
Handwerck, Heinrich 171
hanger 157
Hardel, Brooklyn J. 149
Hardy Bros. 185
Hardy 182
Haseler, Edwin 177
Hassall 182
hatchli 150
Haviland 144
Haviland, David 146
Haviland factory 146
Haviland, Theodore 146
Haynes, E. Barrington 140
  Glass Through the Ages 140
Heale, Ambrose 146
Hearn 179
Heath, John 84
Heath and Wing 179
helmet, close 156
Hendrix, Jimmy 181
Hepplewhite, George 27, 50
  Cabinet Maker's and Upholsterer's Guide, The 50
Herold C.F. 86
Herold, J.G. 86
Heubach (Gebrüder Heubach) 171
Heubach, Ernst 171
Heylyn, Edward 82
Hill, Jockey 84
hilt 157
Hirado 90
Hoffmann, Josef 146, 149
Hollins, Warburton 87
Holtzapffel 184
Hope, Thomas 50
Hornby 173
Hunebelle 148
Hunger, C.C. 89
hunter 157
Huntley & Palmer 184
hygrometer 126

I

Illingworth, Alfred 185
Imari 56, 84, 90
  Chinese 90
Ince, William 50
  Universal System of Household Furniture, The 50
ironstone 56–7
Ives, E.R. 173

J

Jacob, Georges 50
Jacob-Desmalter, François Honoré 50–1
jambiyah 157
Japanese periods 90
jardinière 57, 96
jasper ware 57
Jenkinson, William 85
Jennens & Bettridge 177
Jensen, Georg 146, 149
jewellery 174–5
  Art Nouveau and Art Deco 149
Jianyao 90
Jizhouyao 90
Joel, Betty 146
Johnson, Mason & Taylor 171
Jones, Inigo 51
jugs
  claret 96
  silver 117
  sparrow-beak 97
Jumeau, Pierre François 171, 173
Junyao 95

K

kabuto 157
kaga 90
Kakiemon 83, 88, 91
Kammer & Reinhardt 171, 173
Kändler, J.J. 86
Kangxi 95
kard 157
Kashmir 150
katar 157
Kayser-Zinn 149
kenare 150
Kent, William 51
kermes 150
Kestner, J.D. 171
kettle hat 157, 161
Khandar 157
khanfar 157
khanjar 157
kilim 150
kindjal 157
Kirchner 182
Kirkby, T. 87
Kley & Hahn 173
Kling, C.F. 172
Klinger, J.G. 87
Knox, Archibald 146, 149
ko kutani 91
Kraak porselein 91

kris 157
Kruse, Käthe 172
kukri 157
Kutani 91

L

Lacloche Frères 146
Lalique, René 146, 148, 149, 176
lamps, Art Nouveau and Art Deco 149
Lardry 148
latten 96
Le Verrier, Max 146
Leach, Bernard 144, 146
lead-crystal 137
Lealand 178
Lehmann 173
Leica camera 180
Leighton, William 138
Leitz 178
Lenci 172
Li shui 91
Liberty, Sir A. L. 146
Liberty's 149
Linthorpe 145
Lister 179
Littler, William 85
Liverpool factories 85
Loetz 146
London & Provincial Antique Dealers Assn. (LAPADA) 7
Longton Hall 85, 86, 87
looking glass 32
Louis-Henri de Bourbon, Prince de Condé 83
lowboy 33
Lowenfinck, A.F. von 86
Lowenthal & Co. 172
Lowestoft 82, 86
Lund, Benjamin 52, 82, 89

M

MacDonald 182
McGill 182
Mackintosh, Charles Rennie 146, 148
MacIntyre's 147
Maddison, Charles 83
majolica 57
Malloch, P.D. 185
mamluk 150
Manchu (Qing) Dynasty 92
Marchand, James 84
Marinot, Maurice 146
Märklin 173
Marot, Daniel 51
marquetry 11
marriages, furniture 18
Marseille, Armand 172
Marsh, Charles 73
Martin 173, 178
Martin Brothers 51, 145, 146–7, 149
Martinware 146–7
matchlock 157, 166, 167
mauchline ware 185
May 182

Mayhew, John 50
mazarine 97
medical instruments 179
Meissen 52, 82, 83, 84, 85, 88, 89
metalware 96–123
  Art Nouveau and Art Deco 149
  glossary 96–7
Metropolitan Museum, New York 6
militaria, general 164–5
  badges, insignia and buttons 164
  ephemera 164
  medals 164
  powder flasks 164
  regalia 164
  uniforms 164
  see also firearms; weapons
Mills, Nathaniel 176
Ming 95
Minton 57, 84, 87, 88, 147
  cyphers 55
Minton, Thomas 87
mir 151
mirrors 32
Molyneaux 179
Montanari, Augusta 172, 173
Montanari, Richard 172, 173
Moorcroft, William 147
Morgan, William Frend de 147
morion 157, 161
Morris, William 50, 51, 147
Moser, Kolomann 147, 149
Moser, Ludwig 147
mouldings 49
Mucha, Alphonse 147, 181, 182
Müller & Strassberger 172
museums 53
musical boxes 180
musket 158

N
namas 151
Nantgarw 84, 89
National Antique and Art Dealers' Association of America Inc. (NAADAAI) 7
needlepoint or needlework 137
Nekola, Joseph 184
Nekola, Karel 183, 184
netsuke 175
New Century 180
Newcastle baluster 137
Newhall 52, 84, 87
Newman, Frederick 177
Nicklin, William 85
Niedermayer, J.J. 89

nimcha 158
Norris 184
nutmeg grater 97

O
oignon 126
Old Sheffield plate 115, 121
Oliver 180
O'Neale, J.H. 83
oriental wares 90–5
orrery 126
over-and-under 158

P
papier mâché 177
patch-box 97
pâte de verre 145, 147
patination 13
pattern numbers 55
Payne 182
pearlware 57
Peche 149
Peck, Mrs Lucy 172
pediments 48
Pegg, "Quaker" 85
Pennington, James 85
Pennington, John 85
Pennington, Seth 85
pepperbox 158
pepperette 97
percussion lock 158, 166, 167
Petruschenck 86
petuntse see porcelain
Petzgold, Dr Dora 172
pewter 121
  American 123
  marks on 122–3
  modern 123
Pewterers' Co. 121, 122
phonographs 180
photographs 179–80
Phyfe, Duncan 45, 51
pier glass 32
Pierotti family 172, 173
pike 158
Pilkington 145
Pilsbury, R. 87
Pinxton porcelain 87
Planche, André 84
Plymouth porcelain 52, 82, 86, 87, 88
Podmore, Robert 85
Pollard 89
poniard 158
pontil mark 137, 138
pop ephemera 181
porcelain and pottery 52–89
  design registration mark 55
  glossary 56–7
  hard-paste 52, 56
  major factories 82–9
  marks 58–81
  Oriental 92–5
  pattern numbers 55
  soft-paste 52, 57
porringer 96, 97

postcards 182
posters 181
potlids 176
pottery see porcelain
pounce box 96
Powell 178
Pratt, Felix 176
Prattware 57
Preiss, F. 147, 148
Presley, Elvis 181
Preston 184
Pugin, Augustus W. 51
punch bowl 97
Pu-Tai 91
Putnam, Grace Storey 172

Q
quality marks 122
quarrel 158
Quezal 149
Qianlong 95
Qing 92, 95

R
railway antiques 185
raku 91
ramrod 158
rapier 158
redware 57
regulator 126
Reid, William 85
Reinicke, Paul 87
Remington 166
Revere, Paul 119
revolver 158, 166, 167
Rhead, Frederick 147
Riesenburgh, B. van 51
Riesener, Jean-Henri 51
rifle 158, 166
  express 156
Rockingham 84, 87, 88
roemer (rummer) 137
Rohde, Johan 146
Rohmer 172
Rollei camera 180
Rose, John 83, 84
Rosenthal 147
Ross 178
Rossignol 173
Rousseau, Clément 147
Roycroft 149
Royal Crown Derby 84
Royal Dux 147
rugs and carpets 150–5
  glossary 150–1
  pronunciation guide 154
Ruhlmann, Jacques-Emile 51
rummer 137
runner 150, 151
ruta kali 151

S
sabre 158
St. Cloud 88, 89
salt 97
salver 97
Samhammer, Philip 172

Samson, Edme 88, 176
sashqua (sashka) 158
Satsuma 91
sauceboats 117
saucepan, brandy 96
savonnerie 151
scabbard 158
Scarlet 179
scent bottles 176
Schilling, Barbara 172
Schilling, Ferdinand 172
Schinkel, K. F. 51
Schmidt, Bruno 172
Schoenau & Hoffmeister 172
Schoenhut Co. 172
scientific instruments 178–9
scimitar 158
sconce 97
"scrambling" 26
sculpture, Art Nouveau and Art Deco 148
Seddon, George 51
sereband 151
settees see sofas
Sèvres porcelain 52, 83, 84, 88, 89
sewing antiques 177–8
SFBJ 172
Shah abbas 151
shako 159
shamsir 159
Shearer, Thomas 51
  Cabinetmaker's London Book of Prices, The 51
Sheffield plate 97, 115, 121
Sheraton, Thomas 16, 24, 30, 51, 129
  Cabinet Dictionary 30
Shufu 91
sideboards 23
Silver, Rex 149
silver 120
  shapes 116–18
  American 119
  marks 98–110, 114
silversmiths, 112–13
Simms, William 179
Simon & Halbig 172, 173
Sinkiang 151
skean-dhu 159
Smith, George 51
Smith, Jesse 87
Smith, Ogden 185
snapha(u)nce 159
snuffboxes 176
Society of Fine Art Auctioneers (SOFAA) 7
sofas and settees 45
Soqui, Monsieur 88
Sorgenthal, K. von 89
sparrow-hawk jug 97
spelter 147
Spiers of Oxford 177, 184
Spode 57, 87
spoons
  apostle 96

caddy 96
  shapes 118
Staartklok 127
standish 97
Steiff, Margarete 172
Steiner 173
Steiner, Hermann 172
Steiner, Jules N. 172
Steuben.149
Stickley, Gustav 147, 148
stiletto 159
stirrup cup 97
Stolzel, Samuel 86, 89
stools 32
stoneware 57
Sung Dynasty 90, 91, 92, 95
Swansea 84, 88, 89
swords 156–159, 162
  broadsword 156
  dress 156
  mortuary 158
  smallsword 159
  sympiesometer 127

T

taaweesh 159
tables 33–4
tachi 159
Taddy & Ainsworth 182
tallboy 27
talwar (tulwar) 159
T'ang Dynasty 52, 95
tankards 97, 116
tanto 159
tazza 137
teapots 116, 119
Thackeray 182
thimbles 177–8
Tiffany, Charles L. 147
Tiffany, Louis C. 145, 147
tikh 151
tingyao 91
tins 184
Tinworth, George 145
tokkuri 91
tools 184
torchère 20
Touch Plates 122
touchmark 97, 122
toys see dolls and toys
Transitional wares 91
treen 185
trefid 97
"trembly rose" painter 86
Troughton brothers 179
Tudric see Liberty
tureen 97
Turner, Thomas 82
typewriters 180–1

U

uniface 97

V

Van Erp 149
Van der Rohe, Mies 51, 148
vases 56, 57, 91

baluster 56
sleeve 91
veramin 151
Verlux 148
vesta case 97
Vever brothers 149
Victoria and Albert Museum 6
Vienna porcelain 89
Vienna regulator 127
Vile, John 50
Vile, William 51
vinaigrette 97
Vincennes 52, 83, 88, 89
Vose 123
Voysey, Charles F.A. 51, 147, 148
Vulliamy family 127

W

Waals, Peter 147
Wain 182
Walker 88
Walker, Izannah 172
walnut furniture 35
Walton, B. & Co. 177
wardrobe 28
watches see clocks
weapons, edged 162–3
  bayonets 158, 162
  daggers and dirks 156, 157, 162
  pole 162
  swords 156, 158, 162
Wedgwood 56, 57
  cypher 55
Wemyss ware 57, 183–4
West Pans factory 85
Wheel-lock 159, 166, 167
Wiener Werkstätte 146–7
Wileman, H. 145
Williams 180
Wilkinson A.J. Ltd. 145
Wiltshaw & Robinson Ltd. 144
Winchcombe pottery 144
wine coolers 35
Wolfe, Thomas 85
Wolfe & Co. 85
Wolfers 149
Worcester 82, 83, 85, 87, 88, 89
  porcelain dates 89
Wright 148

X

Xingyao 91

Y

yataghan 159
Yingqing 95
Yongzheng 95
Yost 180
Yuan Dynasty 95
Yueyao 91

Z

Zaanklok 127
Zach 148
Zeiss 178, 180

ACKNOWLEDGEMENTS

The compilers and publisher are especially indebted to the following Consultants on *Miller's Antiques Price Guide* for their expert advice and help over many years. Their excellent source material for that bestselling annual publication has been invaluable in the planning and preparation of *Miller's Pocket Antiques Fact File* and in ensuring that its scope is both authoritative and wide-ranging.

Robert Bailey; Keith Baker; Ron Beech; John Bly; Roy Butler; Graham Child; Victor Chinnery; David Clark; Roy Clements; Nigel Coleman; Stuart Cropper; Richard Davidson; Tony & Elinor Foster; Mike Golding; Jonathan Horne; Valerie Howkins; Hilary Kay; Chris King; Eric Knowles; Gordon Lang; Ann Lingard; Nicholas Long; Brian Loomes; James Lowe; Nicholas Marchant-Lane; Victoria Mather; Arthur Middleton; Nicholas Pine; Richard Price; Henry Sandon; Christopher Spencer; David Symonds; Lars Tharp; Wing Cdr. R.G. Thomas; Russell Varney; Peter Waldron.

Special thanks are also due to Crown Publishers Inc., New York, for permission to reproduce in the Porcelain and Pottery section of this book a substantial number of marks which appear in their publications *Dictionary of Marks – Pottery and Porcelain* and *Kovel's New Dictionary of Marks*, both by Ralph and Terry Kovel.

Other major source books consulted

American Folk Art,
J. Lipman, Dover
Antique Collector's Handbook,
G. Savage, Spring Books
Antique Collectors' Illustrated Dictionary,
D. Mountfield, Hamlyn
Antique Collector's Picture Guide to Prices,
D. Coombs, Ebury Press
Antiques Directory: Furniture,
J. & M. Miller, Mitchell Beazley
Antique Gun and Gun Collecting,
F. Wilkinson, Hamlyn
Antique Pewter of the British Isles,
R.F. Michaelis, Bell
Antique Weapons & Armour,
R. Wilkinson-Latham, Phaidon
Arms & Armour,
F. Wilkinson, Hamlyn
Art Collector's Handbook,
R.B. Whiffen, Estates Gazette
Arthur Negus Guide to British Silver,
A. Negus & B. Inglis, Hamlyn
Arthur Negus Guide to English Pottery & Porcelain,
A. Negus, Hamlyn
Art Nouveau,
F. Abbate, Octopus
Book of American Furniture,
Doreen Beck, Hamlyn
Book of Carpets,
R.G. Hubel, Barrie & Jenkins
British Cut & Thrust Weapons,
J. Wilkinson-Latham, David & Charles

Britten's Old Clocks and Watches & their Makers,
Britten, Bonanza Books
Buyer's Price Guide to Art Deco,
S. Barton & M. Miller (ed), Millers
Buyer's Price Guide to Chinese Porcelain,
G. Lang, Millers
Buyer's Guide to Continental Porcelain,
J. Miller, Millers
Buyer's Guide to English Porcelain,
J. Miller, Millers
Buying Antique Furniture,
R. Feild, Macdonald
Clocks & Watches,
A. Smith, The Connoisseur
Clocks in Colour,
A. Nichols, Blandford
Collectors' Complete Dictionary of American Antiques,
F. Phipps, Doubleday
Collector's Guide to Militaria,
D.E. Johnson, Wm. Luscombe
Collectors' Illustrated Guide to Firearms,
M. Miller, Barrie & Jenkins
Concise Encyclopaedia of Antiques,
L.G.G. Ramsey (ed.), The Connoisseur
Construction of Period Country Furniture,
V.V. Taylor, Stobart & Son
Continental Porcelain,
J. Cushion, Letts

Dictionary of Antiques,
G. Savage, Barrie & Jenkins

Dictionary of Marks – Pottery & Porcelain,
R.M. & T.H. Kovel, Crown

Directory of American Silver, Pewter and Silver Plate,
R.M. & T.H. Kovel, Crown

Discovering Antiques,
Greystone Press

Dolls: European 1800–1930,
J. & M. Cieslik, Studio Vista

Edged Weapons,
F.J. Stephens, Spur Books

Encyclopaedia of British Pottery & Porcelain Marks,
G.A. Godden, Barrie & Jenkins

English Dolls & Toys,
M. & K. Fawdry, Benn

English Domestic Clocks,
Cescinsky & Webster, Chancery House

English Goldsmiths & Their Marks,
Sir C.J. Jacks, Dover

English Period Furniture,
C.H. Hayward, Evan Bros.

English Silver Hall Marks,
J. Banister, Foulsham

European & American Dolls,
G. White, Batsford

Fine Points of Early American Furniture,
A. Sack, Crown

Field Guide to American Antique Furniture,
J.T. Butler, Henry Holt

Gentle Art of Faking Furniture,
H. Cescinsky, Dover

Glass Through the Ages,
E. Barrington Hayes, Pelican

Godden's Guide to English Porcelain,
G.A. Godden, Hart Davis MacGibbon

Guide to Marks of Origin on British and Irish Silver Plate,
Fredk. Bradbury

Guns,
F. Wilkinson, Hamlyn

Hallmarks & Date Letters,
N.A.G. Press

Historic Furnishing,
N. Truman, Pitman

Illustrated Encyclopaedia of British Pottery & Porcelain,
G.A. Godden, Barrie & Jenkins

Illustrated Guide to Antique Collecting,
A. Ridgway, Wm. Luscombe

Illustrated Guide to Silver,
M. Holland, Phaidon

Is It Genuine?,
J. Bly, Mitchell Beazley

Japanese Porcelain,
S. Jenyns, Faber & Faber

Know Your Antiques,
R.M. & T.H. Kovel, Crown

Kovels' New Dictionary of Marks,
R.M. & T.H. Kovel, Crown

Later Chinese Porcelain,
S. Jenyns, Faber & Faber

Look After Your Antiques,
J. Fitz-Maurice Mills, Ebury Press

Lore of Arms,
W. Reed, Nordbok

Miller's Antiques Price Guide, 1980 to 1988, J. & M. Miller, Millers

Old Pewter, Its Makers & Marks,
H.H. Cotterell, Batsford

Oriental Export Market Porcelain,
G.A. Godden, Granada

Oxford Companion to the Decorative Arts,
H. Osborne (ed.), O.U.P.

Penguin Dictionary of the Decorative Arts,
J. Fleming & H. Honour, Penguin

Pewter Collecting for Amateurs,
K. Ullyett, Fredk. Muller

Pewter of Great Britain,
C. Peal, John Gifford

Pictorial Dictionary of British 19th Century Furniture Design, Antique Collectors' Club

Pollard's History of Firearms,
C. Blair (ed.), Country Life

Price Guide to Antique Edged Weapons,
L. Southwick, Antique Collectors' Club

Price Guide to Clocks,
A. & R. Shenton, Antique Collectors' Club

Price Guide to Collectable Antiques,
J. Mackay, Antique Collectors' Club

Price Guide to 18th Century English Porcelain,
S. Spero, Antique Collectors' Club

Price Guide to 19th and 20th Century British Pottery,
D. Battie & M. Turner, Antique Collectors' Club

Price Guide to 19th Century European Furniture,
C. Payne, Antique Collectors' Club

Price Guide to Pine Furniture & Kitchenalia,
J. & M. Miller, Millers

Porcelain Marks of the World,
E. Poche, Hamlyn

Rugs & Carpets of the World,
I. Bennett, Country Life

Rugs to Riches,
C. Bosly, Allen & Unwin

Short Dictionary of Furniture,
J. Gloag, Allen & Unwin

Shorter Dictionary of English Furniture,
R. Edwards, Country Life

Silver Marks of the World,
J. Divis, Hamlyn

Swords of the British Army,
B. Robson, Arms & Armour Press

Working in Wood,
E. Scott, Mitchell Beazley

World Ceramics,
R.J. Charleston, Hamlyn.